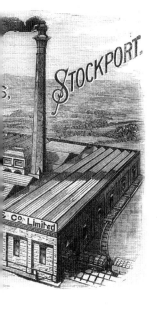

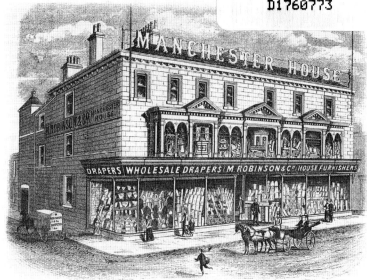

MR. F. J. BOBBY'S GENERAL DRAPERY STORES, MARGATE.

A Guide to

TRACING THE HISTORY OF A BUSINESS

MR. F. J. BOBBY'S GENERAL DRAPERY STORES, MARGATE.

A Guide to

TRACING THE HISTORY OF A BUSINESS

John Orbell

PHILLIMORE

2009

Published by
PHILLIMORE & CO. LTD
Chichester, West Sussex, England
www.phillimore.co.uk
www.thehistorypress.co.uk

© John Orbell, 1987, 2009

ISBN 978-1-86077-575-8

Printed and bound in Great Britain

CONTENTS

Section Three – Information Sources outside the Archives of the Business ✦ . . ✦ . ✦ . ✦ . ✦ 31

LIST OF ILLUSTRATIONS

Illustration Acknowledgements

Reproduced by kind permission of The Baring Archive: 7, 8, 10, 19-20; *The Century's Progress: Yorkshire*, The London Printing and Engraving Company (1893): endpapers; Guildhall Library: 1-6, 26, 29, 31; *Industrial Great Britain Part II, A Commercial Review of Leading Firms Selected from Important Towns of Many Counties*, Historical Publishing Company (1891): frontispiece, endpapers; National Archives: 11-12, 30; private collection: 13-14, 16-18, 23-5, 27-8; reproduced by kind permission of RSA Group Insurance Plc: 9; Suffolk Record Office: 21-2; reproduced by kind permission of the Worshipful Company of Scriveners: 15.

PREFACE

This guide is the successor to *A Guide to Tracing the History of a Business*, published in 1987. Although this new edition adopts the structure of the old, the text has been completely rewritten, extended and brought up to date. It encompasses the extraordinary changes witnessed in the last 20 years.

Since 1987 our ability to access the different categories of information of use in tracing the history of a business has been dramatically enhanced. Digitisation has had, and is having, a major impact on our ability to tap hitherto impenetrable sources such as newspapers. In particular, the digitisation of the *London* and *Edinburgh Gazettes* and of *The Times* has been hugely important. Conversion of archive catalogues to electronic format has transformed our ability to search archive collections for references to a particular business. The emergence of the web has brought digitised copy and archive catalogues to our desktops at home.

At the same time publication of works on the history of businesses has stormed ahead, reflecting a surge of interest by enthusiast historians in everything from family history to genealogy, canals to motorbikes, ceramics to furniture, printing to computers. Alongside this, the academic world has seen steadily rising interest in business history at the expense of other areas of economic history. These developments result in a vastly larger body of monographs and periodical articles, gazetteers and dictionaries all telling the story of specific businesses, albeit in varying detail. Increasingly those wanting to discover the history of a business need look no further than published sources.

Compared with the state of affairs existing in 1987, matters could not be more different. Yet the pace of change shows no sign of slacking; each month we learn of new initiatives, products and publications. Looked at from this perspective, writing this guide is somewhat akin to building on quicksand – but worthwhile nevertheless! Yet there is much more to be done. Take for example the trade press and house journals. These enormously important sources for finding out about a business remain largely impenetrable for want of indexes and on account of the inaccessibility of paper copy.

I am enormously grateful to Richard Storey, Lesley Richmond, Alex Ritchie and Steven Freeth for commenting on certain parts of the text. Notwithstanding their valued help, there will continue to be shortcomings for which I must take responsibility. This is inevitable in a book covering in detail such a wide range of sources; I have used many of them extensively in my research in different places and at different times, but some less so. That said, I have done my best to make the book as accurate as possible.

In revising this book my main port of call has been Guildhall Library and I am also enormously grateful to its most excellent staff.

INTRODUCTION

In the 1980s I worked as Honorary Research Adviser of the Business Archives Council, dealing with a postbag from people invariably seeking historical information about a particular business. I was then conscious of how very little many of my correspondents knew about business history sources; those from abroad were wholly unfamiliar with the library and record office network. This guide is written therefore with that experience very much in mind. It is pitched at both the uninformed and more experienced researcher.

Businesses touch our lives in so many ways. They build and modernise our homes, build the cars we drive and the trains, aircraft and ships we travel in. They lend us money and insure our homes, lives and places of work. They make the furniture we sit on, the crockery we eat off and the clocks that tell us the time. They provide our farmers with fertilizers and tractors, process the food we eat and manage the restaurants and bars we visit. They generate our electricity and deliver our gas and water. They manage our pensions, arrange our funerals, organise our holidays and cut our hair. They own and manage the cinemas and theatres we visit and make the films and produce the plays we watch. Most of us work for them. Some of us have a stake in them either as proprietors or as shareholders. A few of us direct them at the top while most of us work for them at the bottom! And as with us, so it is with our ancestors.

All of this means that the archives created by businesses, together with the huge volume of business-related records and printed material generated by other bodies, are of real relevance to historians, whether academic or enthusiast, professional or amateur. There is something here for each one of us, whether our interests are agriculture or transport; art or architecture; collectibles such as clocks, furniture, ceramics or toys; the performing arts; family or genealogy – or just business and economic history!

It is true that the link between a business and a research topic is often obscure, unlikely or tangential and consequently unrealised or underestimated. Take for example the study of an artist's output, a subject seemingly far removed from the world of business. It might well be enriched by using archives produced by those businesses that provided the artist's canvases, brushes, paints and frames, which exhibited and/or sold his or her pictures or which provided banking and insurance services. As another example, take the writing of biography. This can be enhanced through study of the businesses with which the subject was connected, either as an employee, director, owner, investor, customer or supplier. Of these, customer relationships are often the most varied and the most interesting. Each category of purchases – whether banking or insurance services, legal advice, travel, art, houses, estates, motor cars, clothing, champagne and the rest – is likely to shed intriguing light on different aspects of a subject's life.

The purpose of this guide is to help historians of all sorts and descriptions to locate historical information about a specific business; it is not nearly so concerned with context or the environment in which the business functions. It does not aim to provide great detail or to describe particular collections of material. What it does try to do is, on the one hand, to provide the historian with a route map for use in locating different business archives collections and published histories of businesses. On the other, it describes and explains the main categories of sources available for research. A wide range of research materials are covered, ideas and contacts worth pursuing are suggested and further reading is indicated.

While it does deal with some quite complicated areas, this guide also acknowledges that the requirements of most historians are not over-ambitious and often limited to locating broad details of a specific business. These details might simply be the names under which the business operated; the goods and services it made and sold; the addresses of its offices and factories; the dates of its foundation and demise; and the identity of the people most important in its development. No very profound research is usually required in dealing with these questions, as answers can be found in a small range of secondary sources. However, the needs of some historians are more complex, requiring in-depth research using primary sources for scholarly output. This guide seeks to serve both groups of researchers.

For the avoidance of confusion, the boundary of this guide should be clearly marked out. Its terms of reference are unashamedly historical; it is *not* intended for researchers seeking current or near-current information about a business. If that was its function, an entirely different emphasis and significantly different content would be required. This guide is written by an historian for historians.

The guide has four sections. The first deals with locating broad details of a business. Is the business still alive and well? Is it dormant? Is it defunct? Has it been absorbed by a larger business either by acquisition, merger or takeover? Where is or was it based? What does or did it do? Answers to such questions might, in themselves, satisfy the researcher's needs. If not, they can direct the researcher to the archives of the business, to people associated with it and to secondary source material. Section One, therefore, describes the procedures to adopt and the sources to use in order to discover key information about a business and, in particular, whether it is alive or defunct.

Section Two is more matter-of-fact. It describes sources – whether published or otherwise – for use in locating any surviving archives of a business, especially a defunct one. These sources might be in hard-copy form or in electronic form available via the internet. Archives could be in record offices, academic libraries, national archives or with businesses.

Section Three is much more extensive. This reviews the wide range of secondary sources that shed light on a business; these are especially important if, as is highly likely, the archives of the business have not survived or are substantially incomplete. These sources include the archives of the business's bankers, legal advisers, insurers and other suppliers of goods and services; of the business's customers; of central and local government departments with which the business dealt either on a routine or particular basis; of associations to which the business belonged or with which it had connections such as trade associations, chambers of commerce and trade unions; and published sources such as newspapers, trade press, official publications, annual reports, brokers' reports, prospectuses and the like.

The final section schedules publications and organisations cited in the text. Neither claims to be a comprehensive listing of all possible entities and references of use in tracing the history of a business; these schedules simply serve to support references made in the text.

Finally, it is worth pointing out that this guide is written at a time of immense and rapid change in the way we store and access information. Digitisation and the internet are, in leaps and bounds, extending the availability and use of historical information. This is an enormously exciting time for historians but such is the pace of change that writing this guide is akin to running in order to stand still. However, the task is still worth doing as the overriding objective is to describe sources, suggest strategy and provide ideas. That said, the guide seeks to provide a balanced approach, dealing appropriately with electronic and traditional formats.

SECTION ONE

Locating Vital Information about a Business and Research Strategy

FORMATION, DISSOLUTION, ADDRESSES, ACTIVITIES AND NAME-CHANGES

Introduction

The first and most obvious step to take in tracing the history of a business is to discover if the business is alive or dissolved. If alive, by contacting it the researcher might discover a published history of the business, gain access to its archives or meet people such as directors, shareholders, employees and/or pensioners who can recall historical information or point to sources of information outside the business. If defunct, then a very different research strategy is called for. In order to discover if the business is active or defunct, it is often vital to know about any change or changes in its name. The objective of this section is to describe how these vital pieces of information can be discovered. In achieving this, along the way other core information will inevitably be located, most obviously address and activity.

No single database or reference book lists every business active in Britain today, let alone all those that once existed. However, a few sources used together provide reasonable coverage of all but the smallest entities. Of these, the indexes of Companies House are vital in locating currently or recently registered companies, by far the most common business type in the last 100 years. These indexes are supported by several published reference books and online business information services that derive much of their data from Companies House. These sources are considered in Parts Two and Three of this section.

Part four deals with finding information about defunct or dissolved registered companies. In one form or another, Companies House maintains comprehensive indexes to dissolved registered companies and to changes in their name since the beginning of company registration in the 1840s; only recent dissolutions are listed in online indexes. Otherwise they are recorded in relatively inaccessible card indexes at Companies House. Useful substitutes, however, are the *London* and *Edinburgh Gazettes*, which, since the early days of company registration, have carried notices about registered companies in the process of being wound up. Access to the *Gazettes* has been massively enhanced since their digitisation; notices can now be searched and read online, providing a very effective means of discovering details of registered company dissolutions.

Parts Five, Six and Seven deal with finding vital details about partnerships and individual-trader businesses. Before the 20th century these were the most common forms of business ownership. It is inevitable that the older a business, the more difficult it is to discover information about it and this is so here. Unlike registered companies, no central register of partnerships and individual traders exists but useful sources are, once again, the *London* and *Edinburgh Gazettes* and also trade directories.

Part Eight considers publications carrying core information about registered companies at the time of their registration, such as activities, objectives, address and capital; very often this has been extracted by publishers from Companies House files. For 19th-century formations, the most important source is the annual returns of newly registered companies published in Parliamentary Papers between 1844 and 1907. A number of business journals also published details on a regular basis through to the 1970s.

Finally, Part Nine very briefly refers to published histories of businesses on the basis that the existence of these might make research using the above sources unnecessary! Published histories are considered at much greater length on pp.81-104.

Currently Registered Companies:
Companies House Online Index

Companies House (www.companieshouse.gov.uk) is an executive agency of the Department of Business, Enterprise & Regulatory Reform; it was once more generally known as the Registrar of Companies with principal branches in London, Edinburgh and, sometime, Dublin. It traces its origins to the beginning of company registration in 1844. Today about two million businesses are registered with it; another million businesses formerly registered are now dissolved.

Before 1844 it had been possible to form a company with multi-shareholders largely through recourse to royal charter or specific legislation. But such companies were, relative to partnerships or individual traders, tiny in number and largely restricted to a narrow range of business sectors – most commonly inland navigation, railways, insurance, banking, and gas and water supply. The 1844 legislation changed all of this by making the procedures for the formation of companies routine and therefore inexpensive. Company formation was taken an important stage further in 1855 with the introduction of limited liability.

With some very particular exceptions, since 1844 it has only been possible to form a company through registration with the Registrar of Companies; on registration, the company receives a unique registration number that remains unaltered throughout its lifetime. The Registrar's roles have always been to incorporate and dissolve companies; to receive from them, for the most part annually, on-going information about their affairs for examination; and to store this information during the life of the company and make it available to the general public on request. In undertaking this work, Companies House has always maintained a file on each registered company as well as schedules of name changes and removals from the Register following dissolution.

Today Companies House maintains an online database that holds details of all currently registered companies, all dissolved companies removed from the Register since 1985 and all name changes from at least the mid-1980s (www.companieshouse.gov.uk). It can be searched without charge by name of company or by registration number for basic details including registered address, date of incorporation, type of company, activity, name changes and, where applicable, details of dissolution. It is a very powerful and helpful aid to finding core information about the vast majority of businesses operating in Britain today. Additional information, for example annual returns, is available online but for a payment *see* pp.81-104.

Currently Registered Companies and other Businesses: Online Databases and Reference Books

Profiles of current businesses are available via online information services and in published reference books; both generally derive much of their data from Companies House sources. In due course online services are bound to replace reference books but so far show little sign of doing so. All leading company-profile reference books still seem to be published and, unlike online business services, are generally available in reference libraries. When available, for example via the internet, online services are often charged for. Because of their greater availability to the general researcher, books are covered here in greater detail than online services.

Reference books and online services generally cover quoted and large private companies but some specialise in small private businesses operating at local level, which form the majority. Especially useful are sources that link subsidiaries – even dormant ones – to parents. The following is a selection of well-known books and services; others could have been added. All books appear periodically, usually annually, and have been published over several years so earlier editions may prove useful if the current edition is unhelpful. A comprehensive listing of reference books and online services is available in the periodic *Directory of Business Information Resources*.

Online Databases

Fame
Carries contact, ownership, activity and financial data on 2.5 million companies in the UK and Ireland, together with summary information on a further 1 million smaller businesses. Excellent for contact, activity and financial details.

Marketline Business Information Centre
Provides detailed profiles of 10,000 companies worldwide, including the largest British companies. A general description of the company is provided along with a brief company history and details of products, locations and executives.

Kompass Online
Focuses on products and services produced by a vast number of businesses in 70 countries. Searchable by, *inter alia*, company name, trade name, location and activities.

Amadeus
Lists the top 1.5 million private and public companies in Europe but excludes the vast majority of medium and smaller companies.

One Source
Covers large companies worldwide, giving in-depth company profiles and associated broker reports, press reports. Small and medium companies are dealt with more briefly.

Reference Books

D&B Business Register (Information Services Ltd in association with Dun & Bradstreet Ltd)
Aims 'to meet the needs of all those people looking for reliable information about local

businesses'. Published annually since 1996, the 2007-8 edition extends to 31 volumes and provides, *inter alia*, contact details, status, activity and often date of establishment for a huge number of businesses. Its constituency is businesses having more than five employees or an annual turnover exceeding £250,000.

Britain's Top Privately Owned Companies (Jordans Ltd)
Lists 8,000 private British companies with an annual turnover exceeding c.£7 million. Contact details and financial data are provided. First published 1981.

Kelly's Industrial Directory (Reed Business Information Ltd)
Published for over 100 years, this records contact and activity details for c.90,000 businesses arranged in one alphabetical sequence. Qualification for inclusion is not obvious.

Key British Enterprises (Information Services Ltd in association with Dun & Bradstreet Ltd)
Covers about 50,000 businesses. In 2005 the qualifications for inclusion were 80 or more employees or turnover exceeding c.£8 million or total assets of c.£30 million. Arranged by name of company, it includes, *inter alia*, contact details, date of formation, status, activity, parent company, brief financial data and number of employees. First published 1961.

Kompass Register (Reed Business Information Ltd)
Lists businesses by different criteria in four volumes, viz.: products and services; company information; parents and subsidiaries; and industrial trade names. The parents and subsidiaries volume lists around 200,000 businesses by name of parent for which contact details are given. Dormant and associated companies are included.

Regional Leads Report (Keynote Ltd)
Helps users 'target and evaluate companies in a particular region of the UK or a particular business sector'. It covers about 500,000 entities, arranged by county, in 100 or so volumes. Contact details, activity, date of incorporation, financial details and other data are provided. Qualifications for inclusion are active trading and assets exceeding £25,000. Now in its 20th edition.

Waterlow Stock Exchange Year Book (CaritasData Ltd)
This annual publication 'is the leading reference for companies listed on the London and Irish Stock Exchanges'. Its constituency is therefore relatively narrow. Contact details, principal subsidiaries, previous names, company history, capital history and other details are given for each listed company. The publication traces its origins to 1876 when it was known as *Stock Exchange Year Book*; it was renamed *Stock Exchange Official Year Book* in 1934 and later *International Stock Exchange Official Year Book*. In 1934 it merged with *Stock Exchange Official Intelligence*, first published in 1882 and known as *Burdett's Official Intelligence* until 1899. A connected publication is *The Register of Defunct and Other Companies Removed from the Stock Exchange Year Book* for which *see* p.6.

Waterlow's Unquoted Companies (CaritasData Ltd)
Published annually since 1986 and formerly known as *Macmillan's Unquoted Companies*, it profiles 20,000 leading unquoted British companies.

Who Owns Whom: United Kingdom and Republic of Ireland
    (AP Information Services Ltd in association with Dun & Bradstreet Ltd)
Published annually since 1958, this lists around 150,000 subsidiary companies under the name of their parent whose contact details are given. These subsidiaries, including dormant ones, often go unlisted in other sources. Subsidiaries are defined as businesses in which the parent has at least a 51 per cent interest. No size qualification for inclusion exists.

Dissolved and Renamed Registered Companies

If a business cannot be located in the current Companies House online index or in current reference books, the chances are that it is dissolved, has changed its name or operates in a very small way. Unfortunately, comparatively few sources list dissolved or renamed companies, the most important ones being those at Companies House. Of these, Companies House's online index, referred to above, covers only dissolutions and name changes since the mid-1980s. Indexes in traditional formats have to be consulted in all other cases.

The pre-online indexes of Companies House are either in microfiche or index card form. From the mid-1970s, indexes on microfiche were kept for the first time and could be purchased by users to facilitate remote ordering of documentation. The indexes were for name changes dating from 1976 and for dissolved companies dating from 1963.

In searching for earlier dissolutions and name changes, a card index now kept at the headquarters of Companies House in Cardiff should be consulted. This is no longer directly available to the public but Companies House staff answer written and telephone requests for information from it. This index includes all businesses incorporated, dissolved and renamed prior to the introduction of microfiche; there can be no doubt about its importance in finding details of the fate of registered companies but its relative inaccessibility is an obvious disadvantage.

Dissolved Scottish companies are also included in the Cardiff-based index while, in addition, the National Archives of Scotland holds card indexes for Scottish dissolutions/name changes from the mid-19th century to 1979; it is not known if these are comprehensive.

A less obvious but far more accessible source of information about, *inter alia*, dissolved registered companies is the *London* and *Edinburgh Gazettes* (www.gazettes-online.co.uk). These official government newspapers are discussed in more detail in part six; here it is sufficient to say that their content since the early days of company registration has included notices of dissolution of registered companies, the insertion of these being required as part of the formal dissolution process. The 1844 Act, for example, required publication in the *Gazettes* of notices about the bankruptcy of registered companies, while the 1856 and 1862 Acts required an announcement of the voluntary liquidation of a company and of the final meeting of its shareholders called to approve the liquidator's account. As the *Gazettes* have now been digitised, such notices can be located and read online without charge.

Various reference books published brief details of company dissolutions extracted from the notices published in the *Gazettes*. The most notable was *Stubbs' Year Book and Gazette Index*, published annually from 1870 until well into the 20th century. It listed company dissolutions and gave the appropriate *Gazette* page number. It therefore acted, as its name suggests, as a *Gazette* index. However, copies, especially complete sets, are scarce and difficult to locate. A sister publication was *Stubbs' Weekly Gazette*, formerly known as *Bankrupt and Insolvent Calendar*.

In Liquidation.
In the Matter of the Companies Acts 1862, and
  in the Matter of the Brenkburne Iron and
  Coal Company Limited.

*THE creditors of the above-named Company
  are required, on or before the 11th day
of April, 1870, to send their names and addresses,
and the particulars of their debts or claims,
and the names and addresses of their Solicitors (if
any), addressed to Herbert John Marshall, of Poul-
ton Cricklade, in the county of Wilts, the Liquidator of the said Company, and, if so required by
notice in writing from me, the said Herbert John
Marshall, are, by their Solicitors, to come in and
prove their said debts or claims at such time and
place as shall be specified in such notice, or in
default thereof they will be excluded from the
benefit of any distribution made before such debts
are proved.—Dated this 21st day of February,
1870.*

H. J. Marshall, *Liquidator.*

The Norwegian Copper Company Limited.

*NOTICE is hereby given, that a General
  Meeting of the Shareholders of the above
Company will be held at No. 53, Moorgate-
street, in the city of London, on Wednesday, the
30th day of March, 1870, at eleven of the clock in
the forenoon, for the purpose of having the accounts
produced and laid before them, and hearing the
explanation of the Liquidator thereon, and as to
the manner in which the winding-up has been conducted since the Resolution was passed for winding
up the Company, and to finally wind up the said
Company, and close the accounts thereof.—Dated
this 23rd day of February, 1870.*

William Colman, *Liquidator.*

*AT an Extraordinary General Meeting of the
  Shareholders of the British and Irish
Magnetic Telegraph Company Limited, duly convened and held at the Law Association Rooms,
Cook-street, Liverpool, in the county of Lancaster, on the 4th day of January, 1870, the following Special Resolution was duly passed; and at
a subsequent Extraordinary General Meeting of
the Shareholders of the said Company, also duly
convened and held at the same place, on the 1st
day of February, 1870, the same was duly confirmed:—*

  " That to facilitate the distribution of the
assets, the Company be wound up voluntarily."

W. Langton, *Chairman.*

1   *The official government newspapers, the*
London Gazette *and the* Edinburgh Gazette
*include notices of the dissolution of registered
companies, such as those left, which appeared in
the* London Gazette *on 25 February 1870. As
digitised copy of these newspapers can be searched
online, these notices constitute a convenient means
of discovering if and when a registered company
was dissolved.*

The only other significant reference book for dissolved companies is *The Register of Defunct and Other Companies* (last edition 1990), which listed companies removed from the *Stock Exchange Official Year Book* and its predecessor publications since 1875. It therefore included only the relatively small number of public companies quoted on the London Stock Exchange. Nevertheless, the 1990 edition listed over 25,000 such companies, giving for each registration date, former names, details of capital returned to shareholders, year of winding up and year when removed from the *Year Book*. Subsequent removals are published annually in *Waterlow Stock Exchange Year Book* (see p.4).

Partnerships and Individual Traders

The sources discussed so far relate almost entirely to registered companies, and omit a huge number of other businesses that operated either as partnerships or individual traders. Before the coming of company registration in 1844, virtually all businesses adopted one or other of these forms of ownership, the exceptions being the tiny minority of businesses created by special Act of Parliament or royal charter.

Even after the introduction of company registration, ownership by partnership or individual trader remained the norm for many years. Only in the last decades of the 19th century did registered companies become numerically significant. Therefore, the Companies House's indexes described above only really come into their own when tracing the history of 20th century businesses; other sources have to be found for the earlier period. Two of these are particularly important, one being the official government newspapers, the *London Gazette* and the *Edinburgh Gazette* (*see* Part Six), the other being trade directories (*see* Part Seven). The significance of the *Gazettes* as a source of details for dissolved registered companies has already been dealt with. The information they carry about private partnerships is equally important.

Partnerships and Individual Traders:
Official Government Newspapers as an Information Source

The *London Gazette*, which was established in 1665 when it was briefly known as the *Oxford Gazette*, and the *Edinburgh Gazette*, which first appeared in 1680 (www.gazettes-online.co.uk), were charged with publishing official information on behalf of the Crown and central government. While the *London Gazette* has been in continuous publication ever since, the *Edinburgh Gazette* appeared only intermittently until 1793 but since then has been published without interruption. For much of their history, both were published twice weekly.

The content of the *Gazettes* is wide-ranging, their staple being 'state intelligence' touching on Acts of Parliament, proclamations and orders in council; ecclesiastical, civil and military appointments and promotions; the award of honours and decorations; advertisements for government contracts; and a mass of other intelligence, much of it commercial and business related. Most notable in the present context is the inclusion of notices about bankruptcy and dissolutions of partnerships. Over the years information about insolvency has remained a vital element of their content; they remain the official source of UK personal and corporate insolvency data.

The *London Gazette*, from at least the beginning of the 18th century, published notices about the bankruptcy of individuals and informed creditors and others about subsequent meetings to examine the bankrupt, to prove his or her debts, to make payments to creditors or to otherwise arrange a settlement, and finally to release the individual from bankruptcy. These notices are light on detail, providing not a great deal more than the bankrupt's name, address and occupation, although sometimes details of asset sales and partnership names are given. Lacking in detail they might be, but these notices nevertheless serve as invaluable markers for the demise of early businesses. For archives relating to bankruptcy *see* pp.61-4.

Just as useful are notices of the dissolution of partnerships. These had nothing to do with bankruptcy proceedings; rather they announced to customers and suppliers the winding up of a partnership and the procedure for settling debts and making payments. Once again few, but valuable, details are given – names of partners and partnership, address, activity and date of dissolution. Very occasionally other information is provided such as an explanation for dissolution and the name of a successor partnership.

The number of notices of dissolution and bankruptcy published in the *Gazettes* grew steadily over time. Few partnership dissolution notices appeared before 1750 but by 1800 around 700 were published annually, rising to about three thousand in 1850 and remaining at that level

THE Commissioners in a Commission of Bankrupt awarded and issued forth against William Betts Bird, late of Yarmouth, in the County of Norfolk, Linen-Draper, Dealer and Chapman, intend to meet on the 17th Day of October next, at Twelve o'Clock at Noon, at Guildhall, London, (by Adjournment from the 26th of September instant,) in order to take the Last Examination of the said Bankrupt; when and where he is required to surrender himself and make a full Disclosure and Discovery of his Estate and Effects, and finish his Examination; and the Creditors, who have not already proved their Debts, are to come prepared to prove the same, and, with those who have already proved their Debts, are to assent to or dissent from the Allowance of his Certificate.

THE Commissioners in a Commission of Bankrupt awarded and issued forth against James Andrew, of Manchester, in the County of Lancaster, and Thomas Mason, of Saint Swithin's-Lane, in the City of London, Cotton-Merchants, Dealers, Chapmen, and Copartners, intend to meet on the 24th Day of October next, at Spencer's Tavern, in the Market-Place, in Manchester aforesaid, at Four of the Clock in the Afternoon, in order to receive the Proof of the Separate Debts of the said James Andrew, under the said Commission.

THE Commissioners in a Commission of Bankrupt awarded and issued forth against Jonathan Sherwood, of Birmingham, in the County of Warwick, Sadler, intend to meet on the 4th Day of November next, at Four of the Clock in the Afternoon, at the Public-Office, in Birmingham aforesaid in order to make a Final Dividend of the Estate and Effects of the said Bankrupt; when and where the Creditors, who have not already proved their Debts, are to come prepared to prove the same, or they will be excluded the Benefit of the said Dividend. And all Claims not then proved will be disallowed.

THE Commissioners in a Commission of Bankrupt awarded and issued forth against Thomas Paul, late of North Shields, in the County of Northumberland, Butcher, intend to meet on the 28th Day of October next, at Eleven in the Forenoon, at William Loftus's, the Shakespeare Tavern, in Newcastle-upon-Tyne, in order to make a First and Final Dividend of the Estate and Effects of the said Bankrupt; when and where the Creditors, who have not already proved their Debts, are to come prepared to prove the same, or they will be excluded the Benefit of the said Dividend. And all Claims not then proved will be disallowed.

THE Commissioners in a Commission of Bankrupt awarded and issued against John Elston, of Liverpool, in the County of Lancaster, Merchant, intend to meet on the 22d of October next, at Eleven in the Forenoon, at the Globe-Tavern, John-Street, in Liverpool aforesaid, to make a Dividend of the Estate and Effects of the said Bankrupt; when and where the Creditors, who have not already proved their Debts, are to come prepared to prove the same, or they will be excluded the Benefit of the said Dividend. And all Claims not then proved will be disallowed.

2 *Notices relating to bankruptcy were published, as required in law, in the* London *and* Edinburgh Gazettes. *Examples, appearing in the* London Gazette *in 1801, are reproduced here. The* Gazettes *are a convenient source for discovering details of when and how a business 'disappeared', as they have been digitised and can be searched online.*

NOtice is hereby given, that the Partnership lately subsisting between Thomas Robinson, Robert Robinson, and Joseph Heywood, all of Manchester, in the County of Lancaster, Merchants, carrying on Trade under the Firm of Robinsons and Heywood, was dissolved on the 1st Day of January 1799, by mutual Consent. The Business hath since been and still is carried on by the said Robert Robinson and Joseph Heywood, at Manchester aforesaid, under the Firm of Robinson and Heywood. Witness our Hands the 19th Day of August 1801. Thos. Robinson. Rob. Robinson. Jos. Heywood.

THE Partnership between us Francis Moyser, of Topcliffe, in the County of York, and John Rotherford and John Potter, of Stamford-Bridge Mills, in the said County, Millers, was this Day dissolved by mutual Consent; and all Debts due from or to the said Partnership will be respectively paid and received by the said John Rotherford and John Potter: As witness our Hands this 18th of July 1801. Fras. Moyser. John Rotherford. John Potter.

Liverpool, August 15, 1801. NOtice is hereby given, that the Partnership between Ralph Hewitt, Joseph Woodyer, and James Whiteley, all of Liverpool, under the Firm of Woodyer, Whiteley, and Co. as Grocers and Linen-Merchants, was dissolved on the present 15th Day of August 1801. All Debts owing to and by the said Concern will be paid and received by Joseph Woodyer, who is authorised to settle the same. Witness our Hands this 15th Day of August 1801. Ralph Hewitt. Joseph Woodyer. James Whiteley.

THE Partnership between Meredith Swancott and Andrew Savage, of Foster-Lane, London, Baize-Factors and Partners, is this Day dissolved by mutual Consent. Witness our Hands, this 21st of August 1801. Meredith Swancott. Andrew Savage.

3 *Notices of the dissolution of partnerships were published in large numbers in the* London *and* Edinburgh Gazettes, *although as publication was not required in law not all dissolutions were included. Examples of notices, appearing in the* London Gazette *in 1801, are reproduced here.*

in 1900. As the publication of such notices was not required in law but was done for the sake of good business practice, it is not known what proportion of total dissolutions this figure represents but it is probably quite high. Bankruptcy notices on the other hand were required in law and were more numerous. They were being published from at least the beginning of the 18th century and numbers rose steadily from around two thousand in 1785 to about five thousand annually by 1850, to about ten thousand by 1900.

HOL

1799, Mar. 9—Holbrooke R. farmer, Hendon, Middlesex. [Clarke, Warren street; Fitzroy square], cert. May 21, 99.

1799, Apr. 6—Holder William, clothier, Painswick, Gloucester. [Vizard, Gray's inn; Gardiner, Minchinhampton] cert. June 22, 99; div. Nov. 20, 99; Oct. 20, 04.

1799, June 29—Holmes J. dealer, Newbold-upon-Avon, Warwick. [Fox, Rugby] div. Jan. 9, 02; Sept. 13, 02.

1799, Nov. 23 {Holt Charles jewellers, Hatton wall. {cert. May 13,} div. June and [Gem, Birmingham;} 1800. 21, 03. Edward Davis, Bolton, Temple]

1800, May 24—Holloway Daniel, innholder, Aylesbury, Bucks. [Rose and Co. Gray's inn; Adams. Aylesbury] div. Dec. 1, 00; Dec. 8, 04, final.

1800, June 24—Holland John, butcher, Nottingham. [Holmes, Mark lane; Enfield, Nottingham] cert. Aug. 8, 01; div. July 1, 01.

1800, Oct. 18—Holt James, jun. rope maker, Manchester. [Ellis, Cursitor street; Knight, Manchester].

1800, Dec. 20—Holland William, linen draper, Southwark. [Ludlow and Co. Monument yard] div. Nov. 5, 01; Dec. 22, 04, final.

1801, Jan. 17—Holmes John, ironmonger, Leeds. [Battye, Chancery lane; Wainwright, Leeds] superseded, Feb. 23, 02.

1801, Mar. 7—Holman James-C. money scrivener, Mount street. [Brace, Essex court, Temple].

1801, May 5—Holmes W. drysalter, Pudsey, Yorkshire. [Battye, Chancery lane; Lee, Leeds] cert. June 7, 06; div. June 17, 02; July 29, 02; July 13, 03; Nov. 14, 03.

1801, May 16—Holden Richard, gun maker, Birmingham. [Hore and Cave, Essex street; Smith, Birmingham] cert. Oct. 10, 01; div. Sept. 21, 02.

1801, June 2—Holland Thomas, woollen draper, Bedford bury, Covent garden. [Berry, Mead's court, Soho] div. Sept. 18, 02; Jan. 22, 03; Mar. 25, 06.

1801, July 25—Holmes Thomas, cordwainer, Oxford. [Philpot, Red-lion square; Tubb, Oxford] cert. June 29, 05.

1801, Aug. 4 {Holmes John, army brokers, Craven {cert. Nov. 14, 01,} div. Feb. and street. [Dyne, Ser-} div. Feb. 7, 04, 7, 04. James Palmer, jeants' inn] {cert. Nov. 14, 01,}

1801, Nov. 24—Holmes Samuel, merchant, Thomas street, Southwark. [Carter and Co. Prescott street] cert. June 5, 02; div. Dec. 10, 03.

1801, Dec. 8—Holt Charles, warehouseman, Leather lane. [Abbot, Chancery lane] cert. March 2, 02.

1801, Dec. 22—Holmes William, mercer, Otley, York. [Sykes, New inn; Barrett, Otley] div. Aug. 23, 02.

1802, Feb. 9 {Holmes John-Edward merchants, Crosby {cert. Apr. 14, 04.} div. and square. [Walton,} Jan. William Hall, Girdler's hall] {cert. Apr. 14, 04.} 17, 03.

1802, Apr. 13—Hollyoch William, butcher, Camberwell, Surrey. [Warrand, Arundel street.]

1802, Aug. 10—Holder William-Compton, scrivener, Ross, Hereford. [Taylor, Gray's inn; Holder, Rudford].

1802, Dec. 4—Holloway John-Peter, wine, spirit, and beer merchant, St. Swithin's lane. [Wadeson and Co. Austinfriars] cert. June 25, 03; div. Nov. 8, 03; Jan. 25, 06.

1802, Dec. 7 {Holloway John-Peter, merchants, London. {cert. May 10, 03. and [Marson, Newington,} Michael Curtis. Surrey]

1803, Feb. 15 {Holbrow D.-T. manufacturers of div. James Haynes, chemical prepa- {cert. May 10, 03; Nov. 2, Thomas Haynes, rations, Old {cert. May 10, 03; 03; Sep. and Landmill. [Ga- 22, 04, R. Henderson, bell, Lincoln's inn] {cert. Mar. 4, 06. final.

1803, Dec. 20—Holden George, jun. merchant, Kingston, Hull. [Rosser, Kirby street; Frost, Hull] div. Nov. 15, 05.

1803, Sept. 13—Holmes David, grocer, Liverpool. [Kearsley, Inner Temple; Manly, Liverpool] div. May 8, 05.

1804, Aug. 4 {Holbrow John dealers, Avening, Gloucester. [Bennett, Dean's and court; Chime, Minchinhampton]. William Holbrow,

4   *From the mid-18th century onwards, lists of bankrupts, based on information extracted from the* London *and* Edinburgh Gazettes, *were published commercially on a regular basis. Although the content of the* Gazettes *is now searchable online, these registers remain useful for browsing when, for example, precise details of the business being researched are not known. Precise contents differ from one publication to another but this page, taken from William Smith's List of Bankrupts (1786-1806), is representative.*

The use of the *Gazettes* for historical research has been hugely enhanced by digitisation; copies can be searched and read without charge at www.gazettes-online.co.uk. Otherwise contemporary annual indexes must be used, which is extremely time-consuming. Complete hard-copy sets of the *Gazettes* are not easily come by but are generally available, sometimes on microfilm, in leading reference and academic libraries. For more details about the history of the *London Gazette see* P.M. Handover, *A History of the London Gazette, 1665-1965* (1965).

Lists of bankrupts, based on information extracted from the *Gazettes*, were published from time to time. Several also list partnership dissolutions. The first seems to have been published in the 1770s but only with the arrival of *Perry's Bankrupt and Insolvent Gazette* in 1828 were bankruptcy details published on a regular basis. These publications rarely survive in libraries but the following are available in the British Library and/or Guildhall Library:

Jarvis, J., *An Alphabetical List of All the Bankrupts, from the first of January 1774 to the thirteen of June 1786 inclusive: With the date of the certificates and supersedures to those who have received them* (London, 1786)

Bailey, William, *List of Bankrupts, Dividends and Certificates from the Year 1772 to 1793: both included with the name and residence of the different solicitors under each* (2 vols, London, 1794).

Smith, William, *A List of Bankrupts with their Dividends, Certificates ... from Jan 1 1786 to June 24 1806* (London, 1806)

Elwick, George, *The Bankrupt Directory: Being a complete register of all the bankrupts, with their residences, trades and dates when they appeared in the London Gazette, from December 1820 to April 1843* (London, 1843)

The Bankrupts' Register for the Year 1832 -1847 (London, 1833-48); also lists dissolved partnerships.

Brough's Alphabetical Gazette: A permanent register of bankrupts, insolvents, assignments, sequestrations, dividends, certificates, partnership dissolutions, notable suspensions, etc, for the purpose of reference (London, 1861); covers part of 1861 only.

Perry's Bankrupt and Insolvent Gazette: Containing a complete register of English, Scotch and Irish bankrupts, insolvents, assignments, assignees, dividends, certificates, dissolution of partnerships, etc (London, 1827-61); continued as *Perry's Bankrupt Weekly Gazette* (London, 1862-81) and as *Perry's Gazette* (1882-1964); this appears to have its origins in the monthly *Solicitors', Merchants', Traders' Magazine* (1826).

Seyd, Richard, *Record of Failures and Liquidations in the Financial, International, Wholesale and Manufacturing Branches of Commerce (including drapers and ironmongers, exclusive of small mechanical and retail trades, professional pursuits, etc) in the United Kingdom from 1865 to 1884* (c.1884)

Stubbs & Co's Commercial Year Book and Gazette Index (from 1870); a connection was *Stubbs' Weekly Gazette*.

Partnerships, Individual Traders and other Businesses:
Trade Directories as an Information Source

The second source of information about partnerships and individual traders, as well as registered companies, is published trade directories. These are dealt with more fully later (*see* pp.125-32) and therefore only brief reference is made to them here. Directories listing businesses active in individual counties, cities and large towns began to appear regularly from the mid-18th century and, before the advent of the telephone directory, were a vital means of linking suppliers with customers and vice versa.

The earliest directories were mostly limited to London but from the 1760s they were published on a small scale for other cities. For a brief period in the 1780s and 1790s national directories were published but these were soon defeated by the inbuilt difficulties – not least high costs – of accurate data collection on such a scale. By the early decades of the 19th century, directories were published regularly, if not annually, for virtually all counties and many major cities in Britain. At the same time, they became more accurate and the arrangement of their content more sophisticated, as a simple alphabetical listing of businesses was supplemented in many cases with listings by address and activity.

The usefulness of directories in tracing the history of a business is based on an implicit assumption that the year a business is first listed is the year of its formation and the last listing is its year of dissolution. This, of course, might be misleading if the business was renamed or moved to an address outside the area covered by the directory. However, confirmation one way or the other is sometimes possible through reference to the address and business activity sections of successor directories, while it should also be noted that, at this time, the distant relocation of businesses was rare.

Complementing trade directories are telephone directories and the *Yellow Pages*; indeed, it was the telephone directory that rang the death knell of the trade directory. Local telephone directories were first published in the last two decades of the 19th century when the majority of subscribers were businesses. Their survival rate is generally poor although British Telecom's archives (www.btplc.com/Thegroup/BtsHistory) have a more or less complete set from 1880 which is available from www.ancestry.co.uk. Others can be found in national libraries and in good reference libraries. Guildhall Library also has London and other directories from 1880.

Newly Registered Companies:
Published Information at Time of Registration

Schedules giving core details of newly registered companies were published regularly from the beginning of company registration. These give the date of formation and other core information extracted from Companies House records (perhaps from classified index sheets, for which *see* p.52). However, as cumulative indexes to these schedules do not exist, locating a particular company could be time consuming, especially if an approximate date of formation is not known.

Perhaps the most useful of these sources is the annual returns of newly formed joint stock companies published annually between 1845 and 1906 in Parliamentary Papers (*see* pp.139-41), although no returns seem to have been made for much of the 1850s. These returns were published under the title of 'Return of Companies Formed or Registered ...', or derivations of this title, and include brief details of all companies registered in England, Scotland and Wales in the previous 12 months. While content varied over time, for most years it included, for each new company, date of registration, objects/activity, place of business, number of shareholders and details of capital. Each annual listing is arranged in order of date of registration and indexed by name of company. Guildhall Library has a set of returns, 1866 to 1900 (and also, somewhat oddly, a return for 1856 in typescript), that have been extracted and conveniently bound together in 10 volumes (48 hours' notice for use is required). Digitised copy also exists at www.parlipapers.chadwyck.co.uk, although this online service is chargeable if not accessed via a reference library.

Another source is *Investors' Guardian*, initially known as *Investors' Guardian and Limited Liability Review*, published weekly between 1863 and 1973. Its description of newly registered companies is broadly similar to that of Parliamentary Papers and includes, for each company, registration number, address, amount of capital and details of capital structure, objects/activity, and name and address of subscribers to articles of association. After 1900 this data becomes less detailed but even in the 1950s included activity, address, directors' names, amount of capital, company type and registration number. Although new company details make up most of its content, it also carried reports on company general meetings and leading articles. A company name index was published half-yearly. Its chief competitor was *Jordan's Daily Register of New Companies*, published between 1914 and 1971; when first published its full title was *Jordan's Daily Register of New Companies Compiled from Official Sources*. Its lists closely resemble those of *Investors' Guardian*.

RETURN of Joint Stock Companies, made up to December 1882.—I. COMPANIES Formed and Registered under the Companies Act, 1862, as Limited Companies—*continued.*

No.	Name of Company.	Objects.	Place of Business.	Date of Registration.	Number of Persons who Signed the Memorandum of Association.	Total Number of Shares taken by Subscribers to Memorandum of Association.	Nominal Capital.	Number of Shares into which it is Divided.	Number of Shares taken.	Amount of Calls made on each Share.	Total Amount of Calls Received.	Number of Shareholders in Company at Date of last Return.	Whether still in Operation or being Wound up.
	ENGLAND—*continued.*			1882:			£.			£. s. d.	£. s. d.		
956	Elastic Lock-Stitch Sewing Machine Company (Limited).	Sewing machine makers and machinists.	32, Brown-street, Manchester.	24 Aug.	8	243	2,200	440	410	5 - -	2,050 - -	14	Supposed to be still in operation.
957	Allan and Burnhouse Gill Mining Company (Limited).	Acquiring and working lead and other mines at Ridley, Northumberland.	7, Market-place, Hexham	25 Aug.	7	7	10,000	8,000	2,045	On 1,731, 1 l. 5 s. On 314, 7 s. 6 d.	2,281 10 -	36	- ditto.
958	Aberdna Lead Mines (Limited).	Mining and quarrying for lead, calamine, and other minerals at Llanferras and elsewhere in the counties of Denbigh and Flint.	30, Great St. Helens, E.C.	25 Aug.	7	35	37,500	25,000	12,730	1 10 -	15,482 6 3 (considered as paid).	80	- ditto.
959	Anglo-Norwegian Guano, Phosphate and Isinglass Company (Limited).	Acquiring and working certain letters patent for improvements in the manufacture of isinglass, gelatine, and glue.	Dashwood House, 9, New Broad-street, E.C.	25 Aug.	7	7	100,000	100,000	7	Nil	Nil - -	7	- ditto.
960	Gold Amalgamating Company (Limited).	Acquiring and working letters patent (dated 2nd August 1881) for "ore grinding and amalgamating machines."	Dashwood House, New Broad-street, E.C.	25 Aug.	7	7	150,000	150,000	No return	No return	No return	No return	No information.
961	Jarrow Cement Company (Limited).	Carrying on the business of cement manufacturers, miners, metal extractors, smelters, &c.	Works, Jarrow-on-Tyne	25 Aug.	7	7	30,000	3,000	654	5 - -	2,500 - -	8	Supposed to be still in operation.
962	Finance Syndicate (Limited)	Transacting every kind of banking, discount, bill brokerage, and financial business.	96, Palmerston Buildings, Old Broad-street, E.C.	25 Aug.	7	7	2,000	40	30	30 - -	750 - -	10	- ditto.
963	S. H. Beckles and Co. (Limited).	Acquiring and carrying on the business of Messrs. S. H. Beckles & Co., Lime-street-square, E.C., chemical manufacturers, drysalters, &c.	6 and 8, Lime-street-square, E.C.	26 Aug.	7	2,005	20,000	20,000	6,098	On 93, 5 s.	6,015 8 - (of which 6,000 l. considered as paid, and 5 l. paid in advance of calls).	20	- ditto.
964	Tilbury District Freehold Brick Works (Limited).	Making and selling bricks, tiles, pipes, terra-cotta, &c, at Corringham, Essex.	10, Bedford-row, W.C.	26 Aug.	7	115	30,000	3,000	115	Nil	Nil - -	7	- ditto.

5 *A source for locating details of newly formed registered companies is the annual returns published between 1845 and 1906 in Parliamentary Papers. Once these suffered from being somewhat inaccessible but they have now been digitised, along with Parliamentary Papers generally, and are available online. The above is an extract from the 1882 returns.*

D.
xed

NEW BALLA BALLA COPPER MINES, LD. (69,844).—
Regd Apl. 16, with cap £2,000, in £1 shs, to acquire the bus
of Balla Balla Copper Mines, Ld. (incorpd in 1898) and to cy on
the bus of miners, financiers, agents, contractors, engrs, etc.
No initial public issue. The first dirs are to be appointed by
the Balla Balla Copper Mines, Ld. Regd by Dale, Newman
and Hood, 75-6, Cornhill, E.C.

cap
ank
cy
ers,
and
etc.
res
1
1
1
1
1
1
han
and
egd
ith
rs,
rs,
of

NORTH MIDDLESEX PUBLISHING CO, LD. (69,870).—
Regd Apl. 18, with cap £2,000, in 10s shs, to cy on in London,
Middlesex, Essex and Herts the bus of newspr proprs, printers,
publishers, newsvendors, etc. No initial public issue. The no
of dirs is not to be less than 3 nor more than 5 ; the first are
J. Pedley, H. Nield and G. L. Wilson ; qualn £25. Regd by
Pedley and Co, 28, Bush La, E.C.

OXCROFT COLLIERY CO, LD. (69,845).—Regd Apl. 16,
in £1 shs, to acquire from A. B. Markham, M.P., the benefit of an agmt for the lease from the Duke of
Devonshire of certain mining rights and minerals known as
Oxcroft, situate nr Bolsover, Derby, and to cy on the bus of
coal and ironmasters, iron and steel mfrs, colly proprs, coke
mfrs, miners, smelters, chemical mfrs, etc. The subs are:
                                                    Shares
A .B. Markham, Stuffynwood Hall, Mansfield, M.P. 1
W. B. M. Bird, 58, Cadogan Pl, S.W., gent 1
C. B. B. McLaren, 43, Belgrave Sq, S.W., M.P............... 1
D. Vickers, Banner Cross, Sheffield, steel mfr 1
M. Deacon, Wittington Hse, nr Chesterfield, ironmaster ... 1
F. W. Preston, Barton Latimer, Kettering, ironmaster ... 1
C. W. J. Stoddart, Blenheim Hse, Rotherham, gent 1
   No initial public issue. The no of dirs is not to be less than
2 nor more than 5 ; the first are A. B. Markham, M.P., Sir C.
McLaren, M.P., M. Deacon and W. B. M. Bird ; qualn £2,000 ;
remun £400 per ann and a sh in the profits, div. Regd by
Bird, Moore and Strode, Gray's Inn, W.C.

egd
and
vay
urn
ns,
ra-
ca-
and
rs,
res
100
100

100

100

100
100
100
to
rd,
at-
its,

PATENT SLACK ADJUSTER, LD. (69,846).—Regd. Apl.
16, with cap £18,000, in £5 shs, to adopt an agmt with W.
McLaren and L. B. Peters (trading as G. D. Peters and Co.)
and G. Spencer Moulton and Co, Ld, and to cy on the bus of
mfrs of patent slack adjusters, engrs, mfrs of rolling stock,
boiler mkrs, metal workers, smiths, etc. The subs are: Shs
W. McLaren, Moorgate Wks, Moorfields, E.C., mfr 20
L. B. Peters, Moorgate Wks, Moorfields, engr 20
A. G. Spencer, 77, Cannon St, E.C., engr 20
A. Spencer, 77, Cannon St, E.C., engr 20
W. E. Sheffield, 77, Church St, Stoke Newington, N., clk 20
W. Kimon, 19, Gayton Rd, Hampstead, N.W., acct 1
D. M. Sutherland, 343, Victoria Pk Rd, N.E., clk 1
   No initial public issue. The first dirs are W. McLaren and
L. B. Peters (nominees of G. D. Peters and Co.) and A.
Spencer and A. G. Spencer (nominees of G. Spencer Moulton
and Co, Ld. The first dirs are permt ; qualn £100. Regd by
R. J. Twyford, 69, Moorgate St, E.C.

egd
igs
he-
ney
No
uor
as ;
on,

PERRANPORTH WATER CO, LD. (69,858).—Regd Apl.
17, with cap £8,000, in £10 shs, to supply water to Perranporth, and Mithin, Cornwall, and to cy on the bus of a water-
works co in all its branches. Regd without arts of assn. The
first dirs are J. R. Daniell, J. V. Thomas, E. Andrews, F. K.
Baker, T. S. Lowry, A. A. Richards and T. Negus. Regd by
Robbins, Billing and Co., 218, Strand, W.C.

egd
of
at
and
na-
rs,
olic
ton
00.

RADEMAKER, LD.(69,887).—Regd Apl. 19, with cap £2,500
in £1 shs, to cy on the bus of cocoa and chocolate mfrs. N
initial public issue. Regd without arts of assn. Regd office,
Quinton Rd, Coventry.

SILVERTHORN AND CO, LD. (69,888).—Regd Apl. 19,
with cap £2,000, in £1 shs, to acquire and take over as a going
concern the bus cd on by Elizabeth A. Silverthorn and to cy
cy on the bus of boot and shoe mchts, mfrs and dirs and leather
mchts in all its branches. No initial public issue. The no of
dirs is not to be less than 2 nor more than 5 ; the first are R.
T. Copley and C. Silverthorn, who shall have power to appoint
one other dir before the first general meeting ; qualn £50 ; remun
as fixed by the co. C. Silverthorn is the first managing director. Regd by James Mellor and Coleman, 12, Coleman St, E.C.

pl.
een
and
as
lly
im-
een
all
res
1
1
1
1
1
k 1
1
1
mt
by

SMOKELESS CHIMNEY CO, LD. (69,889).—Regd Apl. 19,
with cap £60,000, in £1 shs, to acquire the patent numbered
22,614 of 1897, known as Lowe's Patent Smoke Preventer, and
any improvements thereon, to take over the bus heretofore cd
on by the Smokeless Chimney Co, Ld, and to cy on the bus
of mfg and dealing in all commodities and things which can
be conveniently manufactured or dealt in by the company in
connection therewith. The subs are: Shs
R. Smith, 6, Bellair Pl, Chorlton-on-Matlock, Manchr,
      cashier 1
F. W. Blakemore, 17, Mackworth St, Hulme, Manchr,
      shorthand writer 1
R. Heywood, 21, Church Rd, Middleton Junction, clk 1
T. Richardson, 79, Church St, Warrington, clk 1
J. Bladow, 16 Lancaster Rd Fallowfield, clk 1

6   *Periodicals published details of newly formed
registered companies on a regular basis. Best known
was the* Investors' Guardian, *published between
1863 and 1973, and an extract from an 1899 issue
is reproduced here. Details tended to become briefer
over time. This source is especially useful – although
it suffers from being relatively inaccessible – after
1906 when returns of newly formed companies were
no longer made to Parliament.*

Published Histories of Businesses

Details of the history of a business may,
of course, have already been published,
obviating the need for research in the
sources described above. Publication
might be in the form of a book, brochure
or periodical article. It might simply be an
entry in a reference book such as a gazetteer
and dictionary. All these publications are
covered in the section on published histories
of businesses (*see* pp.80-5). Taken as a whole,
these publications cover the histories of tens
of thousands of businesses.

APPROACHING THE BUSINESS

Having discovered basic information about a
business, if it still exists then the researcher
might well want to make contact with it.
The business could be helpful in a number
of ways.

It could refer the researcher to a published
house history or to relevant newspaper or
periodical articles or even provide a photocopy
of an unpublished typescript history.
Alternatively it could put the researcher in
touch with others who have already investigated
its history or otherwise create introductions to
retired staff or their families or to members
of the founding family. Not least, it could give
access to its archives. However, before making
any approach to the business, it might be as
well to work out a strategy for it; a second
opportunity might not easily occur after a
botched first attempt. Remember that the
business has no obligation to help and that, in
some instances, data protection requirements
could complicate matters.

A tiny number of businesses manage their
archives in-house through the appointment
of an archivist, who administers access to
archives and responds generally to enquiries.
This group includes some of the largest
businesses in the country; the smallness of

their number is compensated for by the quantity and quality of their archives together with the archives of their active and defunct subsidiaries.

At least some corporate archives are listed in ARCHON, the online directory to record offices maintained by the National Register of Archives (www.nra.nationalarchives.gov.uk). The most recently published hard-copy directory is the now somewhat dated Janet Foster and Julia Sheppard, *British Archives* (2002). The Business Archives Council formerly published on a regular basis a directory of the 90 or so of its corporate members that maintained archive facilities. The last edition, Lesley Richmond and Alison Turton, *Directory of Corporate Archives* (1997), is now substantially out of date but continues to give a good overview of this group of business archives.

The majority of businesses, of course, make no formal provision for the care and administration of their archives, which means that, *inter alia*, their archives are neither listed nor centralised and the significance of them probably goes unrecognised. That said, it is fair to say that most businesses attempt to be as helpful as possible to researchers although some will doubtless view co-operation as unproductive and distracting. Others may feel uneasy about issues of confidentiality. In approaching a business, the following hints might prove helpful, viz:

- Applications are often best made in writing and should indicate the reasons for seeking access and the questions to which answers are sought. They may well be more effective if addressed to a senior manager by name. A telephone call could follow up a letter.

- Requests for a great deal of help – at least in the first instance – might cause reluctance to co-operate simply because the business cannot provide the level of support required. Ask for a little to start with, more later.

- Remember that access is a privilege and not a right and that an assertion of a 'right to see' can cause irritation.

- Advantages to the business through co-operation could be stressed. Often businesses themselves can make productive use of the results of a researcher's work. Potential uses are set out in 'The Uses of Business Archives', *Record Aids* (1984) and in Alison Turton, 'The public relations uses of business archives' in Alison Turton (ed.), *Managing Business Archives* (1991).

- Co-operation might be more forthcoming if the researcher offers to show research results to the business for reading and comment prior to publication.

Issues touching on access, as seen from the archivist's side of the counter but which also offer insight to the researcher, are dealt with in John Booker 'Access policy', in Alison Turton (ed.), *Managing Business Archives*.

SECTION TWO

Locating Archives of the Business

INTRODUCTION

The sources described in Section One enable a researcher to discover core information about a business operating in the 19th and 20th centuries; given the somewhat meagre sources available for before 1800, less may be known about earlier businesses. For post-1800 businesses, especially ones still active, the chances are that their location is now known. If the business is defunct, the reason for its disappearance may well have been established. Along the way, useful information may have been gleaned about dates of formation and dissolution, name changes and activities. Such basic facts may satisfy the needs of many, if not most, researchers but some will want to know more.

One means of discovering more is to consult the business's archives. If the business is still active it may have retained historical archives, although perhaps uncatalogued, dispersed, uncared for and even unknown! Alternatively, its archives may have been deposited in a record office and be available there for research. The purpose of this section is to deal with issues surrounding the location of archives.

But before setting out to use and find archives it makes sense for the researcher to consider whether access to archives is, in fact, necessary. This is because archive-based research is often time consuming and requires some pre-knowledge of business archives in order to be successful. It may well be vital in academic research leading to scholarly output yet it is equally true that the relatively straightforward needs of most people can be met through use of secondary sources described in Section Three.

In searching for archives it is worth bearing in mind that before the paper explosion of modern times, small and even medium-sized businesses created few archives. Before the mid-19th century, and perhaps even later, the costs of paper and writing materials, widespread illiteracy and innumeracy, and an unsophisticated and undemanding legal and administrative system, except perhaps for businesses dealing in dutiable goods or trading internationally, resulted in minimal record keeping. So even if they survive, the 18th- and 19th-century archives of a typically small business may have limited value. John Armstrong and Stephanie Jones, *Business Documents: Their origins, sources and use to the historian* (1987) deals in its introductory chapter with factors influencing document creation. More generally, this describes and explains the main types of document created by businesses and is useful introductory reading for anyone using business archives.

It should also be borne in mind that the archives of most defunct businesses have not survived. This is largely because the value of business archives for historical research has only been recognised in the last 50 or so years; earlier, very little consideration was given to the preservation of the archives of old businesses when they closed down. But since then, and especially in the last 30 or so years, local and national record offices have made strenuous, if not heroic, efforts to rescue business archives in danger of destruction although, on account of the sheer scale of their task and the finite resources available to them, much will inevitably have been missed.

It is also worth remembering that the archives of a defunct business may well survive in the archives of another organisation. The most obvious instance is when a business is acquired by another – either by purchase, merger or take over – and then wound up or otherwise absorbed so that it does not continue as a separate entity. However, while a business disappears, its archives remain, often lying forgotten in attics and cellars. The banking sector forms an excellent example. In the 19th and 20th centuries, Britain's clearing banks grew to a large extent by acquisition or merger so that their archives today comprise the archives of the hundreds of private, joint stock and other banks they acquired at that time.

A defunct business's archives may also survive amongst the archives of a company that was responsible for its management. An example of this is an investment management company holding the archives of an investment trust company. The archives of solicitors, accountants and other advisers may contain the archives of defunct businesses that they once managed or otherwise advised on behalf of a third party. Other archives of defunct businesses may be held by firms of accountants who acted as liquidators, or by the courts in which they were displayed as exhibits (*see* pp.64-5), or by the business's founding family (*see* p.147).

A word of warning is in order here. Many businesses, especially banks, solicitors and accountants, are rightly concerned to protect the confidentiality of their customers' affairs and this influences their policy regarding access to archives by third parties. Banks, for example, are usually prepared to open up customer records only when they are 100 or more years old; access to more recent archives might be given if the permission of the customer or the customer's successor is forthcoming. Some of these issues – which are not easy to articulate – are considered by John Booker, 'Access policy' in *Managing Business Archives* (1991) and less comprehensively by R.W. Suddards, 'The lawyer and the archivist went down to the filing room', *Archives* (1981).

The archives of many businesses, both defunct and active, are held in record offices. These publicly funded institutions store, organise and catalogue records of historical interest, ensure their preservation and make them available for research. They vary in their focus but no one record office in Britain has specialised in collecting business archives at national level. In other words, no national business archive exists, although some argue for the creation of one to hold the archives of businesses whose activities are nationally or internationally spread and whose archives therefore fall outside the scope of local or regional record offices. So far as business archives are concerned, record offices fall into five broad categories – local, academic, museum, association and national.

Guides to Record Offices

Contact details of all British record offices are available via ARCHON (www.archon.nationalarchives.gov.uk), otherwise 'Archives On-Line', maintained by the National Archives. This is the most important listing and online gateway to UK institutions that collect and/or administer historical archives. It provides contact details of over 2,000 UK institutions including record offices, museums and libraries as well as schools, universities, professional bodies, charities, learned societies and businesses. ARCHON links to record office websites and to multi-level descriptions of their archive holdings, as recorded on the National Register of Archives website, and is a particularly useful feature. ARCHON also lists some 500 overseas repositories in around 50 countries.

Janet Foster and Julia Sheppard (eds), *British Archives* (4th edn, 2002) is the most comprehensive hard-copy guide to UK institutions holding archives; it offers more information per record-holding institution than ARCHON but it is now significantly out of date. Like ARCHON, it covers not just local, specialist and national record offices, but also private holders including businesses. Details of address, specialisation, major collections, publications and guides are listed for each institution. A single consolidated index covers repositories, predecessor organisations and collections.

REGISTERS OF BUSINESS ARCHIVES

In searching for the archives of a particular business, two registers of archives provide a useful starting point.

National Register of Archives (NRA)

The NRA (www.nationalarchives.gov.uk/nra), part of the National Archives, was established in 1945 to act as a central collecting point for information about archival sources for British history. Over half a century later it holds details of the archives of around 200,000 entities, including some 30,000 businesses. Much of this information is taken from catalogues submitted by record offices but some is based on information gleaned from annual reports, newsletters and guides.

The NRA's online indexes cover corporate, family, personal and place names and can be searched to provide collection-level descriptions. Searches for corporate entities can be structured by sector and sub-sector but at present only the final name, not previous names, under which the entity operated is searchable. Online access to the NRA's hard-copy reports is not possible, but where a report has been converted to an electronic format, say via the Access to Archives initiative (q.v.), a link to the new format often exists. Historically, an important feature of the NRA has been its library of hard-copy catalogues or listings which give detailed descriptions of particular collections. These are usually provided by the institution holding the archives and latterly have been received at the rate of around 1,000 new catalogues/listings each year in addition to revisions of catalogues already held.

Each year *Accessions to Repositories* (www.nationalarchives.gov.uk/accessions) is published online, listing deposits notified to the NRA in the previous year. Alex Ritchie, 'Business history and the National Register of Archives', *Business Archives* (2000) provides a useful if slightly dated overview.

National Register of Archives for Scotland (NRAS)

The NRAS (www.nas.gov.uk/nras), which is part of the National Archives of Scotland, operates on similar principles to the NRA; indeed the NRA's online index includes details of collections registered with the NRAS. Its library contains some 4,000 hard-copy catalogues or listings of archive collections in or relating to Scotland and summaries of them can be consulted online. Some catalogues – in particular of archives in private hands – have been compiled by the NRAS itself as part of a longstanding drive to locate and ensure the preservation of

Scottish archives in private hands. Most catalogues have been contributed by Scottish record offices, libraries and, in the case of business archives, by the Business Archives Council of Scotland. The Register's search room is in Edinburgh although copies of all NRAS reports are also held by the NRA in London and by the National Library of Scotland, also in Edinburgh. Summaries of new additions are included each year in the annual report of the Keeper of the Records of Scotland.

ONLINE ACCESS TO ARCHIVE CATALOGUES

Many initiatives are underway to provide online access to information within archive collections. Three of the most notable for business archives are Archives Hub, Scottish Archives Network and Archives Network Wales, but most important of all is Access to Archives.

Access to Archives (A2A)

A2A (www.a2a.org.uk) provides online access to digitised archive catalogues rather than to summary descriptions of them. It is a highly important resource in tracing the history of a business as it not only allows archive catalogues to be consulted on screen but allows simultaneous searching across a huge number of archive catalogues for details of specific businesses. This makes it a very powerful tool indeed, although its usefulness and the effectiveness of searches across it are a function of the level of detail in the individual catalogues digitised. This varies significantly both over time and between record office.

Promoted, *inter alia*, by the National Archives and British Library, this project digitised many thousands of archive catalogues belonging to 400 record offices, libraries and other institutions in England and Wales before being wound up in early 2008. However, many catalogues were not included and access to these will continue to be via paper copy at the National Register of Archives (which has become responsible for A2A maintenance). The basis for prioritising catalogues for inclusion is touched on in Liz Rees, David Tyrell and Sue Wood, 'Picks and pistons: The industrial history of the North East online', *Business Archives* (2003).

Archives Hub

Archives Hub (www.archiveshub.ac.uk) provides a single point of access to around 20,000 archive collections held by 160 institutions, mostly universities and other places of higher education in the Britain. For the most part, this site holds collection-level descriptions, but in some cases entire catalogues. There are search facilities for people, places and subjects. Participating institutions include many with important business archive collections such as the Universities of Warwick, Glasgow, Liverpool, Leeds, Manchester and Dundee.

Scottish Archive Network

The Scottish Archives Network (Scan) (www.scan.org.uk), promoted, *inter alia*, by the National Archives for Scotland, is a major online source of information about the content of 20,000 or so archive collections held by over 50 Scottish record offices and university libraries. It holds summary descriptions of collections, enables simple searching and has record office contact details. Scan is also concerned with digitisation of archives, especially those of interest to genealogists and family historians. Its notable project to date has been the digitisation of Scottish wills which are now available at www.scotlandspeople.gov.uk.

BUSINESS ARCHIVES
DEPOSITED IN RECORD OFFICES

Local Record Offices

Each county and many cities in Britain maintain at least one publicly-funded record office; Birmingham, Chester, Coventry, Glasgow, Liverpool, Portsmouth and not least the City of London and Westminster are excellent examples of the latter. The archives they collect are essentially of local interest and include not only those of businesses but also of local authorities, schools, churches, charities, professional associations, landowners and individuals. Each office is likely to hold archives of a wide range of local businesses; a sense of the nature and extent of business collections in local record offices can be gleaned from online sites such as those of Manchester City Archives (www.manchester.gov.uk) and Bolton Archives (www.boltonmuseums.org.uk). Hard-copy guides, such as *Calderdale Archives 1964-89: An illustrated guide to Calderdale District Archives* (1990), are still useful but detailed ones have been made superfluous by the internet.

When a record office is responsible for a district or city in which a particular industry is concentrated, so its collections become specialist and thereby develop a national or even international significance. An outstanding example is Guildhall Library (www.cityoflondon.gov.uk) in the City of London. Although local in character, the geographical area for which it is responsible coincides with the greatest concentration of financial institutions in the world. It has therefore accumulated archives of banks, insurance companies, discount houses, trading companies, security and commodity brokers, financial markets and others, creating an unrivalled resource for the study of international financial history.

Take also, for example, the Tyne and Wear Archive Service (www.tyneandweararchives.org.uk) at Newcastle upon Tyne. The historical specialisation of Tyneside and Wearside in heavy engineering is well-known and results in its record office holding many valuable archives of shipbuilding and marine engineering, most notably Swan Hunter and Armstrong Whitworth. Extensive archives of shipping companies are in record offices in Glasgow and Liverpool where much of Britain's shipping industry was once headquartered. Record offices in the West Midlands have strong collections created by the metal-processing and motor industries. Those in West Yorkshire, Lancashire and Greater Manchester have excellent textile industry collections. The same story is repeated across Britain.

Academic Record Offices

Many higher education institutions collect materials to support their teaching and research programmes. Their collections are generally not local in character but reflect wider interests and include business archives along with the archives of businessmen. Their websites generally provide collection level descriptions.

Glasgow University (www.gla.ac.uk/archives), more than any other, has specialised in collecting archives of business reflecting its strong tradition of business history teaching and research. Its collections, while covering Scotland as a whole, were largely created when Glasgow's industries formed the workshop of the Empire. The University holds hundreds of collections, including those of Babcock & Wilcox, boiler makers; House of Fraser, department store retailers; John Brown & Co., shipbuilders; North British Locomotive Co. and its predecessors; and Coats Paton, cotton thread manufacturers of Paisley. These and other collections are comprehensively described on its website and its earliest deposits are dealt with in Peter Payne, *Studies in Scottish Business History* (1967) and in Michael Moss, 'Forgotten ledgers, law and the business historian: Gleanings from the Adam Smith Business Records Collection' *Archives* (1984). Glasgow University also holds the extensive Scottish Brewing Archive – formerly at Herriot Watt University – comprising the archives of over 50 Scottish breweries (www.archives.gla.ac.uk/sba), for which an online catalogue is also available.

Another academic institution, University College, London (www.ucl.ac.uk/library), has accumulated a collection of archives of British businesses connected with Latin America, particularly those of commercial and merchant banks and merchant houses. Archives of the Bank of London & South America, the Peruvian Corporation, Balfour Williamson and Frederick Huth & Co. are of particular note. The University of Reading's Museum of English Rural Life (www.merl.org.uk) houses major collections relating to farming, agricultural support and food processing, including those of agricultural engineers such as Ransomes, Sims & Jefferies, David Brown Tractors and John Fowler & Co., and of food processors including Rank Hovis McDougall. The museum also houses farm archives. Reading University's Library (www.library.reading.ac.uk) is the leading UK centre for archives of publishing, printing and other book trade activities; its collections cover leading houses such as George Allen & Unwin, The Bodley Head, Macmillan & Co., Routledge & Kegan Paul and Longman Group. The collection is well described on the library's website and, in the early stages of its development, in J.A. Edwards, 'Publishers' archives at Reading University', *Business Archives* (1979).

Warwick University's Modern Records Centre (www.warwick.ac.uk), established in 1973, has emerged as the leading collector of archives of British industry and labour with a focus on late 19th- and 20th-century industrial relations. The archives of hundreds of British trade unions and related organisations, in particular the TUC, and of employer associations form the core of its collections. The latter range from the Water Companies' Association to the Engineering Construction Industry Association. More notable are the extensive archives, dating from the early 20th century, of the Confederation of British Industry (CBI) and its predecessor bodies including the Federation of British Industries, the British Employers' Confederation and the National Association of British Manufacturers.

In addition, around 100 collections of business archives touch on the mechanical engineering industries of the West Midlands. These include, for example, the archives of Rubery Owen, motor vehicle component manufacturers, and of numerous motor vehicle manufacturing companies which, for a relatively short period, were grouped within British Leyland and which are now held by British Motor Industry Heritage Trust. Other important holdings relate to the motor transport industry and include, for example, applications and decisions of licensing authorities in respect of carriage of goods by road, 1934-89, lodged by the Kithead Trust. This trust, formed by the National Bus Company, holds, *inter alia*, various classes of quasi-public records as well as archives of individual bus operating companies. All the Modern Records Centre's archives are well-described on its website where subject guides can also be found. The Centre's hard-copy publications include *The Confederation of British Industry and Predecessor Archives* (1997) and *The Trades Union Congress Archive, 1920-60* (1992) and *1960-70* (1998).

Museum Record Offices

Many museums have accumulated business archives to support their collections and exhibition programmes. Their collections may be specific or general as industrial museums record industry over a wide area while local museums focus on local history. In particular, museums tend to have strong collections of photographs and trade literature, especially trade catalogues (*see* pp.138-9), as these have particular relevance to their object collections.

London's National Maritime Museum (www.nmm.ac.uk) holds collections associated with ships and the sea, in particular those of shipping, shipbuilding and marine insurance companies, such as P&O, Lloyds Register of Shipping, Royal Dockyards and the Registrar General of Shipping and Seamen. Many are described in R.J.B. Knight (ed.), *Guide to the Manuscripts of the National Maritime Museum, Vol 2: Public records, business records and artificial collections* (1980). The Royal Air Force Museum's (www.rafmuseum.org.uk) collections deal with air transport and aerospace; most noteworthy are those of aircraft builders Fairey Supermarine and Handley Page. The collections of Manchester's Museum of Science and Industry (www.msim.org.uk) include archives relating to, *inter alia*, electricity generation and supply and electrical and mechanical engineering. Businesses that have lodged their archives there include Ferranti and Metropolitan Vickers. The Science Museum (www.nmsi.ac.uk/library) houses fewer collections but some are for notable businesses such as Pearsons, the international contractors, and Chubb, the safe and lock makers.

The Victoria & Albert Museum's National Art Library (www.vam.ac.uk) has in its Archive of Art and Design archives of individual designers, of associations connected with design and of businesses involved in the creation, manufacture and retail of 'designed' products. Collections are wide-ranging and include, for example, those of Heal & Son Ltd, bedding and furniture manufacturers and retailers; Habitat Ltd, household goods retailers; Edward Barnard & Sons, manufacturing silversmiths; Holland & Sons Ltd, cabinet makers; Tom Smith Group, novelty makers; and James Powell & Sons, stained-glass manufacturers. They are described in Elizabeth Lomas, *Guide to the Archives of Art and Design, Victoria & Albert Museum* (2001) and in Eleanor Gawne, 'A not so unusual place to find company records; business archives at the Archive of Art and Design', *Business Archives* (1995).

Association Record Offices

The History of Advertising Trust (www.hatads.org.uk), which has strong support from the media sector, holds archives of many advertising/public relations agencies and of advertising/public relations departments of businesses managing strong brand names. Its collections include archives of leaders such as J. Walter Thompson, Ogilvy & Mather, Charles Barker and Saatchi & Saatchi. These are supported by a strong library, advertising copy, trade literature and TV commercials.

In some instances professional associations and employer-related bodies collect archives relating to the industries and professions they serve, although their focus tends to be papers of individuals rather than archives of businesses. Especially notable is the Institution of Engineering & Technology (formerly the Institution of Electrical Engineers) which, apart from its own archives and papers of distinguished electrical engineers, holds technical and manufacturing archives within its National Archive of Electrical Science and Technology (NAEST) (www.theiet.org). Its archives catalogue is available on its website while NAEST is surveyed in Lenore Symons, 'Archives and records of the Institution of Electrical Engineers', *Archives* (16, 1983). Other professional institutions, notably the civil (www.ice.org.uk) and mechanical (www.imeche.org.uk) engineers, also hold membership archives, papers of distinguished past engineers, documents relating to major engineering projects and a few business archives. All these resources are described on their websites. On a greater scale is the British Architectural Library of the Royal Institute of British Architects (www.architecture.com) which holds Britain's largest collection of papers of architects, architectural organisations and related groups. In 2004 this collection was moved to the Victoria & Albert Museum and is described in Angela Mace, *Architecture in Manuscript, 1601-1996: Guide to the British Architectural Library manuscripts and archives collection* (1998). Angela Mace, *The Royal Institute of British Architects: A guide to its archives and history* (1986) focuses on the Institute's professional and administrative archives (which remain with the Institute).

National Record Offices

These comprise the London-based National Archives and the National Archives of Scotland in Edinburgh as well as the Public Office of Northern Ireland. They hold archives of central government and its agencies and of courts of law and, in the cases of Scotland and Northern Ireland, non-public collections of 'national' as opposed to 'local' importance. The National Library of Wales holds a few classes of public records but mostly non-public archives. The National Archives (www.nationalarchives.gov.uk), formed in 2003 following the renaming of the Public Record Office and its assumption of tasks formerly undertaken by the Historical Manuscripts Commission, also maintains the National Register of Archives (NRA) (*see* p.17).

The National Archives in London does not collect archives created by non-government entities but it nevertheless holds some archives of businesses as a result of the actions of government and the courts. Especially notable are archives of railway companies nationalised in the 1940s (*see* p.65) and business archives lodged as evidence in court of law (*see* pp.64-5). As well as these business-specific collections, the National Archives has a vast accumulation of archives created by government departments in the course of their work in registering and regulating businesses; purchasing goods and services; promoting economic and business development; managing publicly-owned assets; owning nationalised companies; collecting duties and taxes; and so on (*see* pp.49-70).

The National Archives website provides online access to its catalogue, which is organised by administrative structure, and to histories of different central government departments and agencies. Searching and browsing is possible. Also accessible via this website is a series of wide-ranging research guides some of which touch on business-related topics such as bankruptcy, apprenticeship, company registration, architecture, the legal profession and, not least, business history. It also gives access to other databases connected with the National Archives, for example ARCHON (*see* pp.16-17), the National Register of Archives (*see* p.17), census returns (*see* pp.152-3), various digitised document series such as wills (*see* pp.147-51) and Access to Archives (A2A) (*see* p.18).

The National Archives of Scotland (www.nas.gov.uk), once known as the Scottish Record Office, is responsible for administering the archives of central government in Scotland. Historically it has enjoyed a much wider remit than its London counterpart as it also holds privately-created collections of significance to the whole of Scotland. Its central government collections, as with the National Archives in London, include many series that touch directly or indirectly on business. Its non-government holdings include many notable business collections, especially those created by the Scottish iron and steel, shipbuilding and coal mining industries. Most important, it manages the National Register of Archives for Scotland (NRAS) (www.nas.gov.uk/nras) (*see* pp.17-18).

Its catalogue, available via its website, describes wide-ranging collections. Some of its first business collections are also outlined in two somewhat dated publications, J.H. Sime 'The

Records of Engineering Firms and their Treatment in the Scottish Record Office' *Archives* (1983) and Peter Payne, *Studies in Scottish Business History* (1967). Hard-copy publications include *Guide to the National Archives of Scotland* (1995), *Tracing Your Scottish Ancestors: A guide to ancestry research in the National Archives of Scotland* (3rd edn, 2003) and *Tracing Scottish Local History: A guide to local history research in the Scottish Record Office* (1994).

The National Library of Wales (www.llgc.org.uk) holds a relatively small number of public archives relating to Wales such as wills and tithe maps. Its real strength by far is its collections of non-public archives of significance to the Principality as a whole and these will include some business archives.

Business Archives Council and Business Archives Council of Scotland

The Business Archives Council (BAC) (www.businessarchivescouncil.org.uk), a registered charity with a membership drawn from business, record offices and academia, promotes the preservation of business archives and the study of business history. Until recently it undertook surveys of archives held by businesses, sometimes on an ad hoc basis, but mostly as part of special business sector surveys which have included the banking, shipbuilding, brewing, pharmaceutical and veterinary science industries and the chartered accountancy profession. In addition, the archives of the earliest 1,000 companies on the Register of Companies in 1980 were surveyed by the Council in the early 1980s; these were all registered between 1856 and 1889. Publications resulting from this work are referred to below. Reports arising out of its ad hoc surveys were supplied to the National Register of Archives and are included in their indexes and registers. A journal, *Business Archives*, is published twice yearly by the Council along with a quarterly newsletter.

The Business Archives Council of Scotland (BACS) (www.archives.gla.ac.uk/bacs) operates in a similar way to the BAC but has specialised in undertaking ad hoc rather than sector-based surveys (although it is currently undertaking one of the North Sea oil and gas industry). Its survey officer is based in Glasgow University Archives and its numerous survey reports are supplied to the National Register of Archives for Scotland.

Published Guides to Archives

Introduction

Many hard-copy guides to business archives have been published. Some deal with a single business but most cover business sectors or geographical areas and are to be found in good reference libraries, record offices and local studies libraries. In addition, specialist journals, most notably *Business Archives*, list archives newly-deposited in record offices.

Journals and Occasional Publications

Business Archives: Sources and History

This journal of the Business Archives Council carries summaries of business archives reported to the National Register of Archives in the year prior to publication. These collection-level descriptions are classified by business activity and, for the most part, are based on the National Register of Archives online annual publication, *Accessions to Repositories* (www.nationalarchives.gov.uk/accessions).

Business Archives also carries annually a bibliography, arranged by business sector, of recent business history publications but most content deals with source material for business history. Typical articles are:

Victoria Beauchamp, 'The workshops of the cutlery and related trades of Sheffield, 1750-1900: Using archaeology to understand the industry' (1996)

Helen Clifford, 'Accounting for luxury: Some sources and methods for the study of the 18th-century London precious metal trades' (1997)

John Griffiths, 'Exploring corporate culture: The potential of magazines for the business historian' (1999)

Anita Hollier, 'The British Petroleum Archive: What's in it for you?' (1998)

Steve Koerner, 'Business archives relating to the British motorcycle industry' (2000)

Karen Jane Mitchell, 'ICI: A brief history and guide to the archives' (1990)

Spencer Jordan, 'Regional newspapers and prosopography: A neglected source for business history' (1995)

Christine Wiskin, 'Women, business and credit: Sources for the historian' (1997)

Scottish Industrial History

This journal of the Business Archives Council of Scotland was first published in 1976 to succeed the Council's Newsletter. Its contents are broadly similar to those of Business Archives with emphasis on description and use of archives created by Scottish businesses. Article titles are listed on BACS's website (www.archives.gla.ac.uk/bacs).

Monographs: Business Sectors

Architects:

Rebecca M. Bailey, *Scottish Architects' Papers: A source book* (1996). This presents the results of a survey of archives of 114 Scottish-based firms of architects, consulting engineers and quantity surveyors undertaken in the early 1990s. Descriptions are largely at series level although more detail is occasionally given. Other sections cover archives deposited in record offices and with professional bodies. There are extensive indexes.

Banking:

John Orbell and Alison Turton, *British Banking: A guide to historical records* (2001). This Business Archives Council-sponsored book contains series level descriptions of archives of *c*.700 banks operating since the 17th-century. For the most part these archives remain with the banks but some important collections are deposited in record offices. The banks include goldsmiths, country and London private banks, joint stock banks, clearing banks, merchant banks, discount houses and British-owned overseas banks. Each entry includes a short history of the bank varying in length from about 100 to 500 words. There are extensive indexes and a bibliography. This replaced L.S. Pressnell and John Orbell, *Guide to the Historical Records of British Banking* (1985).

Book Trade:

Alexis Weedon and Michael Bott, *British Book Trade Archives, 1830-1939: A location register* (1996). This provides series level descriptions of archives of book trade businesses, viz.

publishers, printers, bookbinders, booksellers, stationers, literary agents and professional associations. Archives of *c*.500 entities are included. All are held in record offices or libraries; none are privately held. No cumulative index.

J.A. Edwards, 'Publishers' archives at Reading University', *Business Archives* (1979). This covers the content of the Archive of British Publishing ten years after its foundation. Although now somewhat dated, it continues as a useful general commentary on publishers' archives.

Brewing:

Lesley Richmond and Alison Turton, *The Brewing Industry: A guide to historical records* (1990). Another Business Archives Council-sponsored publication, this provides series level descriptions of the archives of *c*.650 brewing businesses operating in England, Scotland and Wales. Each entry is introduced by a history of the brewer. Archives included are held both by businesses and record offices. There are extensive indexes.

Chartered Accountancy:

Wendy Habgood, *Chartered Accountants in England and Wales: A guide to historical records* (1994). This describes at series level the archives of *c*.200 active or defunct firms of chartered accountants in England and Wales. The archives date from about 1800 to the late 20th century and are held by firms or record offices. Each entry includes a short history of the firm. The book carries the results of a survey of archives sponsored by the Institute of Chartered Accountants in England and Wales and the Business Archives Council.

Chemicals:

Peter J.T. Morris and Colin A. Russell, *Archives of the British Chemical Industry, 1750-1914: A handlist* (1988). This describes mostly at series level the pre-1914 archives of *c*.180 active and defunct businesses at work in all areas of the chemical industry – alkali, dyestuffs, fertilizer, gunpowder, soap, oxygen, sulphuric acid, pharmaceuticals and very much more. Archives deposited in record offices or remaining with businesses are included. Each entry begins with a detailed history of the business and includes a comprehensive bibliography. The book is based on a three-year survey undertaken in the mid-1980s by the Open University.

Civil Engineering:

A.W. Skempton, *British Civil Engineering 1640-1840: A bibliography of contemporary printed reports, plans and books* (1987). This is not a guide to archives but to printed material and is included because it covers civil engineering projects (but not the construction process). The book is organised by name of engineer and projects include construction of drainage, river navigation, canals, docks, harbours, bridges, roads, railways and water supply.

Coal Mining:

John Benson, Robert G. Neville and Charles H. Thompson, *Bibliography of the British Coal Industry: Secondary literature, parliamentary and departmental papers, mineral maps and plans and a guide to sources* (1981). This is not organised by name of business but by four categories of source material – secondary sources, parliamentary papers, mineral maps and plans, and primary sources – and within those by subject or geographical area. Primary source material is arranged by location of archives. The volume was published prior to the privatisation of coal mining so does not take account of the dispersal of the National Coal Board's archives to record offices. No histories of individual businesses are included but there are name, place and subject indexes.

Engineering and Metal Processing:

Royal Commission on Historical Manuscripts, *Records of British Business and Industry, 1760-1914: Metal processing and engineering* (1994). This describes at series level the archives of *c.*1,200 businesses. Sectors include metal processing; mechanical engineering; instrument and scientific engineering; and electrical engineering. Particular activities include the production of motor vehicles and components, railway equipment, iron and steel, ships, coaches, cables, gramophone players and so on. The archives included are held by record offices or remain with the businesses that created them. Business and place name indexes are included but there are no histories of businesses.

Information Technology:

Geoffrey Tweedale, *The National Archive for the History of Computing Catalogue* (1990). A copy is posted at www.chstm.man.ac.uk/nahc. This lists materials held in the Archive, many of which are business related. It also contains details of archives held elsewhere and useful bibliographies.

Serena Kelly, *Report of a Survey of the Archives of British Commercial Computer Manufacturers, 1950-70* (unpublished typescript, 1985). This very dated survey of archives in the hands of manufacturers and individuals associated with the early computer industry continues to have value. It was funded by International Computers Ltd and carried out by the Institution of Electrical Engineers. It pointed to the vulnerability of the industry's archives.

Insurance:

H.A.L. Cockerell and Edwin Green, *The British Insurance Business: A guide to its historical records* (2nd edn, 1994). This describes at series level the archives of *c.*300 British insurance companies in all branches of the industry – fire, life, accident, marine and so on. Lengthy chapters cover the development of insurance generally and its different specialisations in particular. Arranged by name of business, each entry also gives date of formation, specialisation and details of takeovers and mergers.

Maritime Industries:

Rita V. Bryon and Terence N. Bryon, *Maritime Information: A guide to libraries and sources of information in the United Kingdom* (3rd edn, 1993). This describes in general terms the holdings of *c.*500 libraries, record offices and institutions that cover Britain's maritime industries. Most of the material referred to is historical but the level of detail varies between entries. Somewhat out of date but useful.

Peter Mathias and A.W.H. Pearsall, *Shipping: A survey of historical records* (1971). This provides very general details of the records of *c.*35 shipping companies, each entry being introduced with a short history of the business. It is very much out of date but the histories remain useful.

L.A. Ritchie, *The Shipbuilding Industry: A guide to historical records* (1992). This Business Archives Council-sponsored publication describes at series level the archives of *c.*200 shipbuilders and repairers and marine engineers in England, Scotland and Wales. Each entry includes a history of the business ranging from 100 to 500 words in length. There is a short bibliography. It replaced L.A. Ritchie, *Modern British Shipbuilding: A guide to historical records* (1980).

Motor Vehicle Industry:

Steve Koerner, 'Business archives relating to the British motorcycle industry' *Business Archives* (2000). This journal article describes in general terms the surviving archives of motorcycle manufacturers.

Jane Lowe, *Guide to Sources in the History of the Cycle and Motor Industries in Coventry, 1880-1939* (1982). This guide is in two sections. The first describes archives in record offices including the National Archives. The second covers secondary materials, especially periodicals and local press articles. Dated but still useful.

Richard Storey, *Automotive History Sources in Coventry Archives* (Modern Records Centre, 1996). This covers archives relating to the motor industry held by archives, museums and heritage trusts located in Coventry.

Pharmaceuticals:

Lesley Richmond, Julie Stevenson and Alison Turton, *The Pharmaceutical Industry: A guide to historical records* (2003). This is arranged by name of business. It describes at series level the archives of *c.*300 active and defunct businesses, each entry being introduced by a history of the business ranging in length from 100 to 1,000 words. Archives held by businesses and record offices are included and there are name, place and subject indexes. It is another Business Archives Council survey, carried out in late 1990s with support of The Wellcome Trust. The resource is also available online at the Wellcome Library for the History and Understanding of Medicine (www.wellcome.ac.uk).

Railways:

Cliff Edwards, *Railway Records: A guide to sources* (2001). This does not describe the archives of individual railway companies but is a general guide to them, focusing in particular on materials in the National Archives where many railway archives are to be found. Its sections include where to find archives; nature of railway company archives; general papers relating to government policy and control of the railway industry; staff records; maps; technical drawings; and photographs.

George Ottley, *A Bibliography of British Railway History* (2nd edn, 1983), *A Bibliography of British Railway History: Supplement* (1988) and Graham Boyes, Matthew Searle and Donald Steggles, *Ottley's Bibliography of British Railway History: Second supplement* (1998). These guides schedule around 20,000 separate printed items and include much that is specialist and business-specific. This includes trade catalogues, instruction manuals, legal cases, shareholder documents, parliamentary reports, trade press articles and so on. There is a substantial index to corporate bodies, authors, subjects and places.

Road Transport:

Richard Storey, *Road Haulage History Sources* (Modern Records Centre Information Leaflet, 1996). This outlines the Centre's extensive motor transport holdings including records of the Road Haulage Association, Transport Development Group, etc.

Textiles:

Royal Commission on Historical Manuscripts, *Records of British Business and Industry, 1760-1914: Textiles and leather* (1990). This describes at series level the archives of 1,200 businesses. Entries are arranged by sub-sector – wool; cotton; linen, flax and jute; silk; lace; textile finishing; clothing, hosiery and knitwear; and leather including footwear. There are indexes to businesses and places but no historical details of businesses are provided.

Pat Hudson, *The West Riding Wool Textile Industry: A catalogue of business records from the sixteenth to the twentieth century* (1975). This provides detailed descriptions of the archives of about 125 textile businesses located in the former West Riding of Yorkshire, historically the premier wool textile manufacturing district of Britain. It covers only archives in record offices and is somewhat dated but very detailed. Businesses include weavers, spinners, clothing merchants and manufacturers. No histories are included but bibliographical references are useful.

Terry Wyke and Nigel Rudyard (eds), *Cotton: A select bibliography on cotton in North West England* (1997). This is an extensive bibliography and guide to archives relating to the cotton industry in North West England from its rise in the 18th to its decline in the late 20th century. Its detailed descriptions of business, trade union, employer association and family archives are arranged by repository. Indexed by name and subject.

Veterinary Science:

Pamela Hunter, *Veterinary Medicine: A guide to historical records* (2004). This gives series level descriptions of archives of businesses, associations, individuals, government departments, etc, and is arranged by name of business. As with other Business Archives Council surveys, each entry is introduced by a short history. Name, place and subject indexes are included. The project was funded by The Wellcome Trust.

General:

Lesley Richmond and Bridget Stockford, *Company Archives: The Survey of the records of 1,000 of the first registered companies in England and Wales* (1986). This summarises the results of a four-year Business Archives Council survey of the archives of the earliest surviving companies on the Register of Companies for England and Wales in 1980. Six hundred and seventy-four companies registered between 1856 and 1889 are covered including businesses from the iron and steel, engineering, transport, hotel, overseas trading, property, brewing and food processing sectors. Other entries are for professional associations, charitable organisations, educational institutions and political and social clubs that had registered company status. Archives of subsidiaries are also included; altogether *c*.1,600 business archives are described. Descriptions are at series level and a history of each registered company is given.

Articles and some Online Guides: Single Companies

Babcock & Wilcox Ltd (electrical engineering): Alison Turton, 'Babcock & Wilcox Ltd. An
    engineering company's archive', *Scottish Industrial History* (1992)

Baring Brothers & Co. Ltd (investment banking): John Orbell, *Guide to the Baring Archive at
    ING Barings* (1997)

Bank of England: www.bankofengland.co.uk

British Insulated Cable Co. Ltd (electrical engineering): Gordon Read, 'The BICC archives
    and artefact collection', *Business Archives* (1989)

BP Plc: Anita Hollier, 'The British Petroleum Archive: What's in it for you?', *Business Archives* (1998)

Burmah Oil Co. Ltd: Bridget Stockford, 'Burmah Oil Co. Ltd. History and archives to 1966'
    Business Archives (1989)

Cable & Wireless (telecommunications): www.porthcurno.org.uk

Eagle Star (insurance): Isabel Syed, *Eagle Star: A guide to its history and archives* (1997)

Hadfields Ltd (iron and steel): Geoffrey Tweedale, 'The records of Hadfields Ltd' *Business
    Archives* (1987)

House of Fraser Plc (retail): Alison Turton, 'The archives of the House of Fraser', *Business
    Archives* (1980)

HSBC Plc (banking): Edwin Green and Sara Kinsey, 'The archives of HSBC Group', *Financial
    History Review* (1996)

ICI Plc (chemicals): Karen Mitchell, 'ICI: A brief history and guide to the archives' *Business
    Archives* (1990)

Post Office: Jean Farrugia, *A Guide to Post Office Archives* (London, 1987)

Ransomes, Sims & Jefferies Ltd (mechanical engineering): D.R. Grace and D.C. Phillips,
    Ransomes of Ipswich: A history of the firm and guide to its records (1975)

Rowntree Mackintosh (confectionery): Judith A. Burg, *A Guide to the Rowntree and Mackintosh
    Archives, 1862-1969* (1997)

N.M. Rothschild & Sons Ltd (investment banking): *The Rothschild Archive: A guide to the
    collection* (2000); *see also* www.rothschildarchive.org

Royal Bank of Scotland: *A Guide to the Historical Records of the Royal Bank of Scotland* (London,
    2000); *see also* www.rbs.com

Rubery Owen Holdings Ltd (mechanical engineering): Richard Storey (ed.), *Rubery Owen
    Holdings Ltd Archive* (1997)

WH Smith Plc (retail): T.E. Baker-Jones, 'The archives of WH Smith & Sons Ltd' *Business
    Archives* (1987)

Somerfield Plc (food retail): Gareth Shaw, Louise Curth and Andrew Alexander, 'A new
    archive for the history of retailing: The Somerfield Collection' *Business Archives* (2002)

John Swire & Sons Ltd (international trading): Elizabeth Hook, *A Guide to the Papers of John
    Swire & Sons Ltd* (1977)

Monographs: Geographical Areas

Australia, New Zealand and Pacific:

Phyllis Mander-Jones, *Manuscripts in the British Isles relating to Australia, New Zealand and
the Pacific* (1972). This covers archives relating to all aspects of political, social and economic
history but some businesses are included. The publication is now very dated indeed.

British Dominions:

Charles A. Jones, *Britain and the Dominions: A Guide to Business and Related Records in the United Kingdom Concerning Australia, New Zealand and South Africa* (1978). This covers a large number of businesses involved in a surprisingly wide range of activities, but focuses in particular on their dominion connections. Entries are organised by institution holding the archives; they include many businesses. Descriptions are largely at series level. Indexed by collection and by name/place. Now dated.

Judy Collingwood, *A Guide to Resources for Canadian Studies in the UK and Ireland* (3rd edn, *c*.1998). This lists some business records held both publicly in record offices and privately by businesses. Arranged by institution and indexed by subject and type of material.

Far East, Middle East and Africa:

Noel Matthews and M. Doreen Wainwright, *A Guide to Manuscripts and Documents in the British Isles Relating to the Far East* (1977); *A Guide to Manuscripts and Documents in the British Isles Relating to the Middle East and North Africa* (1980); *A Guide to Manuscripts and Documents in the British Isles Relating to Africa* (1971); and *A Guide to Western Manuscripts and Documents in the British Isles Relating to South and South East Asia* (1965). Each volume contains references to a few collections of business archives but these studies are now very dated.

Latin America:

Peter Walne (ed.), *A Guide to Manuscript Sources for the History of Latin America and the Caribbean in the British Isles* (1973). This contains details of many business archives but the study is now very dated.

North America:

John W. Raimo, *A Guide to Manuscripts Relating to America in Great Britain and Ireland* (1979). Some business archives, either held in record offices or with businesses, are referred to but the study is dated.

United Kingdom:

Avon and Somerset: Jennifer Green, Philip Ollerenshaw & Peter Wardley, *Business in Avon and Somerset: A survey of archives* (1991). This lists at series level the archives of *c*.200 businesses, large and small, engaged in wide-ranging activity. There are also sections on employer and labour organisations.

Coventry: Joan Lane, *Register of Business Records of Coventry and Related Areas* (1977). This provides a detailed description of the archives of *c*.30 Coventry businesses, mostly drawn from the mechanical engineering sector. A thumbnail history is given for each business included.

Suffolk: Christine Clark and Roger Munting, *Suffolk Enterprise: A guide to the county's companies and their historical records* (2000). The archives of *c*.80 leading Suffolk businesses, past and present, are described at series level. Each entry begins with a short history. Some archives are privately held.

SECTION THREE

Information Sources outside the Archives of the Business

ARCHIVES OF SUPPLIERS OF GOODS AND SERVICES

Suppliers and Customers

The archives of suppliers and customers – *if* identifiable – can be of real importance in tracing the business's history, although the extent of their importance depends greatly on the nature of the underlying goods and services. These archives might shed light on a wide range of issues such as costs, prices, consumption of inputs, output, products, market share, credit, margins, discounting, agency agreements, cross-shareholdings, vertical integration and so on.

The roles of supplier and customer are, of course, closely interrelated: every business has both and is itself a supplier and a customer so far as other businesses are concerned. Goods purchased and sold embrace energy, raw materials, components and finished goods; they also include services but these are dealt with at greater length below. The more routine the goods – for example iron and steel, clothing, food, even electricity – the less easy it is to identify specific suppliers or customers. The larger and/or more valuable the goods – for example ships, locomotives, manufacturing plant, scientific instruments, jewellery – the easier the task, the more useful the archives.

The sheer variety of supplier and customer relationships means that this is a particularly diffuse source in tracing a business's history. On account of this, it is only dealt with here in broad terms and by means of example. At the end of the day the researcher has to proceed on the basis of common sense but also play the role of detective.

Here are some examples of customer/supplier relationships. One is an iron and steel producer that purchases coal and iron ore as well as manufacturing plant such as furnaces and rolling mills. In tracing its history, the archives of local colliery and iron ore mining companies and of specialist plant manufacturers may well be useful. These mining businesses, of course, might well be subsidiary companies.

Another example is shipbuilders. These purchase iron and steel, ship engines and components such as propellers, compasses, anchors and navigation equipment, from a large group of suppliers and sell their ships to a fairly narrow range of customers comprising mostly shipping companies and navies. A wide range of businesses are potentially relevant but difficult to identify on the supply side, but on the customer side they will be relatively few and probably easily identifiable. Also, here the archives of government departments such as the Admiralty, held in the National Archives, may help if the shipbuilder supplied warships. Additionally, once again, the shipbuilder might turn out to own (or be owned by) suppliers such as iron and steel producers or even the shipowning customer.

Motor car manufacturers buy sheet metal and components from a wide range of manufacturers and dispose of their output to a huge customer base via what has become a relatively small number of garages and dealerships. Once again, a wide range of difficult-to-identify suppliers is suggested, while the dealership customers should be quite easy to locate. Archives of the ultimate customer, the car owner, might be in the form of diaries, maintenance accounts, marketing material and the like. At another level, market surveys and reports of specialist marketing and consumer organisations may also prove useful.

Of course, the real challenge here is the identification of customers and suppliers. Where the goods traded are sophisticated and valuable, this might be quite straightforward but hugely difficult when they are not. There is no easy solution to this. Very often identification is only possible through access to the archives of the business whose history is being traced but often it is the absence of such archives that has instigated the search for supplier/customer archives! Failing this, a search by the business's name in the A2A website (see p.18) and in the National Archives/National Archives of Scotland websites (see pp.17-18) might produce some results. Business sector trade directories (see pp.129-32) – which in some cases list both makers of components and of finished goods within a particular business sector – might also suggest linkages.

Banking Services

Bank archives shed light on business customers. On the one hand they detail banking facilities received – or not received – by the customer. On the other, they sometimes include character, credit or other reports analysing the standing/credit worthiness of a business and providing a snapshot of it at a point in time. Relative to most business sectors, bank archives have a generally good survival rate, although customer accounts and reporting records tend to be piecemeal. It should be remembered that many small businesses probably did not have significant bank relationships until the 20th century.

Banks have provided services to British businesses since at least the 17th century although for most not on a significant scale until well after 1800. These early services were fairly basic until the emergence of modern joint stock banking from the mid-19th century and included holding deposits, making payments, discounting bills of exchange and making small advances. At this time, borrowing from family, friends and business connections, often secured by mortgage, was very common.

As business processes became more complex and as trading became more long distance, so routine services came to include overdrafts and advances on a much greater scale, guarantees, foreign exchange facilities, payments and collections outside the UK, more sophisticated deposit management and so on. Specialised activities by the late 19th century included the provision of long-term finance by means of issues and placements of shares and debentures and corporate and financial advice, say on structuring finance and arranging takeovers, mergers and acquisitions.

In the history of British banking several distinct groups of banks can be identified. The first comprises private banks owned by small partnerships; their origin can be traced to London in the 17th century and they flourished in the provinces in the late 18th and early 19th centuries

7   Bank archives contain many details of business customers. Among the most useful are customer reports – often held in character, information or interview books – which give brief customer profiles, although their survival rate is generally poor so relatively few exist. This mid-19th-century report on Fruhling & Goschen, well-known but long-dissolved London merchant bankers, is greatly illuminating but far more detailed than most.

8   This 1907 bankers' report on a firm of Liverpool cotton traders is quite typical of the business customer reports to be found in bank archives.

when most country towns usually had at least one bank and sometimes several. Private banks based in London's West End provided banking services principally to individuals while those in the City dealt largely with businesses, especially merchants.

Joint stock banks emerged as successors to private banks from the 1820s although in Scotland their origins date back to the early eighteenth century. These banks were owned by multi-shareholders, had larger capital than private banks and were much more capable of handling the requirements of big business. Another key feature was their branch networks. Many joint stock banks expanded aggressively through acquisition of private and smaller joint stock rivals, a process that ultimately resulted in domination by a comparatively small group of very large banks with nationally spread branch networks and head offices based in London or Edinburgh. On account of their large size and wide geographical spread, they prescribed careful and relatively sophisticated record-keeping systems detailing their customers and the services provided to them.

Two other bank groups are important. One comprises British-owned overseas joint stock banks, which provided general banking services in overseas countries, especially British colonies, invariably through a branch network and mostly from the mid-19th century onwards. British businesses with interests outside Britain inevitably received routine banking services from them. The other group is merchant banks (or investment banks as they have come to be known). In the 18th and 19th centuries these financed, largely via acceptance credits, the commodity trade of international merchants, many based in the City of London, and, increasingly from the late 19th century, the requirements of large British manufacturers and other companies trading internationally. Much more significant, again from the late 19th century, were their issue of shares and debentures for public companies and their provision of corporate financial advice on takeovers, mergers, acquisitions and reconstructions. Acceptance finance, issuing and financial advice were mainstays of their business for most of the 20th century, although latterly the management of investment portfolios, especially pension funds, was significant.

The customer-related archives created by these activities are diverse but broadly similar between bank types. The most routine include signature books, security registers, safe custody registers and customer account ledgers although problems, especially costs, of storage over the years mean that the survival of continuous sets is uncommon. The survival rate of customer account ledgers is particularly poor, although there are notable exceptions. Other useful series include interview, character and information books, which provide reports on customers, their resources and standing, and the facilities provided to them. Minute books give details, *inter alia*, of large loans approved at senior level and of customers in difficulty.

Correspondence files cover day-to-day relationships with customers as well as the major transactions undertaken for them and are a characteristic of 20th-century bank archives.

David Thoms, 'Bank records and the early history of the Coventry motor car industry', *Business Archives* (1992) provides a helpful case study of the use of bank archives as a business history source. His research into the financing, organisation and leadership of the post-1890 Coventry motor industry located information on around 50 motor vehicle and component manufacturers in the archives of Lloyds TSB and HSBC (Midland Bank) alone.

A general absence of reference sources identifying service providers to a given business is a major and recurring limitation when tracing the history of a business whose archives have not survived. Sometimes reference books come to the rescue but this is not so in the case of banks at least until relatively recent years. Identifying the bankers of an 18th- and 19th-century business is especially difficult, particularly if it was not a large business and was based in a city where many banks operated. In the latter period, clues to the identity of a business's bankers might be gleaned from annual reports, company house returns, prospectuses, the Stock Exchange Year Book and so on. Failing this, a round-robin letter to the relatively small number of bank archivists might produce results.

Most surviving bank archives are today held centrally in the archives departments of Britain's big banks in London and Edinburgh. Banks maintaining historical archives to which researchers are given access include the Bank of England, Bank of Scotland, Barclays, Coutts, HSBC (including Midland), Hoares, ING (for Baring Brothers), Lloyds TSB, Rothschilds and Royal Bank of Scotland (including NatWest). Only a few collections have found their way to local records offices or university libraries. Guildhall Library in the City of London has fine collections of archives of merchant banks and overseas banks. The surviving archives of about seven hundred banks are summarised at series level in John Orbell and Alison Turton, *British Banking: A guide to historical records* (2001). A case study of one particular collection containing, *inter alia*, the archives of Hongkong & Shanghai Banking Corp, Midland Bank and the British Bank of the Middle East is Edwin Green and Sara Kinsey, 'The archives of HSBC Group', *Financial History Review* (1996). Published guides to individual bank archives are listed on p.29.

No authoritative general history of British banking exists although its main components are covered in detail in L.S. Pressnell, *Country Banking in the Industrial Revolution* (1956), Geoffrey Jones, *British Multinational Banking, 1830-1990* (1993), Stanley Chapman, *The Rise of Merchant Banking* (1984), which is now somewhat dated, and S.G. Checkland, *Scottish Banking: A history 1695-1973* (1975). P.L. Cottrell, *Industrial Finance 1830-1914: The finance and organisation of English manufacturing industry* (1980) highlights early links between banks and their business customers.

Details of bank mergers, name changes, dates of establishment and liquidation and place of business, all from the earliest days of British banking, are listed in the annual *Bankers' Almanac*. Similar information for country banks is in M. Dawes and C.N. Ward-Perkins, *Country Banks of England and Wales: Private provincial banks and bankers 1688-1953* (2000), in G.L. Grant, *The Standard Catalogue of Provincial Banks and Banknotes* (1977) and in James Douglas, *Scottish Banknotes* (1975). Fred Wellings and Alistair Gibb, *Bibliography of Banking Histories* (1995-7) is the most comprehensive listing of books and articles relating to British banking history and includes works on specific banks.

Savings banks are not dealt with at length because their customers included few fully fledged businesses. That said, many customers were small tradesmen working independently; as early as 1818 a fifth of York Savings Bank's customers were 'mechanics, journeymen, clerks, little tradesmen and very small farmers'. Savings banks were first established shortly after 1800 and in comparatively recent years their survivors joined together to form the Trustee Savings Bank, which subsequently merged to form Lloyds TSB. Local record offices hold many collections of savings bank archives while others are in the archives of Lloyds TSB. They are described in general terms in Karen Sampson and Katy Green, '"Pounds, shillings and sense:" History and sources of the Trustee Savings Bank', *Business Archives* (1998). For a modern history of the savings bank movement *see* Michael Moss and Iain Russell, *An Invaluable Treasure: A history of the TSB* (1994).

Insurance Services

Businesses were early users of fire, marine and accident insurance to cover all sorts of property and risks – buildings, machinery, ships, cargoes, stock, liability to third parties, credit risk, contracts and much more. At the end of the 19th century businesses began to subscribe to group life insurance and pension schemes marketed by life companies for the benefit of their employees. Insurance company archives might therefore be of considerable use in shedding light on, *inter alia*, the assets, losses and employees of a business.

The usefulness of insurance archives in tracing the history of a business is countered by patchy survival rates. It is also limited by difficulty in identifying the insurance company/ companies used by a particular business if that business's archives have not survived. This last limitation is probably more acute than for any other category of service provider archives. All of this said, when they survive and can be found, insurance archives – especially 18th- and 19th-century policy registers – can be great help.

Fire insurance began at the very end of the 17th century and from the outset was dominated by companies as opposed to partnerships or individual underwriters. The first fire office of real note was the Hand in Hand, established in 1696, followed by the highly important Sun Fire Office in 1710 and the Royal Exchange Assurance and London Assurance 10 years later. These businesses were London-based and their activities were for long focused in South-East England, only gradually extending to the provinces through the appointment of local agents.

9   *Insurance company archives are especially useful in giving details of the assets of their business customers. Insurance policy registers are valuable in describing and valuing,* inter alia, *plant and stock. This 1805 policy valuing the property of a Sussex corn miller for insurance against fire is typical.*

Provincial fire offices were formed in cities such as Bristol, Liverpool and Manchester in the late 18th century followed by many more after 1800.

Initially fire offices' business largely comprised residential property and contents but by the late 18th century included a very large number of industrial, commercial and agricultural buildings, machinery and stock in trade. Surveyors were appointed to assess this more complex range of risks while, as the 19th century progressed, specialist fire offices were created to insure particular classes of risk such as theatres and churches. Robin Pearson, *Insuring the Industrial Revolution: Fire insurance in Great Britain, 1700-1850* (2004) provides a detailed account of the development of this branch of insurance.

In terms of business-specific information, the archives of fire offices are highly important. Insurance policy registers contain descriptions and valuations of all types of business property insured by the likes of distillers, brewers, sugar refiners, paper makers, textile manufacturers, corn millers, retailers and merchants in all trades; only businesses with largely non-combustible assets, such as collieries, were excluded. Other series of fire office archives relate to losses and claims and to the assessment of risk. The former are referred to in claims registers and minute books while the latter include plans of industrial premises and maps of business districts where significant hazards were thought to exist (*see also* pp.145-6). Large numbers of insurance policy registers survive for a handful of companies, but claims, losses and assessment records are far less common.

A typical 18th- or 19th-century fire insurance policy recorded a policy reference number, name and address of the policyholder, his or her occupation or trade, details of any tenant occupying the premises, details of materials used in construction, and a schedule and valuation of premises, machinery and stock insured. Comparison of policies enables a rough judgment to be made of the relative importance of a given business as indicated by the valuation and extent of its property. However, the accuracy and basis of valuation is not always clear and has been much debated by academic historians. The basis could be replacement or current value or historic cost; the debate has tended to favour the former while acknowledging that exceptions exist.

D.T. Jenkins, 'The practice of insurance against fire, 1750-1840, and historical research', in Oliver M. Westall, *The Historian and the Business of Insurance* (1984) discusses the issues involved in this debate. David T. Hawkings, *Fire Insurance Records for Family and Local Historians, 1696 to 1920* (2003) provides a particularly comprehensive description of the content of fire office archives, especially insurance policies; his comments on losses and claims are especially useful. A feel for the content of policies is also provided by the several hundred policies transcribed in Stanley D. Chapman, *The Devon Cloth Industry in the 18th Century: Sun Fire Office Inventories of Merchants' and Manufacturers' Property, 1726-1770* (1978).

Given the poor survival rate of policy registers of most fire offices, it is especially fortuitous that those of some of the industry's leaders – the Sun, Royal Exchange and Hand-in-Hand – have survived in large numbers. They are deposited at Guildhall Library and comprise hundreds of volumes covering much of the 18th century and the first half of the 19th. Altogether they contain around three million policies for domestic, agricultural and business property but their usefulness is tempered by the absence of indexes for pinpointing the policies taken out by a given customer. Contemporary indexes exist only to Hand-in-Hand registers. Searching for the policy of a specific business is like looking for a needle in a haystack – assuming, of course, that the needle is there to be found.

That said, the position has much improved in recent years through the creation of indexes for certain periods. One of these, which is microfiche based and available in academic and municipal libraries, covers the Sun and Royal Exchange registers for the years 1775 to 1787; for an introduction to it *see* D.T. Jenkins, *Indexes of Fire Insurance Policies of the Sun Fire Office and the Royal Exchange Assurance, 1775-87* (1986). Another is a card index, at Guildhall Library, under reference MS17817/1-41, to the Sun registers for the years 1714 to 1731 but it excludes policies for London, Scotland and Wales.

Significant indexing of London tradesmen's policies has been undertaken by the so-called 'Birkbeck College Index'; its index cards are lodged, *inter alia*, in the Museum of London Library. Another initiative, underway from 2003 as an Access to Archives (A2A) project, is the indexing of Sun policies, mostly for London, for the years 1811 to 1835. The project is described at www.history.ac.uk/gh/sun.htm and the indexes are at www.a2a.org.uk. Much more narrowly focused indexes include Barbara E. Adams, 'Ceramic insurance in the Sun Company, 1766-74', *English Ceramic Circle Transactions* (1976) and Ian F. Maxted, *The British Book Trades, 1775-1787: An index of insurance policies* (1992).

For the years when no indexes exist, M.W. Beresford, 'Building history from fire insurance records', *Urban History Yearbook* (1976) provides useful practical hints on how to speed-search for relevant policies. A different approach, possible when the location of the business being researched is known, is to seek out the much less bulky registers of local fire office agents, which contain copies of the policies they submitted to head office for inclusion in central policy registers. The relatively few agents' books to survive are invariably lodged in local record offices and are recorded in H.A.L. Cockerell and Edwin Green, *The British Insurance Business* (2nd edn, 1994) in an appendix. Most, if not all, will also be recorded by the National Register of Archives.

Marine insurance has an earlier pedigree than fire, existing in London at least by the 16th century when it was in the hands of merchants acting as underwriters. The Royal Exchange Assurance and the London Assurance entered the market in 1721 but this sector continued to be dominated by private underwriting, increasingly centred on Lloyd's of London, which traces its origins to the late 1680s. Mutual associations formed by shipowners to insure their fleets were a creation of the late 18th century; they were reconstituted 100 years later as protection and indemnity clubs. In the 1820s the first joint stock companies specialising in marine insurance were established followed in the 1860s by another wave of formations some of which were based in the provinces, especially in Liverpool; associations of underwriters facilitated their business. Notwithstanding these formations, Lloyd's of London remained hugely important in marine insurance and progressively broadened its activities so that by the end of the 19th century almost any type of risk could be underwritten there. It was, however, a market, not a corporate underwriter; its function was to facilitate the business of private underwriters, their agents, and brokers.

Important records created by marine insurance include risk books describing assets such as ships and cargoes insured by a given underwriter on behalf of a named merchant or shipowner. A tiny number survive, mostly created by private underwriters and mostly to be found in Lloyds Library; a schedule of them is published in an appendix in Cockerell and Green. Policy registers that record insurance of ships and cargoes are also infrequent survivors other than in the archives of protection and indemnity clubs. Claim and loss books are more numerous while, as with other branches of insurance, details of major losses, claims and risks are likely to have been recorded in board or other committee minute books.

The wide-ranging historical collection of Lloyd's of London, known as Lloyd's Marine Collection and lodged at Guildhall Library, is worthy of special mention as it is of major importance for the history of ships and shipping business. It comprises materials either created by Lloyd's or acquired by it from other entities such as Lloyd's Register of Shipping (which traces its origins to 1760) and the Board of Trade. The collection includes data accumulated to enable the market to assess marine risks. Major components are Lloyd's Register, an annual list giving extensive details of merchant ships and their owners dating from 1764; loss and casualty records from 1837; the newspaper *Lloyd's List*, and indexes, which carried, *inter alia*, details of ship movements and other commercial information from 1741; voyage records from 1927; and *Lloyd's Confidential Index* from 1886. The collection is comprehensively described in D.T. Barriskill, *A Guide to the Lloyd's Marine Collection and Related Marine Sources at Guildhall Library* (1994), while Guildhall also produces a short research guide, 'Marine Sources at Guildhall', which can be downloaded (www.cityoflondon.gov.uk).

Accident insurance is the most recently established branch of Britain's insurance industry, dating in its modern form from the 1840s. It covers the widest range of risks and in its early days was highly specialised; specialist companies were formed to insure specialist risks. Early on, it focused on personal risk and its first formation, the Guarantee Society, guaranteed the personal sureties required by employers of employees occupying positions of trust. Other early branches, established in the 1850s, insured individuals against injury while travelling on the railways, shopkeepers against the breaking of plate glass windows, and factory owners against the explosion of their steam boilers. A further branch, dating especially from the 1880s, is insurance of legal liability of businesses arising out of accidents suffered by employees and other individuals such as railway passengers and pedestrians. Indemnity insurance for professional people was not far behind and in the early 20th century motor insurance became highly significant. Other branches fully established at the end of the century included theft, credit and contract insurance although they had an earlier antecedence.

The archives of accident insurance as a source for tracing a business's history is therefore obvious and their creation follows the same pattern as other branches of insurance – policy registers for recording risks, claim registers for recording losses and minute books and other series for considering large specific risks and claims. Their survival, however, is generally patchy, an exception being the policy registers of plate glass insurers.

The final branch is life insurance, which, in its modern form, dates from the 18th century. The Royal Exchange Assurance and the London Assurance diversified into this sector in 1721 joining a small band of mutual societies. The important Equitable Life Assurance was established in 1762 and other significant formations of the late 18th and early 19th centuries were National Provident, Norwich Union, Provident Institution, Scottish Widows, Scottish Provident and Sun Life.

The business of life offices was almost entirely focused on individual customers drawn from both the professional and so-called industrial classes; specialist companies emerged for particular market segments such as the legal and medical professions and groups of non-professionals. This constituency was widened by schemes enabling working men to purchase life insurance through small weekly payments; the Prudential, for example, made this an early specialisation in the 1850s. However, life offices also had business customers that purchased insurance for employees, the Post Office being an early example in 1859. These group life insurance schemes were added to in the 1920s by group pension schemes.

Given the extended period of risk, the survival of policy and claims registers is high for the life sector. They provide excellent insight into the health, wealth and lifestyle of individuals and groups both at a point in time and over time, although the need to preserve confidentiality and to ensure proper use influences access to them. Historical archives of life insurance are described in Cockerell and Green. No modern general history of the industry exists although a good overview is obtained from Michael Moss, *The Building of Europe's Largest Mutual Life Company: Standard Life, 1825-2000* (2000). Leslie Hannah, *Inventing Retirement: The development of occupational pensions in Britain* (1986) describes the development of occupational pension provision via life insurance companies.

General histories of British insurance are much wanted. H.A.L. Cockerell and Edwin Green, *The British Insurance Business: A guide to its history and records* (2nd edn, 1994) provides an excellent overview while Harold E. Raynes, *A History of British Insurance* (1964) is more detailed. The annual *Insurance Directory and Year Book*, first published in 1842, lists insurance companies and provides details of amalgamations and closures. Cockerell and Green also describe in summary form surviving insurance company archives, while more up to date information is available in the National Register of Archives (www.nationalarchives.gov.uk/nra). The London-based Chartered Insurance Institute (www.cii.co.uk) has a fine library and ephemera collection relating to the history of British insurance, which is described both online and in the Chartered Insurance Institute's book *Sources of Insurance History: A guide to historical material in the CII Library* (1990). Access is by appointment.

In locating specific insurance claims and loss information in insurance company archives, dates of disaster could possibly be helpful. A large literature exists on disasters of all types – railway, aviation, sea, storm, flood, fire and explosion. For example, Charles Hocking, *Dictionary of Disasters at Sea during the Age of Steam, 1824-1962* (1969) provides dates and other details that may assist in pinpointing information in marine insurance archives; it is arranged by ship's name, gives date of loss and owner's name. Similarly E.L. Jones, S. Porter and M. Turner, *Gazetteer of English Urban Fire Disasters, 1500-1900* (1984) might just help to pinpoint claims in fire office archives.

Legal Services

Few areas of business life are untouched by the legal profession; as one historian put it, solicitors are present at the birth of a business, at its death and at periods of crisis in between. They deal with litigation, arbitration, conveyance, acquisitions and disposals, capital raising, legal opinions and so on. Their links with business pre-date those of any other professional group and their archives, when they survive, are bound to include business-specific papers of obvious use in tracing the history of a business.

As early as the 1560s the legal profession in England and Wales was already 500 practitioners strong, although the first attempt at regulation did not occur until 1728. From then on, solicitors were enrolled following examination by a judge; by then their number totalled some six thousand. In 1740 the first steps were made to self-regulation, which eventually led to the formation of the Law Society in 1792. By then the two branches of the English legal profession – barristers and solicitors – had codified their 'adjacent monopolies', barristers alone being able to address the courts and solicitors alone being able to deal with customers and instruct barristers. The position differed in Scotland with its separate legal tradition where advocates had a monopoly only in the highest courts but shared work in the lower courts with writers. By

1850 almost 3,000 barristers and 11,000 solicitors practised in England and Wales; a further 200 advocates and 1,800 writers and notaries practised in Scotland.

At the end of the 18th century the average firm comprised a professional and, say, two clerks; only about a fifth of London solicitors and less than 10 per cent of those in the provinces were combined in two-man teams and hardly any firm exceeded this number. Thereafter numbers increased steadily both inside and outside London but the imposition of an upper limit of 20 partners restricted the emergence of very large firms until recent times. Firms specialising in corporate business have grown particularly large in the last few decades, both organically and through amalgamation.

While many provincial firms depended until recent years on conveyance and other land-related matters for a large proportion of their fee income, in London and, later, in the emerging industrial cities, there was early specialisation in work for business. These business-related firms, which were among the largest and most prestigious, were concerned with interpreting and applying mercantile, admiralty and corporate law in connection with such matters as ownership and transfer of assets, compensation for losses, establishment of rights, promotion of companies and recovery of debts. They drafted documents, commented upon schemes, briefed barristers, compiled evidence, gave private confidential advice and acted as emissaries. In addition they shared with smaller provincial firms more straightforward tasks, such as drafting trust deeds, witnessing oaths, auditing accounts, acting as clerk to public bodies and trusts, organising mortgages, drafting partnership deeds, collecting debts, acting as financial intermediaries, providing financial advice, assisting in drafting private Acts of Parliament and, certainly not least, undertaking conveyance and dealing with other land-related matters.

The archives of solicitors break down into three broad groups – administration records and accounts, customer-related papers, and documents deposited by customers for safe custody or created in connection with specific extramural duties. Customer papers, which are very much a 20th-century creation, detail the general customer relationship as well as particular projects undertaken; their contents also include copies of documents drafted. Administration archives comprise private and general accounts, fee records and papers relating to partnership matters; minutes of partners' meetings are a rarity until recent years as informal communication between partners in small firms was easy. Many administration archives contain tangential references to customers, especially about fees. Deposited archives cover a huge and unexpected variety of document types and subjects – wills, marriage and other trust deeds, partnership agreements, account books dealing with client assets, property deeds and plans, sale particulars, papers of public bodies and trusts, board minutes and so on.

The British Records Association (www.britishrecordsassociation.org.uk) has for many years specialised in locating and passing to record offices solicitors' archives, most especially deposited archives. However, little progress seems to have been made with large commercial firms, whose archives are only now beginning to find their way to record offices. Solicitors' archives in record offices can be located via the National Register of Archives (www.nra.nationalarchives.gov.uk) by searching under 'business and professional services/legal services'. Judy Slinn, 'The histories and records of firms of solicitors', *Business Archives* (1989) gives some insight into the archives of large firms serving business customers.

A significant body of work has been published on the history of the legal profession, especially in recent years. Peter Mathias, 'The lawyer as businessman in 18th century England' in D.C. Coleman and Peter Mathias (eds), *Enterprise and History: Essays in honour of Charles*

Wilson (1984) deals with the commercial work of solicitors in the 18th century and can be extrapolated with little difficulty to the 19th century. Penelope J. Corfield, *Power and the Professions in Britain 1700-1850* (1995) makes useful comments on the emergence of the profession's structure while H. Kirk, *Portrait of a Profession: A history of the solicitor's profession, 1100 to the present day* (1976) deals with institutional development. Histories of most of the major London commercial firms have also been published, such as Judy Slinn, *A History of Freshfields* (1984) and *Clifford Chance: Its origins and development* (1993), Andrew St George, *A History of Norton Rose* (1995) and Laurie Dennett, *Slaughter & May: A short history* (1989).

As with other service providers, in the absence of a business's archives there are real difficulties in identifying the solicitors that acted for it historically. The position is easier with public companies, as the solicitor's name might well appear on its prospectus and other shareholder documents. Otherwise clues may be available on its Company House file.

Accountancy Services

The archives of firms of chartered accountants providing audit and other accounting services, as well as managing the liquidation process, are of great potential help in shedding light on the history of a business although, as with other service providers, their usefulness is countered by a generally poor survival rate.

While specialist accountants were at work at the end of the 18th century, the accounting profession in England did not start to adopt its present form until the 1840s. Most leading accountancy firms today trace their antecedence to this period and in particular to legislation in 1844 that first permitted the general formation of joint stock companies through registration with the newly formed Registrar of Companies. A requirement of registration was the filing with the Registrar of an annual audited balance sheet for the avoidance of fraud and for the confidence of shareholders and creditors. Although this requirement was temporarily abolished between 1856 and 1900, auditing of many company accounts continued as a matter of good practice; it is reckoned that the accounts of 85 per cent of registered companies were audited by 1885. Other legislation in the 1840s regulated the liquidation of companies and was additional to the 1831 Bankruptcy Act, which required the appointment of an 'official assignee' to liquidate a business on behalf of creditors.

These factors created a substantial stream of auditing and liquidation work for the emergent accountancy profession; when the Institute of Chartered Accountants in England & Wales was formed in 1880 it had 600 members. Membership thereafter increased in leaps and bounds while additional associations of accountants were established as the profession became more specialised. The first firms of accountants, as opposed to single practitioners, were formed in the late 18th century and numbers grew steadily although for many years the size of firms remained small; by 1880 the largest practices still had just six partners. In recent years a small group of very large firms has emerged largely as a result of mergers although small firms and single practitioners continue to thrive at a local level.

While auditing and liquidation comprised the lion's share of accountants' work until relatively recently, other functions developed as the corporate environment became more sophisticated and regulated. These functions included the valuation of assets and calculation of liabilities, the provision of tax advice, especially from the First World War, and general advisory work in connection with flotations, reconstructions, amalgamations, changes in ownership, introduction of new accountancy procedures and interpretation of new legislation.

Accountants' archives can be expected to include customer relationship files touching on financial performance, annual audit, tax, accounting procedures, valuation and winding up. Specific documents include copies of audited accounts and various audit letters and associated working papers, memorandum and articles of association, prospectuses and so on. Until they were barred from doing so in the 1940s, auditors sometimes sat on the boards of customer companies and so board papers and correspondence might also be present. Administration and accounting archives include private and general ledgers, diaries, fee records and, more recently, partners' minutes; many will contain customer-specific information, albeit to varying degrees.

Details of the surviving archives of about two hundred firms are described at series level in Wendy Habgood, *Chartered Accountants in England and Wales: A guide to historical records* (1994). More up to date information is available for Britain as a whole in the National Register of Archives (www.nationalarchives.gov.uk/nra) by searching online under 'business and professional services/financial services'. Both sources confirm that survival of archives is at best patchy with most relating to administration and accounting and not customers although there are notable exceptions. Very few archives of the largest firms have found their way to record offices.

Wendy Habgood's guide contains a useful chapter by Peter Boys on the history of the development of accountancy firms and their functions while Edgar Jones, *Accountancy and the British Economy 1840-1980: The evolution of Ernst & Whinney* (1981) provides greater detail through the experience of one large firm.

There are numerous professional accountancy bodies in the UK, but the oldest and most important, and most relevant in the present context, are the Institute of Chartered Accountants in England & Wales (www.icaew.co.uk), established in 1880, and the Institute of Chartered Accountants of Scotland (www.icas.org.uk), established in 1854. The former has extensive archives of its activities and membership deposited at Guildhall Library and its website contains much historical information. Details of accountancy firms and the partners that belong to them have been published on a regular basis since the late 19th century and current ones are available online at www.icaewfirms.co.uk.

The auditors of active and recently dissolved companies can be identified through consulting the files of Companies House (Registrar of Companies) (www.companieshouse.gov.uk) while details of auditors of many earlier dissolved businesses will be on Companies House files in the National Archives and National Archives of Scotland (*see* pp.50-3). Their identity will also be given in documents such as annual reports and prospectuses and, in recent decades, in reference books for public and large private companies.

Property Services

In tracing the history of a business, the archives of providers of property-related services may well be helpful. The architect is prominent among these, and relatively well documented, but there are other groups ranging from construction and civil engineering businesses to chartered surveyors, from consulting engineers to estate agents. However, should a business's archives not have survived, there is no easy means of discovering the identity of the property service providers it used. Perhaps the best source for noteworthy projects is contemporary reports in the architectural and building press.

The origins of the architect, the engineer and the builder are, of course, ancient, but before the early decades of the 19th century there was no great delineation of responsibility in the building process. Major projects were led by architects or engineers who also managed the building process through to completion. After 1800, however, their different roles became quite separate and distinctive. By mid-century important firms of building contractors were emerging while the architect and engineer staked out their ground as professionals. It was at this time, for example, that institutes such as the Royal Institute of British Architects and the Institutions of Civil and Mechanical Engineers were formed to define their profession and represent its interests.

It might also be added that before 1800 large and sophisticated building projects for trade and industry, calling on specialist expertise, were few and far between. Most large commissions were for residential, ecclesiastical, governmental and educational buildings. Early commercial buildings were limited in scale; they included market halls and exchanges but shops, offices and banks were accommodated in little more than residential buildings. Industrial buildings were generally unsophisticated and/or on a small scale, although some notable exceptions existed, such as grain mills near large cities, royal dockyards, ordnance works and the like. Industrial structures were confined in size by power constraints and in design by cost constraints. The most complex were the work of millwrights who used utilitarian and essentially functional structures to house proven production processes. The big exceptions were transport infrastructure, such as canals, navigable rivers and harbours, and water supply. Major projects for these were underway in the mid-18th century.

The archives of businesses such as architects and building and civil engineering contractors detail the buildings of their customers and the functions and processes carried on within them and shed light on costs of construction and refurbishment and on the underlying decision-making process. They take the form of contracts and specifications, contract registers and accounts, job files, plans and drawings and, not least, photographs. Estate agents' archives include sale particulars for buildings and plant, consulting engineers have plans and technical reports and chartered surveyors valuations and building reports.

Local record offices have strong collections relating to architects, construction companies, chartered surveyors and estate agents and they can be located through the National Registers of Archives (www.nra.nationalarchives.gov.uk and www.nas.gov.uk). The archives of architects are better served than the rest. The British Architectural Library at the Victoria & Albert Museum is a source of expertise and holds some 1,500 archive collections although few appear to touch on business. Its collections are described online (www.vam.ac.uk/collections/architecture) and in detail in Angela Mace, *Architecture in Manuscript, 1601-1996: Guide to the British Architectural Library manuscripts and archives collections* (1998). Angela Mace also describes the professional archives of the Royal Institute of British Architects in *The Royal Institute of British Architects: A guide to its archives and history* (1986). Rebecca M. Bailey, *Scottish Architects' Papers: A source book* (q.v.) lists the surviving archives of Scottish architects and gives useful insight into their nature and content. The archives of the specialised firm of Stott & Son, mill architects of Oldham, are held in Oldham Local Studies & Archives (www.oldham.gov.uk) and were used extensively in Roger N. Holden, *Stott & Sons: Architects of the Lancashire cotton mill* (1998).

The Construction History Society (www.constructionhistory.co.uk) has taken the initiative in encouraging the preservation of the archives of the construction industry; it publishes an annual journal, *Construction History*, and a newsletter. Iain Russell gives insight into sources for construction industry research in 'Researching a company history: The McAlpine project', *Construction History* (2, 1986). The libraries and archives of professional bodies such as the Institutions of Civil Engineers (www.ice.org.uk) and Mechanical Engineers (www.imeche.org) and Royal Institution of Chartered Surveyors (www.rics.org) contain much information about the activities of their individual members, the firms to which they belonged, and wider business.

Edgar Jones, *Industrial Architecture in Britain 1750-1939* (1985) provides an overview of industrial buildings while Lynn Pearson, *British Breweries: An architectural history* (1999) highlights the involvement of architects and engineers in a particular industry. The latter includes an extensive schedule of architects dealing with brewery projects. Also useful is Ian H. Goodall, *Yorkshire Textile Mills 1770-1930* (1992) and Julian Hodder & Steven Parissien (eds), *The Architecture of British Transport in the 20th Century* (2004). Commercial, as opposed to industrial, buildings are not as well covered in the literature. John Booker, *Temples of Mammon: The architecture of banking* (1990) deals with bank buildings and Kathryn A. Morrison, *English Shops and Shopping: An architectural history* (2003) provides a handsome account of the development of retail architecture. H.A.N. Brockman, *The British Architect in Industry 1841-1940* (1974) defines the architect's role in industry. Christopher Powell, *The British Building Industry Since 1800: An economic history* (2nd edn, 1996) gives a comprehensive overview of the construction industry's history while Iain Russell, *Sir Robert McAlpine & Sons: The early years* (1988) provides an authoritative history of a major construction business between the 1870s and 1930s.

Architecture and the construction industry have always been well served by the trade press, which gives good coverage to the completion of construction projects for business customers. *The Builder*, published from 1843 and now known as *Building*, is perhaps the best known. In the 19th century its illustrated articles were read by builders, engineers and tradesmen as well as by architects. An annual index to its content was compiled at the time of publication; subsequently a cumulative index to illustrations has been published as Ruth Richardson and Robert Thorne, *The Builder Illustrations Index, 1843-1883* (1994). Other publications included the *Architects' Journal*, started in 1895 when known as the *Builders' Journal*, and the *Architect*, first published in 1869 as *Architect and Building News*. A strength of these publications is their illustrations. By way of example, the photographic archive of the Architectural Press, publishers of, *inter alia*, the *Architects' Journal*, comprises some 500,000 images dating from the 1830s, and is lodged in the British Architectural Library.

Advertising Services

The historical archives of providers of advertising services to a business have obvious value in shedding light on its history. Advertising has been part of the business scene for as long as modern business has existed. Early forms were town criers and handwritten signs above shop doorways, but a glance at late 18th-century newspapers shows the importance of conventional advertising even at this early date. In the following century, as regional and national markets developed, so advertising and other forms of marketing became especially important.

Newspapers, together with popular and specialist periodicals, remained by far the most important advertising vehicles until well into the 20th century. Also important from the late 19th century were mass-produced advertisements on thin metal sheets, often erected in railway stations and shops; in the 20th century they gave way to posters. Cinema advertising dates from the 1920s and was followed by television and radio advertising in the 1950s and 1970s respectively.

Advertisements and posters were early forms of marketing but they were supported by a wide range of other products appropriate to the nature of the underlying goods or services being sold. Product literature, packaging, publicity brochures, price lists, product catalogues, almanacs, calendars, cigarette cards, recipe books, beer mats and promotional goods all fall into this category. As the range of marketing products increased and as the marketplace grew bigger, so broader advertising and marketing strategies were called for if only for co-ordination purposes.

These developments inevitably resulted in the formation of specialist agencies to assist businesses in their advertising and marketing. Although early on, big businesses, especially those involved in the mass production of consumer goods marketed under nationally recognisable brand names, employed their own specialist advertising and marketing teams, few businesses of significant size had no recourse to advertising and public relations agencies by the early 20th century. The archives of these agencies – as well as the advertisements and marketing products they developed – are therefore useful in shedding light on the history of a business. On the one hand they might illuminate advertising initiatives and, through them, product development, while on the other they might well reveal details of markets, marketing strategy and customer base. In addition, their use in supplying the historian with valuable illustrative material is well established.

Early advertising agencies were little more than space-brokers, acting as intermediaries between advertisers and publishers, especially of newspapers, identifying and purchasing advertising space on behalf of the former and selling it on behalf of the latter. In the last decades of the 19th century, the introduction of mass advertising of branded products ushered in change. Adverting agencies now came into their own, writing and designing advertising copy, developing the underlying strategies and arranging publication in different formats. Sell's Advertising Agency, a British leader established in 1869, promoted brands such as Lipton's Tea and Sunlight Soap and forms a good early example. It handled the general advertising requirements of businesses, municipalities and government departments and managed the advertising content of many periodicals. Other notable early agencies included W.S. Crawford, Dorland Advertising, Samson Clark, Frederick Porter and R.F. White & Sons; the earliest, established in 1783, is reckoned to be Charles F. Scripps of London.

In identifying agencies used by businesses, the annual *Advertisers' Annual* is invaluable; it is sometimes referred to as *The Blue Book*. Published since 1915, it provides much detail about advertising agencies including lists of their accounts. The first issue, for example, largely comprised two schedules, one of around 5,000 businesses that 'habitually use the press' for advertising and the other of advertising agencies, together with the names of their business customers. Other useful directories and periodicals detailing the advertising industry and its business include *ALF*, formerly known as *Account List File* (from 1986), *Advertiser's Weekly*, later *Ad Week* (1913-c.72) and *Advertising World* (1901-c.43). Poster advertising is separately covered in such publications as *United Kingdom Bill Posters Association Directory* (1864-88), *Bill Poster Directory* (1888-1936) and *Bill Posters Advertising Year Book and Directory* (1931-49).

A search of the National Register of Archives (www.nra.nationalarchives.gov.uk) under 'business and professional services/advertising and publicity services' provides details of the archives of some agencies, perhaps the most important being those of Charles Barker & Sons, leading agents from the 19th century. They contain much customer account detail, which is something of a rarity, as well as advertisement copy, which is far more common. The latter comprises series such as guard books of advertisement, photographs, artwork and posters.

The History of Advertising Trust (www.hatads.org.uk) is by far the major source for British advertising history and has been particularly successful in building a collection of archives, books, periodicals, television commercials and other materials. Its holdings include archives of over 20 advertising agencies such as J. Walter Thompson, Bates UK, Charles Barker & Sons and Ogilvy & Mather. Alongside these are the advertising archives of brand-focused businesses such as H.J. Heinz & Co. Ltd, Rank Hovis MacDougal (RHM), SmithKlein Beecham and Rowntrees as well as other archives of industry associations and individual designers and artists. A major component is an accumulation of around 10,000 television commercials dating from the 1950s. For more details *see* Stefan Schwarzkopf, 'Sources for the history of advertising in the United Kingdom: The records of the advertising agencies and related advertising material at the History of Advertising Trust', *Business Archives* (2005). This article also provides a potted history of the development of advertising agencies.

A useful account of the advertising industry's development, containing an extensive bibliography, is T.R. Nevett, *Advertising in Britain: A history* (1982). Numerous publications deal with the history of individual brands including *The Story of Sunlight: Centenary of a famous soap* (1984), Peter Hadley (ed.), *The History of Bovril Advertising* (1972), *The Advertising Art of J. & J. Colman: Yellow, red and blue* (1977) and Jim Davies, *The Book of Guinness Advertising* (1998). Advertising on commercial television is dealt with by Brian Henry, *British Television Advertising: The first thirty years* (1986).

Stockbroker Services

Stockbrokers buy and sell shares and other securities, participate in the flotation of new companies, manage investments and, more recently, provide general financial advice. Their archives, therefore, have potential value in tracing the history of a business. They will, however, only relate to companies that are, or once were, quoted on the London Stock Exchange or, until 1973, on provincial stock exchanges.

Stockbrokers, along with the stock market, have existed in London since the 17th century although, in their early days, were focused on British government securities (gilts) and later, in a much smaller way, on securities of overseas governments. Change came in the early 19th century with an increase in the pace of joint stock company formation, initially in such areas as railways, banking, insurance and utility services. By 1850 around a fifth of all securities quoted in London were those of businesses and the proportion grew steadily as entirely new businesses were floated and as old established partnerships converted to public companies.

As the size of the London stock market grew so too did the number of stockbrokers; for example, between 1850 and 1900 membership of the London Stock Exchange grew from 900 individual members to over four thousand. By the early 1980s some 250 firms existed but they were then dominated by a relatively small group of major businesses, which, during the period of Big Bang, were absorbed into much larger investment banking houses.

The stockbroker's role is fairly easily defined. Historically their routine business was buying and selling securities for accounts of their customers, thereby creating a market. Their most high-profile and business-specific activities came to be company flotations and subsequent security issues. They dealt with smaller flotations themselves; in larger ones, handled by merchant banks, they fulfilled a secondary role in putting together lists of underwriters and investors, advertising the flotation, offering advice on market sentiment and so on. A related group of stockjobbers purchased and sold largely for their own account, dealing direct with brokers and thereby providing the market with liquidity.

Stockbroker archives relating to flotations and new issues should, in theory, include prospectuses and other stock exchange-related documentation, customer correspondence, security registers showing lists of underwriters/subscribers and the extent and nature of their participation, and so on. Other archives could include day books showing sales and purchases of securities undertaken as part of routine dealing activity. However, judged from archives deposited in record offices, the survival rate of stockbroker archives is generally poor.

Several archives can be located in the National Register of Archives (www.nra.nationalarchives.gov.uk) by searching under 'business and professional services/financial services'; they are mostly of London-based firms and are held at Guildhall Library. Well-known names include James Capel & Co., Heseltine Powell, Foster Braithwaite, Mullens & Co., Nathan & Rosselli, Phillips & Drew and Sheppards & Chase. However, their focus is administration and accounting, rather than customer-related transactions.

The identity of a business's stockbrokers can today be identified from several reference books. The *Issuing House Year Book* (1935-70) links issues and issuing houses to brokers on an annual basis. Historically, other sources include prospectuses (*see* pp.115-19, stock exchange records (*see* pp.71-5), press reports and so on.

William M. Clarke, *How the City of London Works: An introduction to its financial markets* (2004) provides a short account of the work of brokers. Ranald Michie, *The London Stock Exchange: A history* (1999) gives a detailed account of their historical role and is complemented by three good house histories. David Kynaston, *Cazenove & Co.: A history* (1991) and W.J. Reader and David Kynaston, *Phillips & Drew: Professionals in the City* (1998) are strong on 20th-century broking by two firms with very different traditions. W.J. Reader, *A House in the City: A study of the City and of the Stock Exchange based on the records of Foster & Braithwaite 1825-1975* (1979) deals well with corporate broking and company promotion in the 19th century.

Details of individual brokers and their firms are recorded in various publications. *List of Members of the Stock Exchange*, later known as *Members and Firms of the Stock Exchange*, was published annually from 1836 until recently. Other annual publications include *Ralph's Stock and Share Brokers Directory* (1851-8) and *United Kingdom Stock and Sharebrokers Directory* (1881-1940).

Of great value in terms of business-specific information are the printed reports on companies, as well as on business sectors and markets, privately circulated by brokers and investment houses to their investor customers and potential customers as a means of generating business. Examples of good-quality broker reports on companies can be found as early as the 1920s, but it was in the late 1950s and especially in the 1960s that brokers became more purposeful in their research production. In the 1970s the flow of reports to investors, ranging from brief buy and sell recommendations to lengthy analytical work, increased very substantially. This early output is quite difficult to find. Some survives with the brokers and houses that published it, but it seems that high storage costs have mitigated against this. Some can be found in national and leading academic libraries via their online catalogue, Copac (www.copac.ac.uk).

Recently published reports held in the British Library can be located via the library's Business Information Database (www.bl.uk). Recent reports are also held in online information services such as Investext Plus (www.galegroup.com); its files date back to the early 1980s but appear to be comprehensive only from the late 1990s. The current output of investment houses is stored and increasingly circulated by them electronically so its long-term survival rate should much improve.

RECORDS OF GOVERNMENT

Introduction

Central government impinges on business in so many ways that its archives are an enormous, wide-ranging and immensely valuable source of information for the history of business activity. Most archive series, however, touch on business at industry level and deal with issues such as performance, regulation, taxation and so on. But in addition to these there are some valuable business-specific series of use in tracing the history of a particular business. These include, for example, the company files of the Registrar of Companies, files relating to the bankruptcy of individual businesses, records relating to the registration of patents, designs and trade makes, registers detailing apprenticeships and so on. It is these business-specific archive series that are dealt with here.

That said, the researcher should be aware that a very wide range of archive series do contain references to individual businesses, although these tend to be big businesses. These archives include files created through the purchase of goods and services by central government, especially capital equipment such as buildings, ships, aircraft, naval stores and roads. Others result from public ownership of businesses involved in, say, railway transport, shipbuilding and repair, electricity and gas production and distribution, water supply and iron and steel production. Files of departments such as the Board of Trade, Treasury, Ministry of Public Buildings & Works, Ministry of Aviation, Ministry of Shipping, Ministry of War Transport, Customs & Excise, etc, provide contextual information as well as business-specific information. These series are far too numerous and diverse to be dealt with here.

Virtually all government archives, including those of the courts, are located either in the National Archives (www.nationalarchives.gov.uk), until relatively recently known as the Public Record Office, at Kew, London, or the National Archives of Scotland (www.nas.gov.uk), formerly the Scottish Record Office, Edinburgh. Very much smaller collections are held by the National Library of Wales (www.llgc.org.uk) and the Public Record Office of Northern Ireland (www.proni.gov.uk). In particular, the National Archives of Scotland holds archives of pre-union (i.e. 1707) Scotland, of the Scottish Office, of Scottish courts and of government agencies in Scotland; almost all other UK public records are at the National Archives.

All these entities have informative websites, especially the National Archives and the National Archives of Scotland; most of their catalogues are available online and a large number of extremely useful research guides to different archive series and subjects can be downloaded. Of great importance in tracing the history of a business is the ability to search across the whole content of these online catalogues by name of a specific business.

The websites to a very great extent have replaced earlier hard-copy guides, the most useful of which, for business history in the modern period, continues to be Brenda Swann and Maureen Turnbull, *Records of Interest to Social Scientists, 1919-1939* (1971); its covering dates mask the fact that it deals with a much broader period. Two journal articles give useful overviews: T. Rath, 'Business Records in the Public Record Office in the Age of the Industrial Revolution', *Business History* (1975) and Charles Harvey, 'Business Records at the Public Record Office', *Business Archives* (1986). John Imrie, 'National archive sources for business history' in Peter Payne (ed.), *Studies in Scottish Business History* (1967), while dated, remains a short but very helpful overview of business sources in the National Archives of Scotland.

Company Registration

Companies House (www.companieshouse.gov.uk) is an agency of the Department of Business, Enterprise & Regulatory Reform and originally a section of the Board of Trade. It incorporates and registers new companies, de-registers dissolved companies and collects, examines, stores and makes available to the public on demand information that all companies registered with it are obliged to file on a regular basis. In undertaking these tasks it aims to promote the proper management of companies for the benefit of shareholders, creditors and the community at large. Its archives have obvious value in tracing the history of a business.

The Companies House has its roots in the Registrar of Companies, sometimes referred to as the Register of Companies, established under the Joint Stock Companies Registration & Regulation Act of 1844. Until the passing of this Act, the vast majority of businesses were owned by partnerships or individual traders, the chief exception being the several hundred companies formed by special Act of Parliament or by royal charter. The 1844 Act enabled for the first time the routine and therefore inexpensive formation of multi-shareholder businesses simply through registration with the London-based Registrar or with an Assistant Registrar in Dublin. Additional Assistant Registrars were established in Edinburgh in 1856 to incorporate Scottish-based companies (the 1844 Act had not applied to Scotland) and, for particular reasons, in Truro between 1862 and 1887 to deal with local mining companies.

The 1844 Act defined a company as one with 25 or more shareholders or whose shares were freely transferable between investors. The concept of limited liability was introduced by the 1855 Limited Liability Act while the 1856 Joint Stock Companies Act, as well as requiring all existing companies to re-register, permitted the general formation of companies with as few as seven shareholders. Many other companies acts followed, significantly extending and consolidating this early legislation. Most notably, the 1907 Act introduced the concept of the private company; up until then no distinction in law had been made between public and other companies.

The Registrar has always kept for each company a file identified by the company's unique registration number. On to the file is put core documentation supplied by the company at the time of its registration and subsequently, for the most part, by means of annual returns. The exact make-up of this documentation has varied over the years according to the requirements of different companies acts but in essence not to any major extent. Generally speaking, it provides details of the full name and address of the company, its directors, its shareholders, its purpose, its constitution, its share capital and debt, and its general financial position as shown by an annual balance sheet and annual profit and loss account. As these details change, so the company must report changes to the registrar. Sometime this is done on an irregular basis – e.g. change of address or constitution – and otherwise on a regular annual basis by means of 'annual returns' – e.g. covering balance sheet, profit and loss and shareholders. The files of dissolved companies include papers relating to winding up and removal from the register.

Perhaps the most important documents on the file are the annual financial returns; in their early state these may be viewed as the forerunners of the present-day annual report and accounts. The 1844 Act required the filing of a balance sheet but this was cancelled by the 1856 Act, although submissions were continued by some companies. The 1907 Companies Act, which for the first time distinguished public from private companies (which, *inter alia*, were limited to a maximum of 50 shareholders), partly reversed this requirement by requiring public companies to file an audited annual balance sheet. This balance sheet was to contain 'a summary of [the company's] capital, its liabilities and its assets, giving such particulars as will disclose the general nature of such liabilities and assets, and how the values of fixed assets have been arrived at'. The requirement to lodge a balance sheet did not extend to private companies, which is unfortunate for the historian as these soon outnumbered public companies. This increase in number partly reflected the enthusiasm of existing family partnerships for conversion to private companies, thereby benefiting from limited liability and a more convenient ownership structure, but at the same time maintaining financial privacy.

Due presumably to an oversight, the 1907 legislation failed to stipulate that public companies needed to submit an up to date balance sheet, so some companies made no submission. This shortcoming was corrected by the 1929 Companies Act, which also required additional disclosure of financial information. Disclosure was taken a step further by the 1948 Companies Act, which obliged private companies to file an annual balance sheet with the exception, until 1967, of 'exempt' companies. After 1967 any company wishing to maintain financial privacy had to register as an unlimited company.

Companies House has always maintained the files of currently registered companies in their entirety but their format has changed over the years. From the mid-1970s, all newly submitted papers were microfilmed on arrival while existing papers were also microfilmed with the exception of annual returns and changes in directors/registered offices that were more than three and seven years old respectively. The microfiche comprises three categories – annual reports and accounts, mortgage documents, and general papers including register of directors, memorandum and articles of association and annual returns of shareholders. Paper-based files kept prior to the microfilming programme continued to be held. From the 1990s microfiche was replaced by electronic format, the result of the submission of documents electronically and the digitisation of others thereby radically transforming access to them.

Indexes to company files/registration numbers are also held in three formats – paper, microfiche and electronic. Today Companies House's website (www.companieshouse.gov.uk) provides schedules of currently registered companies and, for the period from the mid-1980s, of dissolved companies and name changes. These schedules can be searched by company name or registration number. Prior to this, from the early 1970s indexes were accessible on microfiche that could be purchased. These indexes comprised a schedule of currently registered companies, updated quarterly, which gave company name, number, address and date of registration, as well as schedules of name changes from 1976 and of dissolved companies from 1963. Prior to 1976, information was kept on conventional card indexes. Those for England and Wales remain with Companies House, Cardiff and, while not available directly to the public, are consulted by Companies House staff on behalf of researchers. These indexes are supplemented by various printed schedules held in the search room of the National Archives, the one covering companies registered between 1856 and 1920 being the most important. Card indexes are available in the National Archives of Scotland.

The files of dissolved companies are retained by Companies House until about twenty years after dissolution when they are either transferred to the National Archives or the National Archives of Scotland or destroyed. At the National Archives, almost 6,000 files of companies formed under the 1844 Act and under the 1856 Act but dissolved before 1860 are held in series BT41. Virtually all others are in held in BT31; in 2007 they amounted to some 45,000 files. The major exception is the 600 files relating to mining companies formed between 1862 and 1897 within the jurisdiction of the Court of the Vice Warden of the Stannaries, which are held in series BT286. Liquidators' accounts for over 5,000 companies dissolved between 1890 and 1932 are in BT34; prior to 1890 no accounts had to be filed, while after 1932 they are held in the main company file in BT31. The individual files making up all these series are described in the National Archives online catalogue (www.nationalarchives.gov.uk). In the National Archives of Scotland (www.nas.gov.uk), dissolved company files are held in series BT2.

Many files of dissolved companies in the National Archives have been destroyed on account of the high storage costs that would otherwise have been incurred. While all files of dissolved public and non-exempt private companies have been retained in the National Archives, the files of other dissolved private companies have been very significantly reduced, initially in 1950 to a one per cent sample and then to one half of one per cent for dissolutions from 1977 onwards. However the microfilmed files or part-files existing from the early 1970s will be retained in their entirety. All files of dissolved Scottish companies have been retained in the National Archives of Scotland; they total around fifty thousand.

In order to fill partially the gap resulting from the destruction of dissolved private company files, relevant sheets of a so-called Classified Index to files have been retained in the National Archives in series BT95. A sheet exists for each company, which gives broad details about it together with details of the documents it submitted to the Registrar. Sheets for companies dissolved after 1943 remain with Companies House. Much of the information in BT95 will also be found in Parliamentary Papers, the *Investors' Guardian* and *Jordan's Daily Register of New Companies* (*see* p.11). Equivalent records in the National Archives of Scotland are in series BT1 for companies registered from 1856.

The contents of retained files of dissolved companies at the National Archives have been reduced, also as a cost-saving exercise. While complete files are retained for all companies registered under the 1844 Act, only a one per cent sample of all other company files has been retained in a complete state. The first decision to reduce content was made in 1950 when annual returns other than the first, last and every intermediate fifth were weeded out for companies dissolved before 1943; in 1960 content was further reduced to every first, last and tenth return for companies dissolved after this date. Files at the National Archives of Scotland have not been weeded.

Court papers relating to the winding up of companies are found outside the Board of Trade series. Series C26, for example, contains almost 700 files of proceedings and accounts in winding-up actions for the period 1849 to 1910 while series J13 relates to winding up and other proceedings for almost 20,000 companies between 1890 and 1980. Other company-specific files are at J44, J137, B3, B9 and B10.

The National Archives publishes an excellent Research Guide to its holdings of company files called 'Registration of Companies and Businesses' which can be downloaded from its website. Other overviews are provided by Lesley Richmond 'The records of the Registrar of Companies', *Business Archives* (64, 1992) and Christopher T. and Michael J. Watts, 'Company records as a source for the family historian', *Genealogists' Magazine* (21, 1983); the latter includes discussion of how genealogical information can be extracted from this seemingly unlikely source. J.R. Edwards, *British Company Legislation and Company Accounts 1844-1976* (1980) and J.R. Edwards, *Company Legislation and Changing Patterns of Disclosure in British Company Accounts 1900-1940* (1981) deal with company law and financial statements. P.L. Cottrell, *Industrial Finance, 1830-1914: The finance and organisation of English manufacturing industry* (1980) and Peter L. Payne, *The Early Scottish Limited Companies, 1856-1895* (1980) provide historical analysis of company formations and discussion of the legal framework.

Business Names Registration

The Register of Business Names operated from 1917 in response to the government's wish for greater transparency about business ownership at a time of war. Businesses trading under a name other than their formal/legal business name were obliged to register their trading name, the name(s) and nationality of their proprietors, their address and their activities. Initially registration applied to partnerships and individual traders, but was extended to include limited companies from 1947. However, difficulties of enforcing registration meant that perhaps as many as half of those business required to register failed to so. The Register was wound up in 1982.

On abolition, a small sample of the Register's registration files was placed in the National Archives in series BT253. The sample comprises registration documents for a selection of businesses registered in 1916-17, and every 10 years from 1921 until 1981-2. In total there are almost 1,300 files or volumes, a tiny proportion of the original register, which very significantly undermines the value of this source when tracing the history of a specific business.

Registration of Patents

A patent provides a business or individual with exclusive rights to the use and benefits of their invention by preventing its exploitation by others, without permission, for a given period. Over the years many thousands of patents have been applied for and usually granted. Early on, most patentees were individuals; only in the 20th century do businesses become commonplace.

Patents as an historical source have the advantages of relating to an early period, when few other sources of information about businesses exist, and of being relatively easy to access. That said, their content is technical and, for the non-specialist, often not easy to interpret. But patents do give insight into inventiveness and technical awareness, although not necessarily innovativeness. Also they might indicate collaboration with individuals or other businesses and shed light on assets, processes and products. Brian Winship, 'Patents as an historical source', *Industrial Archaeology* (1981) deals with their uses and limitations.

While patent law became more sophisticated in the mid-19th century – leading eventually to the establishment of the Patent Office – patents have a much longer history. The earliest known example dates to 1449 but only in 1624 was the first workable patent law in England introduced; it granted protection for 14 years. Scotland developed its own system, although very few patents were granted there before 1750. The first significant modern legislation, in 1852, established the Patent Commissioners' Office to process all British patents.

In 1875 the Patent Commissioners extended their responsibilities to the registration of designs, which had begun in 1839 (*see* pp.46-9), and trade marks (*see* pp.59-61). Legislation in

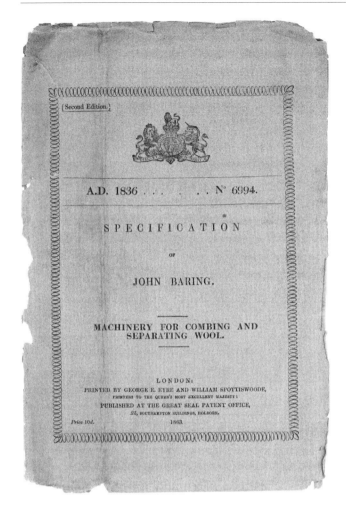

[Second Edition.]

A.D. 1836 . . . . Nº 6994.

SPECIFICATION

OF

JOHN BARING.

MACHINERY FOR COMBING AND
SEPARATING WOOL.

LONDON:
PRINTED BY GEORGE E. EYRE AND WILLIAM SPOTTISWOODE,
PRINTERS TO THE QUEEN'S MOST EXCELLENT MAJESTY:
PUBLISHED AT THE GREAT SEAL PATENT OFFICE,
25, SOUTHAMPTON BUILDINGS, HOLBORN.

Price 10d.   1863.

10   *This patent was awarded to John Baring in 1863. Patents are useful in giving insight into the technical background of a business while also providing an information source that dates back to the early 17th century when business archives are scarce. Patents are supported by numerous printed indexes and abridgements.*

1883 replaced the Commissioners of Patents with the Patents, Designs & Trade Marks Office, where examiners reviewed the validity of patent applications. It was renamed the Patent Office in the 1920s. In 1905 the term of a patent was extended to 16 years; today it is 20 years. Over the years, but especially from the late 19th century, the number of patents filed annually grew substantially, from 450 applications in 1851, to 17,000 in 1884, to 33,000 in 1982.

The Patent Office has published details of patents, and finding-aids to them, in several series of publications. These include the patents themselves, plus abridgements, published journals, papers relating to legal actions and indexes. These and other sources are described in Stephen van Dulken, *British Patents of Invention, 1617-1977: A guide for researchers* (1999). This provides especially useful guidance; what follows here is a brief outline of the major sources available for patents. All are in the Intellectual Property Section of the British Library (www.bl.uk), which incorporates the original Patent Office Library and which today is the major point of access for patent information. The Intellectual Property Section publishes on its website a useful guide to information sources for historical patents.

Soon after the establishment of the Patent Commissioners' Office in 1852 all c.14,500 patents, and abridgements of them, granted in England since 1617 were printed and are available in the British Library. Indexes to them were published under the authorship of the then Superintendent of Specifications, Bennet Woodcroft. They include *Alphabetical Index of Patentees of Inventions from 1617 to 1852* (1854, reprinted 1969), *Chronological Index of Patents of Invention from 1617 to 1853* (1854), which is, in effect, a collection of patent abridgements, *Subject Matter Index of Patents of Invention, 1617 to 1852* (1857) and *Reference Index of Patents of Invention from 1617 to 1852* (1862). Scottish patents prior to 1853 have not been printed (q.v.).

Specifications of patents granted after 1852 were printed, published and indexed as a matter of course, each one being given a unique sequential reference number. Early specifications are typically three or four pages long and supported by diagrams and other illustrations. They describe the invention, provide dates of application and grant, and give the name and address of the patentee. Details of any subsequent amendments are also provided. Abandoned or otherwise unsuccessful applications for patents were not published.

Abridgements of these patent specifications, usually around 100 words in length, were made. They are organised in three main series, each series being arranged by subject category; this can be quite complicated as dozens of different categories exist and sometime categories are subdivided. The first series, extending to about 100 volumes, covers patents granted between 1617 and 1883, the second covers the years 1855 to 1930 in several hundred volumes, and the third covers years 1931 to 1961. Volumes have name and subject indexes. From 1886 until 1930, the Patent Office published its weekly *Illustrated Journal of Patented Inventions Including Abridgements of Complete Specifications Accepted*, which includes short illustrated descriptions of newly granted patents, arranged by date of application. There is an annual patent number index.

Of longer duration was the weekly *Official Journal of the Patent Office*, first published in 1855 as *The Commissioners of Patents' Journal* and continuing today as *The Patents & Designs Journal*. In its early form it included notices of patents sealed, notices of provisional protection and so on, as well as general Patent Office notices. Its content later broadened to include schedules of new applicants, specifications accepted, patents sealed, patents abandoned, and of renewal fees received as well as information about registered designs (*see* pp.56-9).

Various indexes to post-1852 patents exist. An annual name index to applicants for patents was published from 1853 until 1938 and thereafter for every 20,000 applicants, initially under the title *Alphabetical Index of Patentees and Applicants for Patents of Invention* and later as *Names of Applicants and Inventors*. Abridgements of Specifications (q.v.), arranged as they are by subject, provides a useful route to patents relating to a particular subject area; in addition each abridgement volume has subject and name indexes. A cumulative subject index, again arranged by subject class, for 1861 to 1910, was published as *Patents for Inventions: Fifty years subject index, 1861-1910* (1913-16). Other indexes include the annual *Subject Matter Index of Patents Applied for and Granted, 1852-1930* and various chronological indexes.

Disputes concerning patents often ended in the courts and reports on legal cases form another source of business-specific information. Reports on about 800 cases between 1600 and 1883 have been gathered together and published as P.A. Hayward, *Hayward's Patent Cases, 1600-1883: A compilation of the English patent cases for those years* (1987). Reports on cases from 1883 to the present day have been published in annual volumes under the title *Reports on Patent, Design and Trade Mark Cases* (from 1895). Short summaries, arranged by broad subject area and indexed by place name, are provided in *Digest of the Patent, Design,*

Trade Mark and other Cases Reported in … Reports of Patent, Design, Trade Mark and Other Cases 1883-1955 (1959). The National Archives holds papers relating to legal cases in several series but especially LO4, J99, J105 and J130 which include 20th-century papers of the Patent Appeals Tribunal.

Prior to the establishment of the Patent Commissioners, Chancery was responsible for the enrolment of specifications and patents and the issue of patents to patentees. Documents relating to this are found in series C54, C73 and C210 at the National Archives and subject, chronological and patentee indexes to them exist. Archives relating to some earlier patents are in series SO7. The National Archives publishes a research guide, 'Inventions: Patents and Specifications', which describes indexes and deals with search procedures; it can be downloaded from the Archives' website (www.nationalarchives.gov.uk). Other patent sources in the National Archives are listed exhaustively by Stephen van Dulken (q.v.).

Early specifications of Scottish patents are in several series in the National Archives of Scotland (www.nas.gov.uk) including C3, C19 and C20. They are supported by various indexes and calendars. The National Archives in London has two classes, HO105-106, holding information about Scottish patents. All these series end in the 1850s, or thereabouts, when the Scottish, Irish and English patent systems merged to form a unified system based in London under the Patent Commissioners' Office.

While the British Library has by far the best collection of patent-related information, many leading British reference libraries have comprehensive collections of patent specifications, abridgements, journal publications and indexes. Once again, Stephen van Dulken lists these comprehensively.

Useful background information is provided by Neil Davenport, *The United Kingdom Patent System: A brief history* (1979); H. Harding, *Patent Office Centenary: A Story of 100 Years in the Life and Work of the Patent Office* (1953); and Christine MacLeod, *Inventing the Industrial Revolution: The English patent system, 1660-1800* (2002).

Registration of Designs

Archives relating to registration of designs provide details of all sorts of products, especially textiles, manufactured by British businesses, although their potential depends on adequate finding-aids. In particular, they shed light on consumer products that do not survive in great numbers in, say, museums, on account of their short life-span. Not only do they illustrate the products of a business but potentially they show product changes over time, give the date of introduction and enable comparison with the products of competitors.

From 1787 the law offered a measure of protection for the exploitation of original designs, initially textiles, by their owners. Modern design law traces its origins to 1839 and the passing of the Design Copyright Act, which established the Registrar of Designs as a branch of the Board of Trade. In 1875 the Registrar's functions passed to the Patent Commissioners' Office, which in due course became known as the Patents, Designs & Trade Marks Office.

The 1839 Act secured copyright for a 12-month period following the deposit of the article, or more commonly an illustration, model or miniature copy of it, with the Design Registry. Unless the design was registered prior to its publication, it would enjoy no protection. Protection was extended by subsequent acts, especially the 1842 Act, which created 13 classes of design (including earthenware, glass, metal, wood, paper hangings, carpets, shawls, lace and other categories of textiles) and attempted to cover all designed manufactured goods for

11   *Registration of designs became possible in the mid-19th century and today the National Archives hold a vast collection of design representations covering a seemingly limitless range of products. A given business might well register many different designs covering numerous products and will give insight into its output and how this changed over time. The above design relates to door furniture manufactured by William Tonks & Sons of Birmingham in 1875.*

varying periods. From 1843 designs composed of functional as opposed to decorative features were also included.

At the Design Register, representations were generally glued into books, while corresponding series of registers were maintained recording details of ownership. Between 1842 and 1883, 410,000 designs were registered and numbers grew steadily over time; some 368,000 were registered in the much shorter period 1884 to 1901. However, registration, while sensible, was not obligatory and the designs of many businesses went unrecorded. No archives appear to have survived in connection with pre-1839 legislation.

Registers and books holding design representations dating from 1839 to 1990 are held in the National Archives while more recent ones remain with the Patent Office. There are 11 series, BT42-48, 50-53, which extend to several thousand volumes. Access to trade designs is by registration number and, in the absence of this, locating the designs of a business is time-consuming if not impossible. Searching for a business's designs is made more complicated still when registration is in the name of the designer and not the manufacturer. However, some indexes to proprietors' names have survived, for example at BT44/33-38, which covers the years 1839-70, at BT46/5-9 for series BT46 and subjects from 1843 to 1888, and at BT48/3-4 for series BT48. The National Archives' Research Guide, 'Registered designs and trade marks', provides hints for pinpointing designs when indexes do not exist (www.nationalarchives.gov.uk).

The Official Journal of the Patent Office, first published in 1854 as *The Commissioners' of Patents Journal*, from 1878 listed but did not illustrate newly registered designs. The details listed have changed over the years but generally include the name of business or person making the registration, their address, the class of product being registered and date of registration. Arrangement until 1933 is by class/registration number, thereafter by applicant's name. Indexes to registrant names were published yearly or half yearly from 1878 to 1922, while the years 1901 to 1938 are covered in a series of annual name indexes held in the Intellectual Property section of the British Library. Taken together, these are hugely useful in locating the designs of a given business. No name indexes exist for 1939 to 1960, but a card index covers 1961 to 1991.

No illustrations of designs were published until the establishment of *Designs in View* in 1997. Newly registered designs can also be located and viewed at www.patent.gov.uk/design. *The Official Journal of the Patent Office*, today known as *The Patents and Designs Journal*, and *Designs in View* are held on the open shelves in the Intellectual Property section of the British Library. The British Library's website includes a section on registered designs and describes how to search for them (www.bl.uk/collections/patents/designs.html).

From time to time legal cases arise concerning registered designs. From 1883 reports on legal cases have been published annually in *Reports on Patent, Design and Trade Mark Cases* (from 1895). Short summaries, arranged by broad subject area and indexed, are provided in *Digest of the Patent, Design, Trade Mark and Other Cases Reported in … Reports of Patent, Design, Trade Mark and Other Cases 1883-1955* (1959). The National Archives holds papers relating to legal cases in several series but especially LO4, J99, J105 and J130.

For further information about registered designs and their usefulness *see* Sarah Levitt, *Victorians Unbuttoned: Registered designs for clothing, their makers and wearers, 1839-1900* (1986), which reproduces many old designs, and also Sarah Levitt, 'The uses of registered design samples in the Public Record Office, Kew, for the study of 19th century clothing manufacturers', *Business Archives* (1984). 'Here,' she writes, 'are examples or pictures of the most elusive garments, from shirts, collars and neckties, to overcoats, mackintoshes, mantles and all kinds of hosiery. Together they paint a remarkable picture of the clothing trade in the last [nineteenth] century.' Some glass designs registered between 1842 and 1944 are listed on the Great Glass website (www.great-glass.co.uk), while pottery and porcelain designs registered between 1843 and 1883 are listed in John P. Cushion, *Handbook of Pottery and Porcelain Marks* (1980).

It is convenient here to mention also archives created in the early registration of the copyright of literary works, especially books. Before the introduction of copyright law in 1842, protection of copyright was possible through registration of the work at Stationers' Hall, the livery hall of the Worshipful Company of Stationers (www.stationers.org). The Company retains copyright registers for the period 1556 to 1842; transcriptions of those between 1556 and 1708 have been published, while the entire set is available on microfiche. The 1842 Copyright Act confirmed the continuing facility to register at Stationers' Hall, but archives from then until 1924, when formal registration was finally abandoned, have been transferred to the National Archives and are in series COPY 1-3. This great accumulation of information makes the

Stationers' Company's archives the finest source for the history of the book trade. For more information *see* the National Archives' Research Guide 'Stationers' Hall Copyright Records' (www.nationalarchives.gov.uk). *See also* Robin Myers, *The Stationers' Company Archive: An account of the records, 1554-1984* (1990) and 'The Records of the Worshipful Company of Stationers and Newspaper Makers', *Archives* (1983).

Registration of Trade Marks

The Patent Office's trade mark records provide illustrations and other details of trade marks, indicating when they were introduced and how and when they were modified or added to. Many trade marks are quite uninformative, but there are also elaborate ones that might describe products, give the business's date of establishment, indicate the award of prizes and illustrate premises. They also have obvious value of identifying the products of a business, which is useful should they survive, say, in a museum.

The Trade Marks Register was established in 1876 by the Trade Marks Registration Act of 1875, but early on its functions were transferred to the Patent Office, a branch of the Board of Trade then known as the Patents, Designs & Trade Marks Office. However, the origins of trade marks predate this legislation. As early as the 14th century, for example, some livery companies and trade guilds such as London's Worshipful Company of Goldsmiths and Sheffield's Cutlers' Company of Hallamshire, obliged their member tradesmen to mark their output for quality control and prevention of counterfeiting (*see also* pp.77-80).

The new Trade Marks Register had similar objectives – to keep official records of trade marks that would verify that a certain good had been made by a certain business and thereby serve to prevent counterfeiting or other abuse. Once registered, an owner had exclusive use of the trade mark forever, whether it was a name, a design or both. Historically the largest number of marks relate to foodstuffs, textiles and clothing, and medicines.

Examples of historic trade marks are illustrated in a number of publications including Edward Burns, *Scottish Brewery Trade Marks, 1876 to 1900* and *1900-1976* (1986-87); Roger Price and Fraser Swift, *Catalogue of 19th Century Medical Trade Marks, 1800-1880* (1988), which reproduces about 1,300 items; and John Mendenhall, *British Trade Marks of the 1920s and 1930s* (1989), which arranges around 300 marks by subject. Adrian Room, *Dictionary of Trade Name Origins* (1983) provides the background history to almost 1,000 well-known marks.

The surviving archives of early registration are held in the National Archives (www.nationalarchives.gov.uk) in series BT82, BT244 and BT900 and comprise almost 2,000 trade mark registers for the period 1876 to 1938, although many of the marks registered in 1876 had already been in use for many years, some as early as the turn of the 19th century. Altogether these registers hold representations of over 700,000 marks. More recent archives remain with the Patent Office and current and recently expired trade marks – some of which date back to the beginnings of registration – can be searched for and accessed via the Patent Office's website (www.patent.gov.uk/tm).

As part of the registration process, since 1876 proposed trade marks have been advertised in the *Trade Marks Journal* so that objections to them could, if necessary, be raised. The practice still continues. Each trade mark is illustrated and, while associated details have varied over the years, they generally include applicant's name, address and business activity, the class and a description of the goods to which the mark relates and the date when it

12   *Registration of trade marks was possible from 1876 and vast numbers of trade mark illustrations are held in the National Archives. Many trade marks are quite uninformative, but some shed details on products, premises and the like. For example, this trade mark of Robert McClure & Sons of Manchester provides an illustration of their Stockport premises in 1876 and suggests the parts of the world with which they did business.*

was first used. The *Journal* is generally indexed on a yearly or half-yearly basis until 1978, after which databases are available. The *Journal's* index can assist in locating trade marks in the original registers in the National Archives. A complete set of the *Journal* is held on the open shelves in the Intellectual Property section of the British Library and recent issues are available online (www.patent.gov.uk/tm). Trade marks, both applied for and registered, are also listed, but not illustrated, in *The Official Journal of the Patent Office*, first published in 1884 and today known as *The Patents and Designs Journal*. The British Library's website provides a guide to searching for trade marks, albeit with a strong emphasis on current ones (www.bl.uk/collections/patents/tms.html).

Disputes sometimes arose regarding particular trade marks and were settled in the courts. From 1883 reports on legal cases have been published annually in *Reports on Patent, Design and Trade Mark Cases*. Short summaries, arranged by broad subject area and indexed, are provided in *Digest of the Patent, Design, Trade Mark and Other Cases 1883-1955* (1959). The National Archives holds papers relating to legal cases in several series but especially LO4, J99, J105 and J130.

For a detailed account of the history of trade marks *see* the Patent Office's publication, *A Century of Trade Marks* (1976). David Higgins and Geoffrey Tweedale, 'Asset or liability? Trade marks in the Sheffield cutlery and tool trades', *Business History* (1995), analyses their use by the Sheffield metal industry and provides useful background to the pre-1876 use of trade marks. David C. Newton, *Trade Marks: An introductory guide and bibliography* (1991) provides a succinct introduction, but with an accent on recently published material.

Bankruptcy

Bankruptcy archives, created through proceedings against a businessman or woman unable to settle their debts when petitioned by creditors to do so, form another source of business-specific information about a very large number of businesses. The level of debt at which a bankruptcy action could be initiated was sometimes prescribed, for example at £100 or more before 1842 and £50 afterwards. Individuals who were not businessmen were not granted the status of a bankrupt until 1861; they were instead insolvent debtors and liable for punishment. Businessmen, on the other hand, received more lenient treatment; often they reached a settlement with their creditors and continued in business. Archives relating to bankruptcy are therefore of great potential interest in tracing the history of a business, suggesting reasons for failure and shedding light on assets, borrowings, customers, suppliers, networks and business processes, albeit at a particular moment in time. Bankruptcy was not uncommon: about ninety thousand cases are recorded between 1780 and 1842 alone although archives detailing the bankruptcy process for most of them do not survive.

Legislation dealing with bankruptcy dates back as far back as the reign of Henry VIII. For much of the time since then, individual cases of bankruptcy were dealt with by independent commissioners of bankruptcy, who were appointed as a result of petitions by major creditors to the Lord Chancellor or, after 1832, to the newly established Court of Bankruptcy. The commissioners administered the bankrupt's estate, receiving claims from creditors, overseeing the valuation and assessment of the bankrupt's assets, arranging for an equitable distribution to creditors and finally discharging the bankrupt from bankruptcy through the issue of a certificate of conformity. Three classes of certificate were issued, one denoting no blame to the bankrupt for his or her bankruptcy and the other two denoting partial or entire blame. The certificate was replaced after 1861 by an order of discharge. From 1831, full-time official assignees were appointed to prevent fraud, paying the proceeds from the sale of a bankrupt's assets into accounts at the Bank of England. Details of these are held in the Bank of England's archives (www.bankofengland.co.uk/about/history) as well as in National Archives series AO18. In 1842 district bankruptcy courts were established to deal with cases of bankruptcy outside London; after 1869 this function passed to county courts.

There are two main categories of information about bankruptcy. The first is notices relating to the process of a bankruptcy action, which were published from 1684 in the *London Gazette* and the *Edinburgh Gazette*; at least some of these were also published in other newspapers such as *The Times*. They are addressed to creditors and cover meetings called, *inter alia*, to interview the bankrupt about his assets and debts, enable creditors to prove their debts, agree a distribution of monies to creditors, and to confirm the bankrupt's compliance with the creditors' requirements and release from bankruptcy. As the publication of notices was required in law, they are comprehensive. These notices provide core information such as name, location and occupation of the bankrupt, perhaps the name(s) of any associate(s) in bankruptcy such as a business partner, approximate date of bankruptcy, dates of the bankruptcy process, and names of the individuals administering it. Such information is hugely useful for the 18th and early 19th century when business-specific information is scarce. From time to time these notices give additional information, say details of the bankrupt's assets being realised or the trading name of his business.

The *London* and *Edinburgh Gazettes* (www.gazettes-online.co.uk) have now been digitised so that searching for specific pieces of information, such as the name of a bankrupt, is greatly facilitated. In addition to this resource are various registers, published from the 1770s to the 20th century, which name bankrupts and give additional information, such as date of bankruptcy. Their whole content was copied from the *Gazettes* but, despite digitisation of the latter, they continue to be useful, as they facilitate browsing for information about a bankrupt when precise details are wanting. These registers are listed on p.10.

The second source comprises archives held in the National Archives and the National Archives of Scotland. These extend to many series, but are mostly in the form of registers giving summary details of bankruptcies, at least some of which are available in the *Gazettes* and the published registers referred to above. There are, however, some case files covering individual bankruptcies and other files relating to legal cases and these have special importance. Archives relating to bankruptcy are described in detail in two National Archives research guides, 'Bankrupts and Insolvent Debtors 1710-1869' and 'Bankruptcy Records After 1869', both of which can be downloaded from the National Archives' website (www.nationalarchives.gov.uk). These are invaluable aids to finding a route through quite complicated archive series and the writer draws heavily upon them in this section.

Series B3 comprises some 6,000 files covering individual bankruptcies between the 1770s and the 1840s or around five per cent of the actual number of bankruptcies; it indicates a generally poor survival rate of files. Some files contain very limited information while others are extremely bulky. They might contain details about the circumstances of bankruptcy, a balance sheet showing the assets and liabilities of the bankrupt, information about creditors and dividends paid to them, and assignee's accounts. Other case files after 1832 are in series B9; after 1869 most relate to the London area. Archives relating to some ancient commissions of bankruptcy and related matters are in series C54, C66-67 and C217.

Series B4 comprises registers recording, in date order for the period 1710 to 1849, commissions of bankruptcy and, after 1832, of fiats. However, only brief details are given, such as name, address and trade of bankrupt and names of petitioning creditors and bankrupt's agent or solicitor. Most, if not all, such details can be gleaned from published sources such as the *London Gazette*. The registers are generally indexed by bankrupt's name; those that are underlined or ticked denote the existence of a case file in series B3.

Series B6 contains registers for the issue of certificates that discharged bankrupts from bankruptcy. They give the name and address of the bankrupt and date of certificate. They are indexed by name of bankrupt. Series B5 contains enrolled copies of some certificates from 1710 to 1846, as well as some assignments of assets, 1825 to 1834, and appointment of assignees, 1832 to 1851. Series AO18 contains various accounts of official assignees from their first appointment in 1831 mostly until 1836; other accounts after 1844 are in BT40.

Bankruptcy procedure changed after 1869. In London, petitions for bankruptcy by creditors owed in excess of £50 were now dealt with by the London Court of Bankruptcy, which became the High Court of Justice in Bankruptcy in 1883. In the provinces cases were heard mostly by county courts, which received the functions of District Bankruptcy Courts. From 1884, official receivers, supervised by the Bankruptcy Department of the Board of Trade, assumed responsibility for the administration of a bankrupt estate once the court had made a receiving order. The receiver held meetings of creditors, investigated circumstances and sometimes acted as administrator of assets.

These institutions created several archive series although, as with most bankruptcy archives, they generally contain only very brief details, many of which are available in the *Gazettes*. Registers of bankrupts for 1870 to 1886 are at BT40, registers of petitions for bankruptcy, 1870 to 1883, are at B6/184-197 and registers of creditors' petitions for London, 1870 to 1886, are at B6/178-183. The first two groups give brief details, but the latter group is more informative. Registers of petitions to the High Court, 1884 to recent years, are at B11 and registers of the receiving orders it issued from 1887 to recent years, are at B12. A five per cent sample of London and High Court bankruptcy cases, 1869 to recent times, is at B9. Archives relating to bankruptcy cases dealt with by county courts are likely to be held in local record offices.

From 1884 to 1923, Board of Trade registers in series BT293, indexed by name, give details of all persons served with a petition of bankruptcy along with a broad range of other summary information. An incomplete series of estate ledgers at BT294, arranged alphabetically by name and covering the years 1884 to *c*.1950, may show how assets were distributed to creditors. Other Board of Trade series include registers of deeds of arrangement reached privately between debtor and creditors, covering the years 1888 to 1947, in BT39 and some relating case files from *c*.1880 to *c*.1930 in BT221.

The National Archives also holds archives relating to legal actions arising out of bankruptcy. They are held in the archives of many courts, including Chancery, Exchequer, King's Bench and Common Pleas. Case files in respect of High Court legal actions from 1891 are at BT226. Archives relating to issues which commissioners of bankrupts could not resolve or appeals in bankruptcy cases are in series B1 and B7. Appeals are also at J15, J56, J60, J69-70, J74 and J95. Registers of petitions for protection in county court cases are at LCO28.

Like the National Archives, the National Archives of Scotland holds large quantities of archives relating to sequestration, i.e. bankruptcy, in Scotland from the late 18th century; these archives are far more complete and fuller than bankruptcy archives in London. They are located in several series (but usually not dedicated ones) within the archives of the Court of Session, Scotland's premier court, and are very generally referred to in a National Archives of Scotland research guide that can be downloaded from its website (www.nas.gov.uk/guides). Some series have not yet been added to the archives' online catalogue.

Bankruptcy processes until 1838 are held in series CS230; they contain an examination of the bankrupt before the court together with statements of assets, creditors and debtors. They are supported by sederunt books in CS96, which contain a detailed account of the bankruptcy and were kept by administrators of the bankruptcy. Archives to 1838 are accessed via a range of indexes. Post-1838 processes are in CS280, CS318 and CS319 and petitions and appeals are at CS278-9, CS281 and CS284-5. M.S. Moss and J.R. Hume, 'Business Failure in Scotland 1839-1913: A research note', *Business History* (25, 1983) refers to a sequestrations database covering the period 1839 to 1913 constructed by Glasgow University Archives.

From the late 19th century, as more and more businesses took the form of registered companies with limited liability, bankruptcy archives become less important in tracing the history of a business. Other procedures were now available to deal with and wind-up businesses that had got into financial difficulties. That said, B10 contains a selection of about one hundred case files for the years 1857 to 1863 relating to the winding-up of companies registered under early Companies Acts 1856 and 1857. For the archives of the Register of Companies *see* pp.50-3.

Useful insight into bankruptcy archives in the National Archives is provided by Sheila Marriner, 'English bankruptcy records and statistics before 1850', *Economic History Review* (33, 1980). V. Markham Lester, *Victorian Insolvency: Bankruptcy, imprisonment for debt and company winding up in 19th century England* (1995) provides useful insight into the bankruptcy process and Julian Hoppit, *Risk and Failure in English Business, 1700-1800* (1987) analyses some 33,000 18th-century bankruptcy cases. Hugh Barty-King, *The Worst Poverty: A history of debt and debtors* (2001) provides general background.

Exhibits in Courts of Law

The National Archives and the National Archives of Scotland hold important series of court records. Some of these inevitably touch on disputes concerning businesses and some are very ancient. Many series, of course, relate to the conduct of litigation but others, most importantly, hold business records produced before the court as evidence but never reclaimed.

There was a myriad of courts and sometimes it is not easy to distinguish the responsibilities of one from another. Many dealt with business-related matters. In this respect, the Court of Chancery, which dealt with all manner of civil actions, is reckoned to be of particular interest to business historians, but there are many others. The High Court of Admiralty, for example, dealt with cases relating to prizes, salvage and collisions, while the Court of Exchequer was concerned with disputes touching on land, mineral rights, debts, wills and so on.

Court records include papers relating to pleadings, depositions, reports, judgements, appeals and so on, describing the basis of the action, the processes of the court and the final outcome. Court of Chancery records are especially useful as so many of its proceedings were in documentary form: written pleadings by the parties to the case, evidence including sworn statements as well as exhibits, reports drawing on the evidence, written judgements and so on. Its businesses-specific cases must be of great potential interest.

That said, court records are especially difficult to access on account of their volume, the complicated nature of the court structure, the diffuse way in which records relating to a given case were filed, and the poor finding-aids kept at the time, which remain in use. A great deal of perseverance is required although catalogue descriptions gradually improve.

Exhibits are especially useful as these might well be documents created by the business/ businessman involved in the action. While most litigants withdrew such documents from the court at the end of the action, several did not and they remained with and were filed by the court. At the National Archives they are held in several series, the most widely known being C103 to C114 but there are several others including C171, E140, PL12 and J90. Some classes are extremely extensive; classes C103 to C114 contain 3,327 bundles of records dating from 1300 to 1800 (although most will not be business-related). Similarly E140 contains 246 bundles covering the 17th to the 19th centuries. Various Court of Session classes in the National Archives of Scotland contain similar records, especially in CS96, which are well described in the Archives' online catalogue. Some are also listed in P.L. Payne (ed.), *Studies in Scottish Business History* (1967).

The riches of exhibits in court are evident from series J90, which has been well catalogued. This contains many businesses archives of banks, shipping firms, mines, engineers, publishers and the like. The series is described in John Orbell, 'A Note on Series J90 in the Public Record Office', *Business Archives* (1983). Court records as a whole are generally poorly served by published guides, an indication in itself of how complicated they are to pin down. That said, the National Archives publishes several useful research guides on its website, not least 'Chancery masters and other exhibits: Sources for economic and social history' and 'Chancery proceedings: Equity suits from 1558' (www.nationalarchives.gov.uk). *See also* D. Gerhold, *Courts of Equity: A guide to Chancery and other legal records* (1994).

Railway and Canal Companies

The largest group of business-specific archives in the National Archives (www.nationalarchives.gov.uk) and the National Archives of Scotland (www.nas.gov.uk) is located within what is called the British Transport Historical Records. This collection was formed through the centralisation of the historical archives of British railway companies following their nationalisation in 1948. After a period in the care of the British Transport Commission and the British Railways Board, the collection was handed to the two national archives in 1972. Subsequently additional archives have been added.

The collection includes archives created by well over 1,000 railway and canal companies, many of the latter having been purchased by railway companies in the 19th century in order, *inter alia*, to limit competition. The archives range from minutes and accounts to timetables and operating publications, but exclude technical records and photographs, which are lodged in the National Railway Museum at York (www.nrm.org.uk). Some archives not selected for preservation in the National Archives may be deposited in local record offices. Archives created by London's tube and tramway companies are also excluded and are lodged with the London Metropolitan Archive.

In the National Archives, the archives are usually arranged under the name of the company that created them (each series having the prefix RAIL) but some series comprise archives of a particular type irrespective of company. These include, for example, annual reports (RAIL 1110), railway prospectuses (RAIL 1075-1076), canal prospectuses (RAIL 1077), omnibus and other company prospectuses (RAIL 1078), maps of railways and canals (RAIL 1029-1037), agreements for the provision of sidings (RAIL 1167) and papers of welfare organisations (RAIL 1115). Railway and canal company archives in the National Archives of Scotland are in series BR and comprise the archives of about two hundred companies.

Railway and canal company archives are well described in the online catalogues of the National Archives and of the National Archives of Scotland. Those in the National Archives are also described (along with very many other relevant but less obvious series) in Cliff Edwards, *Railway Records: A guide to sources* (2001) and also, much more briefly, in an online National Archives Research Guide called 'Railways: An overview'. Somewhat dated articles, largely about the early organisation of these archives, include L.C. Johnson, 'Historical records in the British Transport Commission', *Journal of Transport History* (1953-4) and 'British Transport Commission archives: Work since 1953', *Journal of Transport History* (1962).

Registration of Shipping and Seamen

The National Archives and the National Archives of Scotland have rich and varied resources for the history of shipping and of the closely associated business of merchanting. At the centre of these resources are the archives of the Registrar General of Shipping & Seamen (RGSS), which contain a vast amount of information about shipowning, ships, voyages, cargoes and crews; their early date makes them particularly useful. They originate in the 17th century, for when business-specific archives are especially uncommon and when shipping and merchanting formed a large component of Britain's economy.

The RGSS's archives are enormous, those within the National Archives alone extending to some 79 series. Some of its other archives have been dispersed to institutions such as the National Maritime Museum, the National Archives of Scotland, county record offices and the Memorial University of Newfoundland at St John's, Newfoundland. On account of their large volume only a greatly simplified account of its archives is given here. Much more can be learnt from a series of research guides published by the National Archives, which can be downloaded from its website (www.nationalarchives.gov.uk); 'Merchant Shipping: Registration of Ships 1786-1994' provides an especially useful overview.

The government, through various departments, had maintained records of shipping since at least 1600, long before the creation of RGSS. The Board of Customs, via its Registrar General of Shipping, had, for example, administered the compulsory registration of British merchant shipping since 1786. In 1835 the General Registrar & Record Office of Seamen was established in the Admiralty to maintain records of seamen; in 1850 it was transferred to the Board of Trade. Four years later, the board was given responsibility for all matters relating to merchant shipping, including the keeping of a register of British merchant ships; in due course, in 1872, it consolidated these activities in RGSS. RGSS was subsequently to become part of, *inter alia*, the Ministry of Shipping and was renamed Register of Shipping and Seamen in 1992.

Ship-ownership archives in the National Archives are diffuse prior to 1786. Port books, kept by customs officials in ports largely in connection with the payment of duties on goods, provide many details of ships, owners, cargoes, ship movements and merchants, although some do not survive, especially for London. Many are held in series E122 and E190 and, with other accounts, date from the 13th to the end of the 18th century. Other port books are held in local record offices. Examples are described in detail in R.W.K. Hinton (ed.), *Port Books of Boston in the Early 17th Century* (1956) and in *The Gloucester Port Books Database, 1575-1765 on CD-ROM* (1998) while the National Archives provides a brief overview in its research guide 'Port Books 1565-1799'.

Other early archives, which shed light on the ownership of ships and the trade of merchants from the 17th century, are shipping returns held in many Colonial Office (CO) and Board of Customs & Excise (CUST) series, especially outport records. Equivalent archives are held in the National Archives of Scotland in E171-2 and E504.

When formal ship registration began in 1786, registration documentation, generally known as 'transcripts and transactions', was kept both centrally by the Customs Houses in London and Edinburgh and locally at ports. The content of these varies over the years but generally includes ship name, registration date, home port, date and place of construction, type and size as well as master's name and, from 1825, details of ownership. The central archives are now in the National Archives (series BT107-111) and the National Archives of Scotland (CE11) and are complete, with the exception of pre-1814 London archives that were destroyed by fire (although the gap thus created is filled by the locally maintained books for London). Duplicate copies kept locally in ports have often found their way to local record offices.

Other series of potential use to the historian of a business include lists of ships registered for the years 1786 to 1955, which are at BT162-163. The Statistical Register of Fishing Vessels, 1887 to 1938, is at BT145. From 1850 ships were obliged to keep official logs largely recording matters relating to crew. They are generally filed with crew lists (q.v.), but some are at BT165; many have not survived, especially for 1880 to 1901. Between 1850 and 1976 the RGSS published the annual *Mercantile Navy List*, the official list of British-registered ships.

Crew lists and agreements give general details of individual crewmen, their ship and, importantly from the perspective of business history, its voyage. Lists were first kept on a systematic basis in 1747; those from then until 1860 are at BT98, but are not indexed and nor are they complete until the creation in 1835 of the General Registrar & Record of Seamen. Lists and agreements from 1861 to 1938 and from 1950 to 1994 are at BT99, but this is only a 10 per cent random sample of the original accumulation. A further 10 per cent sample is held by the National Maritime Museum (www.nmm.ac.uk), others are in the National Archives of Scotland (BT3) and local record offices, and the balance is in the Maritime History Archive of Memorial University, St John's, Newfoundland (www.mun.ca/mha). For more details *see* the National Archives' research guides 'Merchant Shipping: Agreements and crew lists 1747-1860' and 'Merchant Seamen: Agreements and crew lists after 1861', which can both be downloaded from the National Archives' website. The latter describes the holdings of local record offices.

For more details about these and many other archives relating to shipping and seamen in the National Archives and elsewhere *see* C.T. & M.J. Watts, *Records of Merchant Shipping and Seamen* (1998) and C.T. & M.J. Watts, *My Ancestor was a Merchant Seaman* (2002).

Apprenticeship Records

The relative paucity of information relating to individual businesses active before the 19th century means that early sources of information, however narrowly focused, assume very substantial importance. One such source is the apprenticeship books of the Commissioners of Stamps, which cover the years 1710 to 1811. They are held in the National Archives in class IR1.

Apprenticeship books give brief details of a huge number of apprentices and their masters; for 1710 to 1762 alone it is reckoned they carry details of a quarter of a million apprenticeship arrangements. They shed light, *inter alia*, on the training of businessmen and on business networks.

The Statutes of Apprenticeship, introduced in 1563 and revoked in 1814, required individuals entering a trade to complete an apprenticeship with an established master for a period of seven years. The apprentice usually lived and worked with his master who was remunerated by the apprentice's family. The amount of remuneration might be influenced by the master's standing in his trade and by the consequent quality of training and amount of privileged information he was able to provide. The deadline for payment was one year after completion of the apprenticeship.

In 1710 stamp duty became payable by masters in England, Scotland and Wales on apprenticeship monies. Duties were payable to the Commissioners of Stamps and were recorded by them in apprenticeship books dating to 1811. Early on, details included name, address and occupation of master, name of apprentice, year of apprenticeship indenture, period of apprenticeship, details of parents and consideration paid to the master. Unfortunately, from the 1750s many of these details are omitted and so the apprenticeship books become much less useful. It should also be pointed out that not all apprenticeships were recorded in the apprenticeship books, as some apprentices were, for example, taken on at the common or public charge or were trained informally by their fathers/relatives or were the subject of other informal arrangements for the avoidance of duty.

Indexes to masters' and apprentices' names appearing in the apprenticeship books were compiled by the Society of Genealogists between 1929 and 1941 for the years 1710 to 1774. Known as *The Apprentices of Great Britain*, microfiche copies of them are available at, *inter alia*, the National Archives and Guildhall Library.

Other sources of apprenticeship information exist although they are much more piecemeal. Of great importance are the archives of London livery companies and provincial trade guilds; they were closely involved in regulating apprenticeships and the resulting archives both pre- and post-date the National Archives' apprenticeship books. These are discussed in greater detail elsewhere (*see* pp.77-80). Local council archives such as those of Bristol and Coventry are also useful when the council administered, either jointly or wholly, the apprenticeship system. Joan Lane's *Coventry Apprentices and their Masters, 1781-1806* (1983) gives excellent insight into the apprenticeship records maintained by that city.

Some writers, often on behalf of local history and record societies, have indexed and/or abstracted information from apprenticeship books and, by way of example, some of these are listed below; many others, published and unpublished, exist and the relevant local record office or local history library will hold details of them. Sometimes apprenticeship abstracts/indexes have been compiled on an occupational basis and, once again, some examples are given below.

Examples of apprenticeship indentures, i.e. the actual agreements between master and apprentice, from time to time turn up in record offices; the location of several relating to banking, for example, is recorded in John Orbell and Alison Turton, *British Banking: A guide to historical records* (2001). Useful reading includes the National Archives' research guide *Apprenticeship records as sources for genealogy*, which can be downloaded from its website (www.nationalarchives.gov.uk). Joan Lane, *Apprenticeship in England 1600-1914* (1996) provides detailed historical context.

Occupational

Dennis Moore, *British Clockmakers/Watchmakers Apprenticeship Records* (2003)

Ian Maxted, *The British Book Trade, 1710-1777: An index of masters and apprentices recorded in the Inland Revenue registers* (1983)

Donald F. McKenzie, *Stationers' Company Apprentices* [1641-1800], 2 vols (1974-8)

Geographical

Christabel Dale, *Wiltshire Apprentices and their Masters, 1710-1760* (1961)

Anne Daly (ed.), *Kingston upon Thames Registers of Apprentices 1563-1713*, Surrey Record Society (1974)

I. Fitzroy Jones, *Abstract of the Apprentice Books of the City of Bristol, 1600-1630* (1936) [typescript at British Library]

R. Garraway Rice (ed.), *Sussex Apprentices and Masters, 1710-1752, Extracted from the Apprenticeship Books* (1924)

Malcolm Gray (ed.), *Oxford City Apprentices, 1697-1800* (1987)

Henry Hartopp, *Register of the Freemen of Leicester; including apprentices sworn before successive mayors* [1196-1930], 2 vols (1927-33)

Joan Lane, *Coventry Apprentices and their Masters, 1781-1806* (1983)

Winifred M. Rising & Percy Millican, *An Index of Indentures of Norwich Apprentices Enrolled with Norwich Assembly, Henry VI to George II* (1959)

Scottish Record Society, *Registers of Apprentices of the City of Edinburgh* [1583-1800], 4 vols (1906-63)

K.J. Smith (ed.), *Warwickshire Apprentices and their Masters, 1710-1760* (1975)

Clifford R. Webb (ed.), *Surrey Apprentices; being an index of apprentices of Surrey extracted from some London livery company records, 1563-1928* (2000)

Local Authorities

Local authorities in many ways mirror the connections of central government with business but these, while numerous, give rise to very few routinely created business-specific archive series. Instead, business-specific references are widely spread through many series. Local authority archives are held in large numbers in local record offices.

As with central government, local authorities are important procurers of goods and services from business; often they are among the most important procurers within their local economy. The larger the item and the more specialised the service, the more likely they are to be acquired externally. At the top of the list is infrastructure such as roads and schools, municipal buildings and public housing. Local authority archives are bound to contain some business-specific papers relating to their construction such as contracts, plans and photographs.

Another connection touches on the lease of property as it is inevitable that local authorities own, to varying degrees, commercial property portfolios. These might include cattle markets, corn exchanges and market halls but also shops, offices and factories. A few, for example, owned grain mills. Local authority archives might therefore include property deeds, plans and photographs shedding light on business tenants or businesses that were parties to property sales and purchases. Other archives touch on planning issues, perhaps planning permissions for the building or extension of an industrial building, especially if it had environmental impact. Other property-type papers may relate to relocation of businesses or compulsory purchase of their premises.

Other business-specific archives may be created through a local authority's work to encourage growth in, or regeneration of, the local economy through attracting businesses to locate there or supporting those already present. Again this might well give rise to the creation of some business-specific papers, especially regarding big businesses making major local economic impact.

Other archives are created through local regulation of businesses and markets, say regarding weights and measures, hygiene issues and trading standards. Much earlier, some local authorities were involved in the regulation of local trades either solely or in conjunction with a local guild. Such activities gave rise to archives touching on registration of apprentices and masters, trade disputes and so on.

More archives are created through revenue generation. Local authorities generate income through property taxes requiring routine records to be kept of ownership and tenancy as well as valuation and taxes paid. Some such records are likely to be found in local authority archives.

Business-related archives also stem from the trading activities of local authorities. They had since early times taken an interest in harbours, roads and so on but from the mid-19th century were enabled by Parliament to provide utility services such as water, gas, electricity, sewerage, public transport and telephone services; virtually all were 'nationalised' in the late 1940s. Archives relating to these activities shed light on the businesses from which the assets were initially acquired, but also on procurement of equipment from engineering business, motor vehicle builders and so on.

The list of possible connections is as long as its broad. A general absence of guides to local authority archives as a source for business history underlines the extent to which this source is underused.

Records of Associations

Employers' Organisations and Trade Associations

This diverse group of organisations represents the interests of specific industries, either at local or, now more commonly, national level. Each is funded through the subscriptions of member businesses and these determine policy. The functions of employers' organisations and trade associations differ fundamentally, although the roots of both are in the need to combine in order to deal with a common issue or threat such as, early on, the growing power of organised labour. Both types of association emerged, at least at a national level, in the last quarter of the 19th century, although many local associations date back to the early century.

The historic functions of trade associations were to fix prices and production quotas, although other more specific reasons can be identified. The Timber Trade Federation (established 1892), for example, facilitated its members' effective negotiation of inland freight charges while the Society of Motor Manufacturers and Traders (established 1902) promoted the Motor Show. Representation at industry level came to prominence during the First World War, when industries needed to negotiate with government about regulation of production, expansion of strategic plant, supply of raw materials and so on. Since the 1950s, and following strict regulation of price fixing, trade associations have focused on monitoring government policy and proposed legislation; on collecting and making available product information and economic and market intelligence; on compiling technical publications; on organising exhibitions and trade missions; and, not least, on making representations to the government and its agencies. Many maintain information centres and circulate newsletters and journals.

In contrast, historically, employers' organisations have dealt with wage bargaining at either national or local level. Although early formations can be traced to the 18th century, most date from the late 19th century onwards and were responses to the emergence of more effective organisation of labour. Their original function was the fixing or negotiation of wages and conditions of employment across an industry or in a particular district or region. This role was enhanced under wartime conditions and the arrival of industry-wide pay settlements. Their heyday, however, was the period from 1880 to the second half of the 20th century, after which company-based wage settlements came to predominate. A few are still active in wage negotiation but are more likely to focus on advising members about wage trends, dispute procedures, productivity and so on. Arthur J. McIvor, *Organised Capital: Employers' associations and industrial relations in northern England, 1880-1939* (1996) covers their role in detail with special reference to the building, cotton and engineering industries.

The archives of employers' organisations and trade associations – largely minutes, files of papers and publications – shed much light on the environment in which businesses operated and on the performance of the industry as a whole. Also, it is reasonable to expect their archives to contain at least some business-specific information needed for the operation of price-fixing and production quota schemes. Details of labour costs, working conditions, size of workforce and so on may also have been collected for the negotiation of wages.

The Modern Records Centre of the University of Warwick holds a growing collection of archives of these organisations and they are described on its website www.warwick.ac.uk. The National Register of Archives (www.nationalarchives.gov.uk/nra) provides summary descriptions of over 100 collections in its trade and employer association category. Linda Smallbone with Richard Storey (eds.), *Employers' & Trade Associations' History* (1992) lists several hundred collections in record offices as well as published histories of associations, although its information is now somewhat dated. H. Campbell McMurray, 'The records of the Shipbuilders' and Repairers' National Association', *Business Archives* 45 (1979) describes in detail a particular collection now housed in the National Maritime Museum. G.S. Bain and G.B. Woolven, *A Bibliography of British Industrial Relations* (Cambridge, 1979) and G.S. Bain and J.D. Bennett, *A Bibliography of British Industrial Relations 1971-1979* (1985) are also helpful. Contact details of existing organisations are in *Trade Associations and Professional Bodies of the United Kingdom* (periodically from 1962) and *Directory of British Associations* (periodically from 1965); the latter also gives date of formation.

The Confederation of British Industry (CBI) stands at the head of British industrial and commercial representation and traces its origins to three organisations established between 1915 and 1919 – the National Association of British Manufacturers, the Federation of British Industries (FBI) and the British Employers' Confederation. Its archives are also held at the Modern Records Centre and are described in Alan Crookham, Michael Wilcox et al, *The Confederation of British Industry and Predecessor Archives* (1997). An unpublished history of the FBI by Peter Mathias, written in the late 1960s, is available for study at the Centre and at the Business History Unit of the London School of Economics. For the CBI *see* Wyn Grant and David Marsh, *The Confederation of British Industry* (1997).

Stock Exchanges

Market organisations are dealt with generally on p.72, but stock exchanges are considered separately on account of the important business-specific archives they accumulate.

A stock exchange is where investors, invariably through agents, buy and sell shares and other securities and where businesses both inside and outside Britain issue their securities in order to raise funds. It is this last activity that leads to the creation of business-specific archives dealing with matters such as initial flotation, subsequent share or debenture issues, compliance with regulations, temporary suspension of dealings, takeovers and mergers, delisting and so on. Businesses currently quoted on the London Stock Exchange are described in the annual *Waterlow Stock Exchange Year Book*, while most formerly quoted businesses are listed in the *Register of Defunct and Other Companies Removed from the Stock Exchange Official Year Book*, the last edition of which was published in 1990 (*see* p.6).

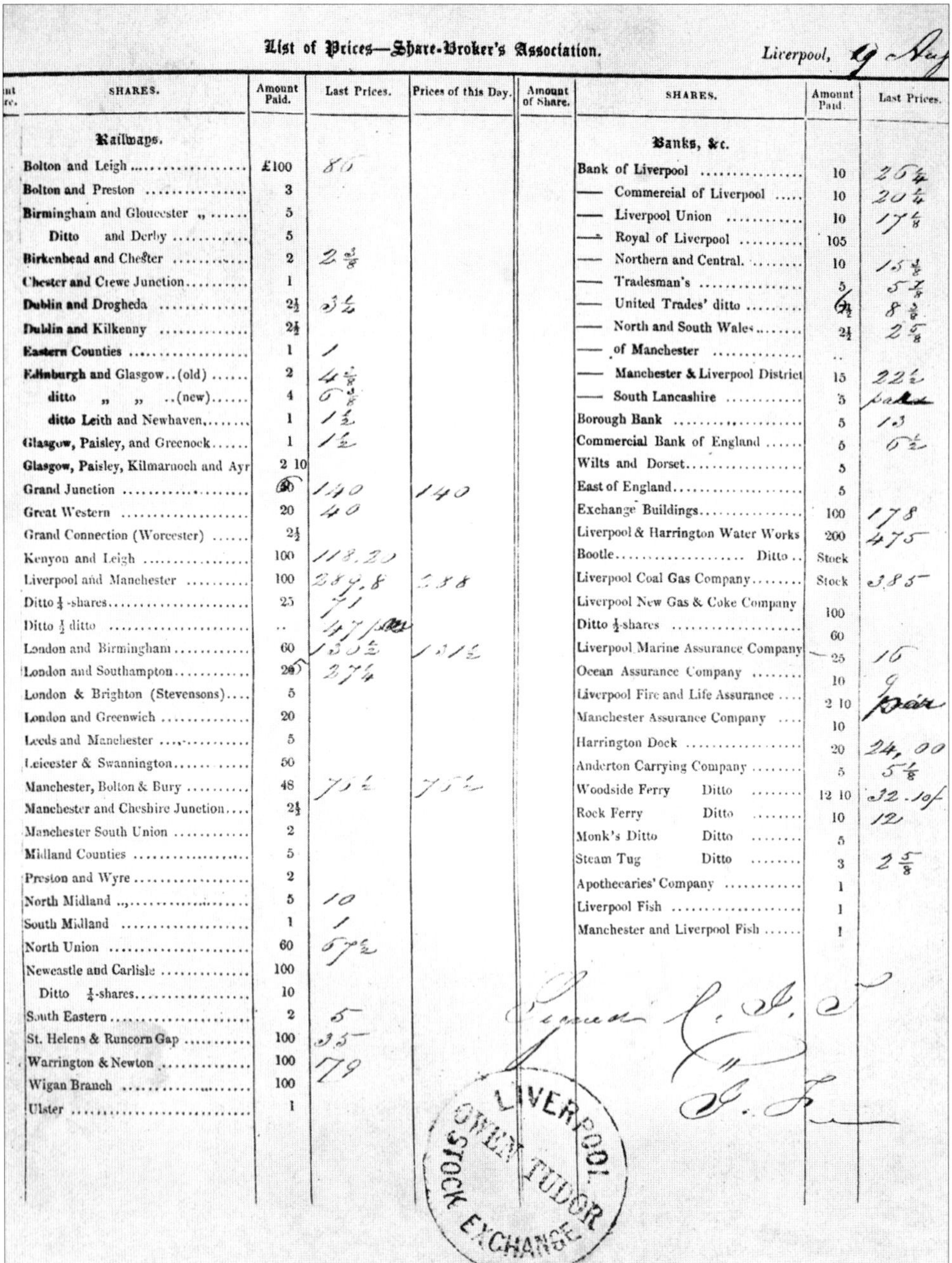

List of Prices—Share-Broker's Association.   Liverpool, *9 Aug*

SHARES.	Amount Paid.	Last Prices.	Prices of this Day.	Amount of Share.	SHARES.	Amount Paid	Last Prices.
Railways.					**Banks, &c.**		
Bolton and Leigh	£100	86			Bank of Liverpool	10	26¼
Bolton and Preston	3				—— Commercial of Liverpool	10	20¾
Birmingham and Gloucester ,,	5				—— Liverpool Union	10	17⅞
Ditto and Derby	5				—— Royal of Liverpool	105	
Birkenhead and Chester	2	2⅜			—— Northern and Central.	10	15¼
Chester and Crewe Junction	1				—— Tradesman's	5	5⅞
Dublin and Drogheda	2½	3½			—— United Trades' ditto	6½	8⅜
Dublin and Kilkenny	2½				—— North and South Wales	2½	2⅝
Eastern Counties	1	1			—— of Manchester	..	
Edinburgh and Glasgow..(old)	2	4⅞			—— Manchester & Liverpool District	15	22½
ditto ,, ,, ..(new)	4	6⅜			—— South Lancashire	5	paid
ditto Leith and Newhaven,	1	1¾			Borough Bank	5	13
Glasgow, Paisley, and Greenock	1	1½			Commercial Bank of England	5	6½
Glasgow, Paisley, Kilmarnock and Ayr	2 10				Wilts and Dorset	5	
Grand Junction	80	140	140		East of England	5	
Great Western	20	40			Exchange Buildings	100	178
Grand Connection (Worcester)	2½				Liverpool & Harrington Water Works	200	475
Kenyon and Leigh	100	118.20			Bootle Ditto	Stock	
Liverpool and Manchester	100	289,8	288		Liverpool Coal Gas Company	Stock	385
Ditto ¼-shares	25	71			Liverpool New Gas & Coke Company	100	
Ditto ½ ditto	..	47 paid			Ditto ½-shares	60	
London and Birmingham	60	303	312		Liverpool Marine Assurance Company } 25	16	
London and Southampton	20	374			Ocean Assurance Company	10	9
London & Brighton (Stevensons)	5				Liverpool Fire and Life Assurance	2 10	par
London and Greenwich	20				Manchester Assurance Company	10	
Leeds and Manchester	5				Harrington Dock	20	24, 00
Leicester & Swannington	50				Anderton Carrying Company	5	5⅛
Manchester, Bolton & Bury	48	75½	75½		Woodside Ferry Ditto	12 10	32-10/
Manchester and Cheshire Junction	2½				Rock Ferry Ditto	10	12
Manchester South Union	2				Monk's Ditto Ditto	5	
Midland Counties	5				Steam Tug Ditto	3	2⅝
Preston and Wyre	2				Apothecaries' Company	1	
North Midland	5	10			Liverpool Fish	1	
South Midland	1	1			Manchester and Liverpool Fish	1	
North Union	60	57½					
Newcastle and Carlisle	100						
Ditto ¼-shares	10						
South Eastern	2	5					
St. Helens & Runcorn Gap	100	95					
Warrington & Newton	100	79					
Wigan Branch	100						
Ulster	1						

13   *Stock Exchange archives shed light on publicly owned companies and indicate performance through share price movements. This circular, issued by the Liverpool Stock Exchange in 1836, shows share prices for different businesses on 9 August.*

14   *(Opposite) Extensive details of companies quoted on the London Stock Exchange have been published since 1876. This page, relating to quoted railway companies, is taken from* the Stock Exchange Year Book, *1884.*

Cleveland Extension Mineral Railway Company.—*Directors:* J. Goodson (Chairman), W. Graham, and J. C. Wakefield. *Secretary:* D. A. Onslow. *Office:* 3 & 4, Great Winchester Street, E.C.—The company was incorporated in 1873. The authorised capital, including loans, is £226,000, and there has been issued £85,630 in ordinary shares of £10, of which £64,695 is paid up. The accounts are made up to June 30 and December 31, and submitted in August and February. Interest at 5 per cent. per annum is to be paid on January 1 and July 1 until August 1, 1884. The line is not yet completed.

Cockermouth, Keswick, and Penrith Railway Company.—*Directors:* J. J. Spedding (Chairman), Sir H. R. Vane, Bart. (Deputy-Chairman), J. Pattinson, Capt. H. Gandy, W. McGlasson, H. C. Howard, E. Waugh, M.P., T. Altham; J. Cropper, M.P., and M. MacInnes (nominated by the London and North Western Company), and Sir H. M. Meysey-Thompson, Bart., and D. Dale (nominated by the North Eastern Company). *General Manager and Secretary:* P. Thompson. *Office:* Keswick, Cumberland.—The company, which was incorporated in 1861, is worked by the London and North Western and North Eastern companies. The capital authorised, including loans, is £377,000, and the several issues are as follow:—£259,000 consolidated ordinary stock, £25,000 preference consolidated 5 per cent. preference stock, £64,250 debenture stock, and £17,100 in loans bearing $3\frac{3}{4}$ to 4 per cent. interest. The accounts are made up to June 30 and December 31, and submitted in August and February. The dividends for the two halves of 1877 were $3\frac{3}{4}$ and 4 per cent. per annum; for 1878, $2\frac{3}{4}$ and 3; for 1879, nil and $2\frac{1}{2}$; for 1880, $4\frac{1}{4}$ and $6\frac{1}{2}$; for 1881, 5 and $6\frac{3}{4}$; for 1882, $5\frac{1}{2}$ and 6, and for the first half of 1883, 4. Reserve fund, £5,607; carried forward £488. Transfers are to be made out on common forms; fee, 2s. 6d. per deed. In transfering any description of stock no fractions of £1 are allowed. Latest prices—ordinary, 101.

Colchester, Stour Valley, Sudbury, and Halstead Railway Company.—*Directors:* C. H. Hawkins (Chairman), W. C. A. Hankey, F. A. Philbrick, Q.C., and W. Quilter. *Secretary:* F. B. Philbrick. *Offices:* 6, New Broad Street, E.C.—The company was incorporated in 1846, and in 1847 it was leased for 999 years to the Eastern Union Railway Company (now part of the Great Eastern undertaking) for a rent which has since been fixed at £9,500 per annum. The capital consists of £30,230 in fully-paid 5 per cent. preference shares of £5, and £228,675 ordinary stock. The accounts are made up to June 30 and December 31, and submitted in July and January. For the second half of 1881 the dividend was £1 13s. 6d. per cent.; for the first half of 1882, £1 13s. 0d; for the second half, £1 13s. 6d.; and for the first half of 1883, £1 13s. Carried forward, £70, an increase on last year of £12. Transfer form, common; fee, 2s. 6d., and 2s. 6d. extra for registration of probate of will. Latest price—ordinary, 82.

Coleford, Monmouth, Usk, and Pontypool Railway Company.—*Directors:* T. Holland (Chairman), and T. Gratrex. *Secretary:* H. S. Gustard. *Office:* Usk.—The company was incorporated in 1853. The capital consists of £160,000 in fully-paid shares of £20 and £50,000 in 5 per cent. debentures (held by the Great Western). The accounts are made up to June 30 and December 31, and submitted in August and February. The line is leased to the Great Western Company for 999 years from 1861 at a rent of £10,764. This is sufficient, after providing for the debenture interest, to pay a dividend of 5 per cent. per annum. Transfer form, common; fee, 5s. per deed.

Coleford Railway Company.—*Directors:* Sir D. Gooch, Bart., M.P. (Chairman), R. Basset, and Sir C. A. Wood. *Secretary:* G. Cottman. *Office:* Paddington Station, London.—The company was incorporated in 1872. The authorised capital, including loans, is £88,000, all of which has been issued, £66,000 being in ordinary shares of £10, and £22,000 in loans at 5 per cent. There are also Lloyd's bonds to the amount of £5,708. The accounts are made up to June 30 and December 31, and submitted in August and February. The line was opened September, 1883.

Colne Valley and Halstead Railway Company.—*Directors:* W. Clarke, M.I.C.E. (Chairman), J. Brewster, R. W. Childs, G. J. A. Richardson, H. J. Tweedy, and J. R. Vaizey. *Secretary and Receiver:* W. G. Bailey. *Office:* 3, Throgmorton Avenue, E.C.—The company was incorporated in 1856. The authorised capital, including loans, is £289,633, of which £61,200 has been issued in ordinary shares of £10, £84,250 in preference shares of £10, contingent on the profits of each year ending December 31, and £58,245 in loans at 5 per cent. The accounts are made up to June 30 and December 31, and submitted in August in Halstead and February in London. No dividend is being paid, nor is loan interest being met. Debit to revenue, £1,526, an increase of £783. To June 30, 1883, there was £90,962 against capital, of which £76,200 had been provided for by the issue of Lloyd's bonds. Transfer fee, 2s. 6d. per deed.

A scheme of arrangement is now under consideration.

Today in Britain public companies are quoted on the London Stock Exchange, which was formally constituted in 1801-2 but whose origins date to the late 17th century. Many provincial stock exchanges, providing services to local businesses, once existed; many of these had been formed in the 1830s and 1840s and the six survivors amalgamated with the London Stock Exchange in 1973. These provincial exchanges included ones at Aberdeen (established 1845), Birmingham (1845), Bristol (1845), Cardiff (1892), Dundee (1879), Edinburgh (1844), Glasgow (1844), Halifax (after 1845), Leeds (1844), Liverpool (1836), Manchester (1836), Newcastle (1845), Newport (1916), Oldham (1875), Sheffield (1844) and Swansea (1903); there were several others.

While provincial exchanges served local businesses, the London Exchange always served a far wider constituency. Early on trading in London was in the securities of a relatively few joint stock companies – there were 150 or so of them as early as the 1690s – and especially in British government securities. Overseas government bonds began to have significance from the early 19th century. However, it was only from the 1820s that trading in the securities of British companies became really important – these securities were the shares and debentures of canal, railway, banking, insurance and utility companies, whose formation had been facilitated by particular acts of Parliament. By the end of the century they were being joined by a much wider cross section of British industry and commerce.

The very extensive archives of the London Stock Exchange are held at Guildhall Library. The most important business-specific series are several thousand 'applications for listing' and 'applications for authority to deal' files covering 1850 to 1965; later files remain with the Stock Exchange. Content and level of detail varies over time and in accordance with Exchange requirements but, even pre-1900, files contain a letter of application giving details of objects, capital, voting rights, borrowing powers, procedure for increasing capital, etc, and often articles of association, prospectus, specimen allotment letter, share certificate, agreements relating to assets and so on. Files are held off-site and 48-hour notice is required for access.

Other business specific information is contained in such series as report books (1881-1938), Quotation Panel minutes (1946-83) and Sub-Committee on New Issues and Official Quotations minutes (1930-63), etc. Companies also had to file each year with the Stock Exchange at least one copy of their annual report; those for the years 1880 to 1965 are also held at Guildhall Library (*see* pp.110-15) as is the Exchange's prospectus collection for the period 1824 to 1964 (*see* pp.115-19). Other series give details of broker and jobber members of the Exchange from 1802 onwards.

Archives of provincial exchanges are very much less complete and invariably relate just to committees and administration. All surviving archives appear to be lodged in record offices and can be located via the National Register of Archives (www.nra.nationalarchives.gov.uk).

Exchanges also regularly published information about security prices, useful for the history of a specific business by providing a measure of performance and investor perception over time. The first list was published in 1698, when generally known as the *Course of Exchange*, while daily information appeared from 1844 in what came to be known from 1867 as *The Daily Official List*. Other listings were published by provincial exchanges. *The Stock Exchange Weekly Intelligence* was published from 1882 onwards, initially as the *Weekly Official Intelligence*. Prices, including those of businesses quoted on provincial exchanges, also appeared in the daily press.

Ranald Michie, *The London Stock Exchange: A history* (1999) provides a detailed account of the emergence and functions of the London Stock Exchange while Elizabeth Hennessy, *Coffee House to Cyber Market: 200 years of the London Stock Exchange* (2001) is shorter and less analytical. W.A. Thomas, *The Provincial Stock Exchanges: Their history and function* (1973) is obviously helpful for provincial exchanges. Ranald Michie, *Money, Mania and Markets: Investment, company formation and the stock exchange in 19th century Scotland* (1981) deals with Scotland while histories of individual exchanges, a somewhat dated mixed bag, include *Records of the Glasgow Stock Exchange Association, 1844-1926* (1927) and Stanley Dumbell, *The Centenary Book of the Liverpool Stock Exchange, 1836-1936* (1936). Guildhall Library (www.cityoflondon.gov.uk) publishes a helpful leaflet titled 'Records of the Stock Exchange, London, at Guildhall Library'.

Chambers of Commerce and Trade

Historically, chambers of commerce and chambers of trade represent the interests of a particular business community in, say, a city or town, the former representing the whole community, the latter focusing on the distributive trades. Some chambers trace their origins to the 18th century but many are 19th-century formations. By the late 1970s, 10 regional and 90 local chambers of commerce existed, along with over 800 chambers of trade. In recent years numbers have shrunk due to merger.

In the mid-19th century the functions of chambers were described as promoting measures for the benefit of the local business community, representing its interests in local affairs, collecting data touching on business performance, and settling disputes between members. They continue to provide a forum in which local businesses discuss matters of mutual importance and to make representations, especially to local authorities. At a more practical level, they might organise trade missions and marketing and training events, arrange documentation especially for exports, and provide central facilities such as translation and information technology services.

The archives of chambers provide details covering the local environment in which businesses operated, how this environment affected particular businesses, and the contribution of a particular business or businessman to the chamber's affairs. Archives largely consist of committee minutes and membership records and sometimes newspaper cuttings and newsletters/journals. In the largest chambers, such as those in big cities like London, Liverpool and Manchester, a specific business sector was represented by its own sub-committee, which kept minutes and produced reports.

The National Register of Archives (www.nationalarchives.gov.uk/nra) holds summary details of about one hundred collections while over 20 collections are described in Lesley Richmond and Bridget Stockford, *Company Archives* (1986). The London Chamber of Commerce, whose membership peaked at over 9,000 businesses in the 1930s, probably has the largest archives. Contact details of current chambers are listed in the *Directory of British Associations*, published periodically since 1965, which also gives date of establishment. Online details of some are available on the British Chambers of Commerce website (www.britishchambers.org.uk).

No general history of this sector exists although A.R. Ilersic, *Parliament of Commerce: The story of the Association of British Chambers of Commerce* (1960) has general interest. Histories of specific chambers form a mixed bag but perhaps the most insightful is the somewhat dated *Leeds Chamber of Commerce* (1951) by Maurice Beresford.

Trade Unions

The archives of trade unions may shed light on the contribution of the workforce in the history of a business. Much information is contextual, highlighting the environment in which the business operated and providing insight into education, training, age, sex and health; wages and benefits; working conditions; management/labour relations; and so on. The larger the business and the greater its influence in its sector, the better the chance of finding business-specific information on such issues as wage bargaining, industrial action, redundancy, closed-shop, working practices, productivity and so on. Archives of union representatives and committees operating at local – say company or site level – will be especially useful.

Trade unions in Britain date back at least to the mid-18th century and longer in the case of some ancient guilds. Modern unions trace their origins to formations in the 1850s; by 1860 membership exceeded 500,000 and rose to almost two million, or 13 per cent of the workforce, by 1900 although in industries such as coal mining and engineering the proportion was higher. By 1918 almost 40 per cent of the workforce was unionised while other workers, especially white-collar, were represented by staff associations. Early on, unions were concerned to control admission to trades, protect craft practices and provide mutual aid but, from the mid-19th century, wage-bargaining and improvement of working conditions came to the fore.

In recent years the number of unions has declined steadily due to merger and as they became more centralised so representation at regional, branch, company and site level became more important. The Trades Union Congress (TUC), a federation of unions, has historically been the main focus of union co-operation since its beginnings in 1868.

The archives of trade unions typically comprise minute books, annual reports and, less frequently, contribution and membership registers. Useful insight is provided by Tom Donnelly and Martin Durham, *Labour Relations in the Coventry Motor Industry 1896-1939: A guide to the records of the AUEW (1988)*. This sheds light on business-related information contained in the archives of Coventry District Committee of the Amalgamated Union of Engineering Workers (AUEW).

Since the 1970s significant progress has been made in the location, centralisation and cataloguing of trade union archives. The Modern Records Centre of Warwick University (www.warwick.ac.uk) has led this consolidation since 1973 and holds the archives of several hundred unions including giants such as the Transport & General Workers' Union and the National Union of Railwaymen as well as the TUC's archives. All these collections are described on the centre's website and in John Bennett & Richard Storey (ed.), *Trade Union and Related Records* (1991), which is now somewhat dated. Descriptions of others are available via the National Register of Archives website (www.nationalarchives.gov.uk/nra) and A2A (www.a2a.org.uk). The deposited TUC archive, 1920 to 1970, is described in two sources booklets: Sarah Duffield and Richard Storey, *The Trades Union Congress Archive, 1920-60* (1992) and Alan Crookham, *The Trades Union Congress Archive, 1960-1970* (1998).

Arthur Marsh and Victoria Ryan, *Historical Directory of Trade Unions* (1980-94) provides potted histories of a huge range of labour organisations and Joyce M. Bellamy and John Saville, subsequently Keith Gildart and David Howell (eds), *Dictionary of Labour Biography* (1972-ongoing) gives biographical sketches of leading figures in the labour movement. Royden Harrison, Gillian B. Woolven and Robert Duncan, *The Warwick Guide to British Labour Periodicals, 1790-1970: A checklist* (1977) lists trade union periodicals such as journals and newsletters.

H.A. Clegg, A. Fox and A.F. Thompson, *A History of British Trade Unions, 1889-1951* (1964-94) provides a particularly comprehensive history of organised labour while Derek H. Aldcroft and Michael J. Oliver, *Trade Unions and the Economy, 1870-2000* (2000) is a modern account linking unions to industry. Contact details for present unions are available via the TUC's website (www.tuc.org.uk) or in the Directory of British Associations.

Market Organisations

Wholesale markets are at the heart of trade in all kinds of goods, especially raw materials and agricultural output and including financial products. Some are ancient foundations that may have passed over time into the ownership or management of local authorities. Others, especially commodity markets, date from the 19th century and were the result of the emergence of a modern international economy. Their promoters included potential participants in the market, such as brokers or even sellers and/or buyers, who sometimes used a registered or joint stock company for the purpose.

They embrace local cattle, meat, fish, vegetable and flower markets; market halls for general retailing; corn exchanges in country towns; cotton and wool exchanges in traditional textile districts such as Lancashire and Yorkshire; international commodity markets based in the City of London dealing in such goods as metals, coal, oil, agricultural output and foodstuffs; and not least financial markets dealing in securities (*see* pp.71-5), insurance (*see* pp.38-9), ship charters and like. Well-known names that illustrate the breadth of activities involved include London Metal Exchange (established 1877), Lloyds of London (1680s), the Baltic Exchange (*c.*1744), Smithfield Meat Market (1638), Billingsgate Fish Market (1698), Manchester's Cotton Exchange (18th century), Liverpool Cotton Exchange (1808), London Coal Exchange (*c.*1750s), London Corn Exchange (1747) and Covent Garden fruit and vegetable market (1656).

Markets are managed by market organisations that might construct and manage the premises in which the market functions, good retail examples being local market halls for the sale of local produce such as vegetables, fruit, flowers and meat. Of greater interest is the involvement of the market organisation in management and regulation of market trading, which meant dealing with issues such as admission (or expulsion) of members, establishment and policing of trading regulations, settlement of transactions, resolution of disputes, compilation and publication of market information such as prices and volumes, and so on.

The archives of market organisations shed light on the brokers or sellers who operated in them, perhaps giving details of dates of involvement, disputes, relative importance, role in the market's management, etc. As with other groups of associations, their archives might well provide contextual information about prices, volumes and trading conditions. The National Register of Archives (www.nationalarchives.gov.uk/nra) contains summary details of the archives of around 100 market organisations.

Livery Companies and other Trade Guilds

The archives of London's livery companies and of other trade guilds in the provinces date back to medieval times. They are of particular value in tracing the history of a business because they cover a period for which few business-specific sources exist. Moreover, they relate largely to individuals, which is highly relevant when the typical business unit was based on a single craftsman or, at the most, a tiny number of them working together.

15 *The archives of livery companies and trade guilds provide details of members and their apprentices. Many, especially those of London's livery companies, date back to early times when few other sources of business-related information exist and therefore are especially useful. This illustration is taken from a 1770 apprenticeship register of the Worshipful Company of Scriveners.*

Although many livery companies and guilds had social and/or religious origins, these were gradually superseded during the Middle Ages by economic functions, in particular the regulation of a craft for the benefit of local craftsmen who formed their membership. They sought to control a range of factors influencing entry to the craft, the training of apprentices, quality of output, wages and costs, and so on. They existed in particular in areas of strong economic activity.

London's livery companies were by far the most powerful, the influence of a few extending far into the provinces; much of what follows is based on their experience. However, many provincial guilds existed in cities such as Bristol, Coventry, Glasgow, Sheffield and York. By the mid-18th century, the influence of most was in rapid decline although, even as late as 1856, any person practising a trade (a definition that excluded commerce and the professions) in the City of London was still required to hold membership of a livery company. Many livery companies – in fact nearly all of those extant in the late 17th century – and provincial guilds survive, although with greatly modified functions. Details of present-day livery companies are available at www.fishhall.co.uk.

Extensive record keeping was vital for effective regulation and over the years vast archives accumulated, many of which have survived. Of those London livery companies with historical archives, over half have at least some material created before 1500. Minutes and accounts feature prominently and, although these deal primarily with administration, they also touch on individual craftsmen in cases of dispute between members, infringement of regulations, imposition of fines and so on.

By far the most important archives containing information about specific businessmen are membership and apprenticeship registers. The latter may include name of apprentice; date of apprenticeship; father's name, address and occupation; and name of master. Likewise, membership registers give details of craftsmen on completion of their apprenticeship (otherwise expressed as having received their 'freedom' from apprenticeship) and may provide name, date of admission, sometimes address, father's name and apprenticeship details. Cliff Webb's ongoing series called *London Livery Company Apprenticeship Registers*, published since 1996 and now extending to 44 volumes, abstracts and indexes livery company apprenticeship archives and is a hugely important finding aid. Guildhall's particularly useful online guide, 'Searching for Members or those Apprenticed to Members of City of London Livery Companies', explains how to locate an individual in livery company archives (www.history.ac.uk/gh).

Other livery company and trade guild archives relate to regulation of trade practices, which in practice meant the identification of inferior produce or dishonest weights and measures. Where possible, such regulation was facilitated by craftsmen's use of distinctive marks to identify their output. These marks were recorded in 'mark books', which survive in the archives of several companies including the armourers and braziers, coopers, cutlers, goldsmiths, pewterers and playing-card makers. Today, they are vitally important in linking craftsmen to their surviving output.

The authority of London's livery companies was largely restricted to the City of London but the influence of a few companies extended to non-members outside the City and sometimes nationally. Among the best known are the Goldsmiths' Company, which assayed and marked gold and silver products, the Stationers' Company, which, prior to the introduction of copyright, possessed a monopoly of registration of printed books, the Gunmakers' Company, which proofed small arms and the Society of Apothecaries, which, from 1815, was the examining body nationally for a new professional exam, the Licentiateship of the Society of Apothecaries.

The archives of well over a hundred provincial guilds and livery companies are lodged in record offices and are recorded in the National Register of Archives (www.nationalarchives.gov.uk/nra) and the National Register of Archives of Scotland (www.nas.gov.uk/nras). The greatest concentration of livery company archives is at Guildhall Library, where 75 collections are to be found; some are extensive. A few companies have chosen to appoint archivists to administer their archives on their own premises. The Guildhall's holdings are described in *City Livery Companies and Related Organisations: A guide to their archives in Guildhall Library* (1989) as well as in its catalogue (www.cityoflondon.gov.uk/librarycatalogue) and online guide (www.history.ac.uk/gh).

A useful overview of the content of livery company archives is C.R.H. Cooper, 'The archives of the City of London livery companies and related organisations', *Archives* (1984), while the archives of single companies are discussed in Susan M. Hare, 'The records of the Goldsmiths' Company', *Archives* (1984) and Robin Myers, 'The records of the Worshipful Company of Stationers and Newspaper Makers 1554-1912', *Archives* (1983). William F. Kahn, *The Development of London Livery Companies: An historical essay* (1959) provides a short historical account of the evolution of livery companies.

Quite separate from livery company archives, the Corporation of the City of London kept registers and supporting papers of 'freemen' of the City of London, a qualification that until 1856 was necessary for them to trade within the City. Individuals were admitted to the City's freedom as a result of the completion of apprenticeship or through patrimony or redemption. Registers and their supporting papers survive in their entirety from the late 17th century and have particular importance when livery company archives do not survive. Formerly available in the Corporation of London Record Office, they are now in the London Metropolitan Archives (www.cityoflondon.gov.uk/lma). Many are well indexed. They are explained in depth in Vivienne E. Aldous, *My Ancestors Were Freemen of the City of London* (1999).

Although overshadowed by London's livery companies, provincial guilds were also hugely important and their archives, which are usually lodged in record offices, can be traced through the National Registers of Archives. Activities varied from guild to guild but regulation of entry to the craft and of craftsmen's output are common themes. The Cutlers of Hallamshire regulated Sheffield's cutlers, for example, while Glasgow's trade guilds covered groups ranging from hammermen (i.e. metal workers) to bakers, from coopers to weavers.

PRINTED SOURCES

Published Histories of Businesses:
Monographs, Articles, Brochures, Reference Books

It goes without saying that a published history is the most immediate and uncomplicated source of information for tracing the history of a business. They exist in abundance and variety. Some are conventional histories, in book or brochure form, perhaps commissioned by the business to commemorate an anniversary or written by an enthusiast historian. Others are articles published in scholarly journals, trade press, house journals and newspapers. A rapidly growing source is information posted on the internet. In addition, dictionaries, directories and gazetteers carry historical details or essays about individual traders or businesses in a particular trade or business sector. This section reviews all these publications as well as the bibliographies of use in locating them.

Internet-based Information

In finding historical information about a business, an invaluable starting point is to type its name into Google or other search engine and see what turns up. A very large proportion of active businesses post at least some historical information about their origin and development on their corporate website; how much depends, *inter alia*, on their resources, the length of their history and their sense of themselves. Other information, either company- or sector-specific, is posted by collectors and enthusiasts in such areas as road transport, shipping, ceramics and clocks. Encyclopaedias, such as Wikipedia, are helpful for big businesses. However, the unstructured and transient nature of much internet-based information, together with the lack of certainty about its reliability, creates problems as to location and use; it not dealt with at length here. Stuart A. Raymond, *Family History on the Web: An internet directory for England and Wales* (6th edition, 2007) is helpful in locating some sites.

Published Business Histories

The earliest-published business histories date back to the very end of the 19th century but the number grew very substantially from the 1940s. Most businesses of significant age have published some account of their history, either for marketing, public relations or employee and management information, or sometimes simply out of curiosity and enthusiasm. Formats extend beyond books and brochures to unpublished essays and fact sheets. Some publications are written by academics for a scholarly or management readership but most are the work of non-specialist writers, staff members or enthusiasts and are aimed at a general readership. Many are published to mark anniversaries, moves to new premises or are used as an opportunity to take stock at a time of corporate change. Some are more lightweight and less accurate than others but all are surely useful especially if the business is defunct and has left no archives.

Many books and brochures are privately printed and circulated among a fairly narrow readership, such as shareholders, staff, customers, friends and members of founding families. This implies short print runs and a failure to lodge copies in copyright libraries. An extremely useful finding-aid for such monographs is Copac (www.copac.ac.uk), the combined online catalogue of copyright and leading academic libraries.

The trade press (*see* pp.134-5) and house journals (*see* pp.133-4) as well as scholarly periodicals such as *Business History, Business History Review, Scottish Industrial History* and *Business Archives* carry articles on specific businesses; this last group uses them as case studies from which to make conclusions of wider importance. Articles in the first two groups are numerous but difficult to locate for want of indexes, especially cumulative indexes.

Collections of Business History Publications and Bibliographies

The major collection of publications relating to specific businesses is at the Centre for Business History in Scotland (www.gla.ac.uk/centres/businesshistory). This incorporates the former library of the Business Archives Council and extends to about 5,000 items; its collection of

The North of England Carpet Shaking and Cleaning Co., 22, Upper Duke Street, Liverpool. Telephone 2,486.—Householders in the city and suburbs of Liverpool are indeed fortunate in the possession amongst them of an institution of the calibre of the above; for by taking advantage of the services of this company many a pound can be saved, and the home rendered bright as well as wholesome. This company was projected in the year 1875, under the auspices of its present proprietor—Mr. R. Thornton—whose premises consist of a compactly built three-storied edifice, with capitally appointed offices at the entrance and works at the rear, elaborately equipped with special patent machinery; the whole of the arrangements being under cover. The machinery is driven by steam

power, and effectually cleanses the carpet or rug of every particle of dust, by shaking without in any way injuring the article. All this is done expeditiously and at strictly economic rates, the carpets being called for and delivered by the company's servants free of any further charge. In addition to this the company operate on an extensive scale as cleaners and finishers of lace curtains, blankets, and counterpanes; and also undertake the cleaning and dyeing of Madras, guipure, Swiss, and other delicate fabrics. Since its foundation the business has literally developed by leaps and bounds, and is now under the control of an able manager, who employs a large staff of experienced workers. The company is manifestly thus in a most prosperous condition, and this must be directly attributed to the highly creditable manner in which every detail of the undertaking has always been carried out.

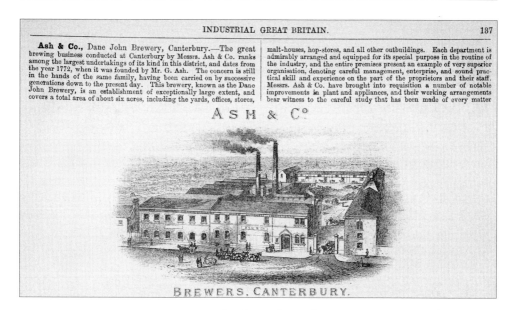

INDUSTRIAL GREAT BRITAIN. 137

Ash & Co., Dane John Brewery, Canterbury.—The great brewing business conducted at Canterbury by Messrs. Ash & Co. ranks among the largest undertakings of its kind in this district, and dates from the year 1772, when it was founded by Mr. G. Ash. The concern is still in the hands of the same family, having been carried on by successive generations down to the present day. This brewery, known as the Dane John Brewery, is an establishment of exceptionally large extent, and covers a total area of about six acres, including the yards, offices, stores, malt-houses, hop-stores, and all other outbuildings. Each department is admirably arranged and equipped for its special purpose in the routine of the industry, and the entire premises present an example of very superior organisation, denoting careful management, enterprise, and sound practical skill and experience on the part of the proprietors and their staff. Messrs. Ash & Co. have brought into requisition a number of notable improvements in plant and appliances, and their working arrangements bear witness to the careful study that has been made of every matter

ASH & Cº

BREWERS, CANTERBURY.

17   See also *16 (opposite)*.

brochures is especially strong and its catalogue can be searched online. Guildhall Library and the libraries of Bristol University and the London School of Economics all have good holdings, as do the British Library and other national and copyright libraries. Their collections can be searched via Copac (*see* above). The libraries of professional bodies and trade associations, especially the former, often have full collections covering the sectors they represent. Their catalogues are often accessible online and several are willing to give visitors access to their libraries on request.

Three specialist bibliographies exist. Francis Goodall, *Bibliography of British Business Histories* (1987) lists about four thousand books, articles and theses relating to specific businesses; it gives a library location for most. A much enlarged version is being prepared for publication. Stephanie Zarach, *British Business History: A bibliography* (2nd edn, 1994) covers around 2,000 publications but excludes works under 50 pages as well as certain sectors such as railways, publishing and co-operative societies. Francis Goodall, Terry Gourvish and Steven Tolliday, *International Bibliography of Business History* (1997) concentrates on scholarly works and is annotated. Two leading online general history bibliographies, with large business and economic history content, are *Royal Historical Society Bibliography* (www.rhs.ac.uk/bibl) with over 400,000 records and *London's Past Online* with over 40,000 records (www.rhs.ac.uk/bibl/london.asp); the latter has its origins in Heather Creaton, *Bibliography*

16   *(Opposite) A vast quantity of historical information has been published about individual businesses. Some is in the form of published histories, while more is in the form of entries in old reference books. An example of the latter is this 1892 entry, relating to the North of England Carpet Shaking Co. of Liverpool, appearing in* The Century's Progress: Lancashire, *one in a series of similar volumes published at the turn of the 19th-20th centuries (see pp. 100-4 for a list). It contains entries for around 400 businesses. Another example is an entry for Ash & Co., brewers of Canterbury, one of 700 entries appearing in* Industrial Great Britain *(1891).*

of *Printed Books on London History to 1939* (1994). The former is hugely important as, in addition to books and brochures, it lists periodical articles and, in the case of multi-contributor publications, individual chapters.

These publishing initiatives have not supplanted a small number of more specialised bibliographies published earlier and which often include obscure local references in journals and newspapers. They include Joyce M. Bellamy, *Yorkshire Business Histories: A bibliography* (1970), D.J. Rowe, *Northern Business Histories: A bibliography* (1979) and Sidney Horrocks, *Lancashire Business Histories* (1971). Other bibliographies are business sector-based such as George Ottley, *Bibliography of British Railway History* (1983) and *Supplements* (1988-98); Fred Wellings and Alistair Gibb, *Bibliography of Banking Histories* (2 vols, 1995-7); J. Benson, R.G. Neville and C.H. Thompson, *Bibliography of the British Coal Industry* (1981); John Armstrong, 'An annotated bibliography of the British coastal trade', *International Journal of Maritime History* (1995); and A.W. Skempton, *British Civil Engineering, 1640-1840: A bibliography of contemporary printed records, plans and books* (1987). John Greenwood has published five industrial archaeology bibliographies (for example *Industrial Archaeology and Industrial History of London* (1988)), each covering a separate English region and these include many business history titles. Other specialist bibliographies can be found on the web, sometimes in unlikely places, such as one for co-operative societies at www.chelmsford-tuc.org.uk.

Reference Books

A small number of reference books, published either annually or periodically as a series, provide short historical essays or brief factual data on the history of specific businesses. One dealing with big business is the ongoing *International Dictionary of Company Histories* (1988-, 74 vols), which carries *c.*3,000-word essays on international – not just British – businesses that are leaders either on account of their size or because they punch above their weight. In recent years size criteria has been defined as an annual turnover in excess of $25 billion. Over 8,000 entries have been published but many are revisions of earlier entries.

A very different publication from an earlier era is the annual *Red Book of Commerce or Who's Who in Business* (1906-39). This provides thumbnail sketches – not histories – of businesses large and small, although the criteria for inclusion are unclear. The first issue, published in 1906, carried about two thousand entries, a number that rose progressively to 5,000 by the 1920s. A typical entry runs to 200 words and covers function, products, address, date of establishment, previous names, employee numbers, directors' names, plus sometimes a brief historical narrative. Comparison of one issue with another provides useful insight into a business over time.

Another publication, hard to find, is *Histories of Famous Firms*, published on a periodic basis from *c.*1954 to 1960. It provides detailed essays, usually on leading businesses based in the provinces. Its first issue for 1957 contains a schedule of 150 businesses covered. Some issues are in the British Library.

A further group of publications, published at the turn of the 20th century and having a common content and 'look and feel', provides more thumbnail sketches of individual businesses. These were the work of publishers such as Historical Publishing Co., and cover businesses in a particular city or region; a typical example is *Illustrated London and its Representatives of Commerce* (1893). This contains descriptions of about five hundred rank and file businesses, ranging from department stores to hat manufacturers, from wine merchants to umbrella makers. An entry might run to several hundred words and deal with current business activity and historical background; many are illustrated with engravings of premises. Articles tend to be unduly self-congratulatory as inclusion was based on subscription. Very few copies survive and those that do are well scattered among reference and academic libraries. Those identified by the writer are listed in Appendix Two; others must surely exist. Taken together, they provide accounts of many thousands of business in the years either side of 1900.

Published Gazetteers and Directories covering Business Sectors

In recent decades many publications, variously described as gazetteers, dictionaries or directories, have covered the history of individual businesses within particular business sectors. Often they are directed at collectors and enthusiasts. Those known to the writer are listed in Appendix One in three separate categories although, at the margin, the distinctiveness of each category is somewhat blurred. Taken together, they provide historical details of many thousands of businesses.

The first category deals with craftsmen such as goldsmiths, silversmiths, potters, printers of books and bookbinders who often worked as individual traders producing handcrafted goods of high quality; many of them were at work before the mid-19th century. Content, which is usually derived from trade directories, apprenticeship records, guild archives, insurance policies and the like, includes name and name changes, dates of establishment and closure, activities/output and address and address changes. In many senses these businesses pre-date modern industry. Other occupational listings are well-covered in Stuart A. Raymond, *Occupational Sources for Genealogists* (2nd edn, 1997).

The second category comprises historical biographical directories. Specialist ones are invariably of professional people such as architects and engineers. These are in addition to more wide-ranging works such as the *Oxford Dictionary of National Biography*, the *Dictionary of Business Biography* and the *Dictionary of Scottish Business Biography*, which are described more fully in the section on Business Biography (*see* pp.105-7).

The third group provides short texts on relatively modern businesses – invariably registered companies – operating in such sectors as banking, brewing, insurance, pharmaceuticals and shipbuilding. These publications provide potted histories of individual businesses and from time to time include details of surviving historical archives.

APPENDIX ONE

PUBLISHED GAZETTES AND DIRECTORIES AND SOME WEBSITES CONTAINING HISTORIES OF BUSINESSES

a) Gazetteers/Dictionaries of Early Craftsmen

Barometer Makers:

Edwin Banfield, *Barometer Makers and Retailers, 1660-1900* (1991). This provides very brief details, mostly only a few words but sometimes much longer, of *c.*6,000 craftsmen or firms at work in Britain and Ireland. Gives location, time span, other occupations, etc. Unindexed.

Nicholas Goodison, *English Barometers, 1680-1860: A history of domestic barometers and their makers and retailers* (2nd edn, 1977). This gives lengthy essays on *c.*45 leading makers and a schedule of several hundred lesser makers, for which very brief details such as name, time span, location, etc, are given.

Bell Founders:

H.B. Walters, *Church Bells of England* (1912). This provides a general account of the history of church bells but includes a substantial appendix listing *c*.700 bell founders, giving for each address, time span and source of information. Indexed by name and place.

Book Trades:

Scottish Book Trade Index. See www.nls.uk. This site (National Archives of Scotland) provides details – name, address, activity, time span, etc – of individuals engaged in the Scottish book trade between the beginning of printing in Scotland and *c*.1850. Many hundred printers, publishers, booksellers, bookbinders, printmakers, stationers and papermakers are included.

Exeter Working Papers in British Book Trade History. See www.devon.gov.uk/localstudies. This site presents a mass of information about British book trade members, apprentices, bankrupts, etc. Much is derived from the published work of Ian Maxted (*see* below).

H.G. Aldis et al, *Dictionary of Printers and Booksellers in England, Scotland and Ireland and of Foreign Printers of English Books, 1557-1640* (1910). This gives name, address, time span and specialisations – bookseller, printer, bookbinder, publisher, stationer – and any other known biographical details. The *c*.1,750 entries are in essay form and usually 100 words in length, sometimes considerably longer. Indexed by London address, by places outside London and by London signs.

Philip A.H. Brown, *London Publishers and Printers, c.1800-1870* (1982). This comprises brief entries in a standard format for *c*.1,500 tradesmen and firms including name, addresses and time span. No indexes.

Tony Copsey, *Book Distribution and Printing in Suffolk, 1534-1850* (1994). This provides brief details of *c*.500 Suffolk booksellers, binders, printers and stationers.

E. Gordon Duff, *A Century of the English Book Trade: Short notices of all printers, stationers, bookbinders and others connected with it from the issue of the first dated book in 1457 to the incorporation of the Company of Stationers in 1557* (1905). This provides short essays on *c*.700 tradesmen, some as short as 50 words. No indexes.

Ellic Howe, *List of London Bookbinders, 1648-1815* (1950). This has entries for *c*.1,000 London bookbinders. Businesses are listed in alphabetical sequence and details provided include name, address, time span and apprenticeship. Unindexed.

Ian F. Maxted, *The British Book Trades, 1710-1777: An index of the masters and apprentices recorded in Inland Revenue registers at the Public Record Office* (1983). This is a schedule of individuals involved in the book trade in such capacities as printers, stationers, papermakers, booksellers, bookbinders and engravers. Each entry, which is in a standard format, gives name, address, occupation of the master and details of the apprentices that worked under him, including start date. The source is Inland Revenue apprentice registers held in the National Archives (*see* pp.67-9). No indexes.

Ian F. Maxted, *The London Book Trades, 1735-1775: A checklist of members in trade directories and Musgrave's Obituary* (1984). This continues Maxted's earlier work of listing tradesmen engaged in the London book trade but using entirely different sources. Entries adopt a standard format and give name, occupation, addresses, date of death if known, time span as deduced from directories. About a thousand tradesmen are included. No indexes.

Ian F. Maxted, *The London Book Trades, 1775-1800: A preliminary checklist of members* (1977). This continues Maxted's work in scheduling members of the London book trades, this time using a much broader range of sources. It lists c.4,000 tradesmen in brief factual entries, which include name, addresses, time span and other biographical details. No index.

Maurice Packer, *Bookbinders of Victorian London* (1991). This covers bookbinders at work between 1837 and 1901 in the Cities of London and Westminster. Gives name, address, time span and any other activities, e.g. bookselling and stationery, undertaken. Indexed by street.

Henry R. Plomer, *Dictionary of the Booksellers and Printers who were at Work in England, Scotland and Ireland from 1641 to 1667* (1907). This gives name, address, approximate time span, specialisation, publications and any other known information for c.800 tradesmen. Entries are in essay form and most extend to 100 words; some are significantly longer. No indexes.

Henry R. Plomer, *Dictionary of Printers and Booksellers who were at Work in England, Scotland and Ireland from 1668 to 1725* (1922). This is similar to the above publication and contains c.1,500 entries. Indexed to places outside London.

Henry R. Plomer et al, *Dictionary of the Printers and Booksellers who were at Work in England, Scotland and Ireland from 1726 to 1775* (1932). This is similar to the above publications, although there are individual sections for each country. Entries cover c.2,500 firms or individuals and range in length from 50 to 1,000 words. Indexed by place. This publication completed a project of the Bibliographical Society to publish details of all publishers and printers at work in the Britain from the beginning of English printing to 1775.

Charles Ramsden, *London Bookbinders, 1780-1840* (1956) and *Bookbinders of the United Kingdom (Outside London), 1780-1840* (1954). These volumes provide short factual entries covering several hundred bookbinders at work in England, Ireland, Scotland and Wales between 1780 and 1840. Name, addresses and time span are provided with other details when available. Unindexed.

William B. Todd, *Directory of Printers and Others in Allied Trades, London and Vicinity, 1800-1840* (1972). This provides name, address and time span of c.3,500 printers and allied tradesmen such as publishers, engravers, press manufacturers, type founders, booksellers and auctioneers. A variety of sources are used but most important are returns made under the 1799 Seditious Societies Act, which are available in local record offices. Entries are short and follow a standard format. Unindexed.

Chronometer Makers:

Tony Mercer, *Chronometer Makers of the World; with extensive list of makers and craftsmen* (2004). This contains brief accounts of several hundred makers, a large proportion being British-based.

Clock and Watch Makers:

Database of Antique Clock Clockmakers' Names and Dates – see www.antiqueclockpriceguide.com. This carries brief details of clockmakers and is available by subscription.

G.H. Baillie, *Watchmakers and Clockmakers of the World* (1951) and Brian Loomes, *Watchmakers and Clockmakers of the World, Vol. 2* (1976). The former lists c.35,000 individuals and firms involved in clock and watchmaking and associated trades. Typical entries extend to only a few words and include name, location, approximate time span and specialisation. Most makers listed were at work before 1825. So far as London makers are concerned, the work largely duplicates *Britten's Old Clocks and Watches and Their Makers* (q.v.). Brian Loomes seeks to complement Baillie, extending the period to 1875 and having *c*.35,000 entries that are additional to or modifications of Baillie entries. Unindexed.

G.H. Baillie et al, *Britten's Old Clocks and Watches and Their Makers* (1982). This includes entries for *c*.25,000 makers, most of whom were London-based and at work up to 1875; some overseas makers are included. Associated trades include case makers, escapement makers and watch jewellers. Entries are short and comprise name, address, specialisation, approximate time span, apprenticeship information and other details. Unindexed.

Brian Loomes, *The Early Clockmakers of Great Britain* (1981). This covers *c*.5,000 clock and watchmakers and makers of mathematical instruments operating in Britain – 80 per cent of whom were London-based – before 1700. The author is a revisionist of errors in Baillie (q.v.) and Britten (q.v.) and his major source is the archives of the Worshipful Company of Clockmakers. The entries give details of name, location, approximate time span, apprenticeship and any other details known to the compiler. Typical entries are a few sentences long but, in the case of well-known names, extend to a few hundred words. Unindexed.

Publications listing details of local clockmakers are too numerous to list. The following serve as examples:

C.F.C. Beeson, *Clockmaking in Oxfordshire 1400-1850* (1962)
J.K. Bellchambers, *Somerset Clocks and Clockmakers* (1968)
J.A. Daniell, *The Makers of Clocks and Watches in Leicestershire and Rutland* (1952)
Brian Loomes, *Lancashire Clocks and Clockmakers* (1975)
Brian Loomes, *Clockmakers of Northern England* (1997)
Iorwerth C. Peate, *Clock and Watchmakers in Wales* (1975)

Firearm and other Personal Weapon Makers:
De Witt Bailey, *British Board of Ordnance Small Arms Contractors, 1689-1840* (1999). This provides very brief details – name, location, materials supplied and covering dates of supply – for *c*.600 suppliers of barrels, locks, bayonets, ramrods, complete arms, etc.

De Witt Bailey & Douglas A. Nie, *English Gunmakers: The Birmingham and provincial gun trade in the 18th and 19th centuries* (1978). This provides location and time span for *c*.4,500 gun and gun-component makers operating in England, outside London, from the 18th century. Entries for important firms are considerably longer. No indexes.

Richard H. Bezdek, *Swords and Sword Makers of England and Scotland* (2003). Gives name, location and lifespan of businesses at work between 17th and 19th centuries.

Howard L. Blackmore, *Dictionary of London Gunmakers, 1350-1850* (1986) and *Gunmakers of London Supplement, 1350-1850* (1999). These list several thousand tradesmen, usually in very brief entries, often giving address, other occupations, approximate time span and apprenticeship details. No indexes.

Robert E. Gardner, *Small Arms Makers: A directory of fabricators of firearms, edged weapons, crossbows and polearms* (1963). This mostly relates to US makers but includes makers in other countries including the UK. The summaries are about twenty words long and usually give just location, function and lifespan. No indexes.

Leslie Southwick, *London Silver Hilted Swords: Their makers, suppliers and allied trades; with directory* (2001). This contains quite lengthy accounts of *c*.300 firms based on information extracted from wills, rate books, trade cards, etc.

John Walter, *Greenhill Dictionary of Guns and Gunmakers* (2001). An international dictionary including short accounts of varying length and detail for British firms. No indexes.

Charles E. Whitelaw, *Scottish Arms Makers: A biographical directory of makers of firearms, edged weapons and armour in Scotland from the 15th century to 1870* (1977). Basic detail about several hundred craftsmen arranged by town and indexed by name. Includes gunmakers, armourers, bowers, arrowmakers, dagmakers, sheathmakers, etc.

Furniture Makers:

Geoffrey Beard & Christopher Gilbert, *Dictionary of English Furniture Makers, 1660-1840* (1986) and Angela Evans, *Index to the Dictionary of English Furniture Makers, 1660-1840* (1990). This lists *c*.40,000 firms and tradesmen involved in furniture making and allied trades such as makers of picture frames, clock and barometer cases, spinning wheels and boxes. Entries include name, address, time span and other details gleaned from a wide range of sources. Most entries extend to *c*.20 words although some are much longer. Indexed by name and place.

Francis Bamford, 'A dictionary of Edinburgh wrights and furniture makers, 1660-1840', *Furniture History* (1983). This lists *c*.2,000 cabinet makers, upholsterers, wrights, turners, furniture dealers and others connected with the making of furniture in Scotland between 1660 and 1840. Entries cover name, address, time span, specialisation and other details and are mostly a couple of sentences long. No indexes.

Goldsmiths and Silversmiths:

Kenneth Crisp Jones, *Silversmiths of Birmingham and their Marks, 1750-1980* (1981). A general history with a gazetteer covering *c*.50 firms in entries of *c*.200 words.

John Culme, *Directory of Gold and Silversmiths, Jewellers and Allied Trades, 1838-1914* (1987). This provides essays, some several hundred words long but mostly much shorter, on *c*.4,000 tradesmen and firms. Largely based on information taken from the makers' marks registers held by the Worshipful Company of Goldsmiths and from trade directories and include names, addresses, time span and other occupations carried on. No indexes.

Margaret A.V. Gill, *Directory of Newcastle Goldsmiths* (1980). Factual entries on several hundred craftsmen arranged in an alphabetical sequence.

A.G. Grimwade, *London Goldsmiths, 1697-1837: Their marks and lives from the original registers at Goldsmiths' Hall and other sources* (1990). Name, address, apprenticeship, marks, approximate time span and any other information known to the author are given for *c*.3,000 goldsmiths. A prime source is the mark registers of the Worshipful Company of Goldsmiths. No indexes.

Ambrose Heal, *The London Goldsmiths, 1200-1800: A record of the names and addresses of the craftsmen, their shop signs and trade cards* (1935). This lists *c*.3,000 goldsmiths and some silversmiths giving for each address, approximate time span and specialisation. No indexes.

I. Elizabeth James, *The Goldsmiths of Aberdeen* (1981). Contains essays, *c.*200 to 300 words, on *c.*250 craftsmen.

Hugh Murray, *Directory of York Goldsmiths, Silversmiths and Associated Craftsmen* (1998). Covers *c.*1,000 businesses in brief factual entries.

Gunfounders:

Charles Ffoulkes, *The Gun Founders of England* (1937). This includes a schedule of European makers giving location and time span.

A.N. Kennard, *Gunfounding and Gunfounders: A directory of cannon founders from earliest times to 1850* (1986). This international directory contains many entries for UK-based individuals and firms. Makers of forged iron guns as well as some retailers and merchants are included. Shot founders are excluded. The 1,000 entries give details of name, address and approximate time span, as well as known output. Most entries are only a few words long. Unindexed.

Medallists:

L. Forrer, *Biographical Dictionary of Medallists, Coin, Gem and Seal Engravers, Mint Masters, etc, Ancient and Modern with Reference to their Works, BC500 – AD1900* (1904-16). This monumental work covers a huge time span and includes medallists from many countries. Entries run from a few words to several pages but cover relatively few British makers in the modern period. J.S. Martin, *Index to Biographical Dictionary of Medallists by L. Forrer* (1987) provides an index to people, places and subjects.

Metallic Tickets, Counters, Etc., Makers:

R.N.P. Hawkins, *Dictionary of Makers of British Metallic Tickets, Checks, Medalets, Tallies and Counters, 1788-1910* (1989). This provides lengthy entries giving name, location, time span, output and other details of several hundreds of makers of metallic discs largely based in Birmingham and the West Midlands. The discs were used as, *inter alia*, membership tickets, admission passes, tradesmen's advertisements and counters for use in education and gaming in an age when cheap and durable card and paper was unavailable. Indexed by names, places and subjects.

Musical Instrument Makers:

❧   Organs:

Lyndesay G. Langwill & Noel Boston, *Church and Chamber Barrel Organs: Their origin, makers, music and location* (1970). An assemblage of information covering *c.*150 businesses.

John Norman, *The Organs of Britain: An appreciation and gazetteer* (1984). This contains a 15-page gazetteer covering *c.*80 firms/individuals in very broad and eclectic detail. Entries are typically 20 to 30 words long.

Laurence Elvin, *Family Enterprise: The story of some North Country organ builders* (1986). This contains lengthy essays on *c.*12 builders in Bradford, Lincoln, Newcastle, Rochdale and York.

Laurence Elvin, *Pipes and Actions: Some organ builders in the Midlands and Beyond* (1995). Lengthy essays on *c.*35 builders

☙ Pianos:

Martha N. Clinkscale, *Makers of the Piano [1700-1860]* (2 vols, 1993, 1999). An international dictionary covering many hundreds of makers with an assemblage of basic information – address, time span, etc – and lengthy accounts of their products.

Philip B. James, *Early Keyboard Instruments from their Beginnings to the Year 1820* (1930). This provides very brief details of *c*.200 makers.

☙ Stringed Instruments:

A large number of publications exists, many of which cover the same ground, more or less. The following is a selection:

Donald H. Boalch & Charles Mould (eds), *Makers of the Harpsichord and Clavichord, 1440-1840* (3rd edn, 1995). International in scope, this provides assemblages of information on *c*.1,000 makers – time span, dates, location, products, etc.

Brian W. Harvey, *The Violin Family and its Makers in the British Isles: An illustrated history and directory* (1995). Very short entries on *c*.1,500 makers.

William Henley, *Universal Dictionary of Violin and Bow Makers* (7 vols, 1959-69). International directory with short entries on several hundred makers.

William C. Honeyman, *Scottish Violin Makers: Past and present* (1910). Essays on 80 makers but somewhat dated.

Karel Jalovec, *Encyclopedia of Violin Makers* (1968). An international encyclopaedia that covers several thousand makers and provides a short assemblage of information for each – time span, products, location, etc.

W. Meredith Morris, *British Violin Makers: A biographical dictionary of British makers of stringed instruments and bows and a critical description of their work* (1904, 3rd edn 2006). This provides essays on *c*.1,000 violin makers at work in Britain from the 16th century, giving as a minimum location, time span and details of output. No index.

☙ Wind Instruments:

William Waterhouse, *The New Langwill Index: A dictionary of musical wind instrument makers and inventors* (7th edn, 1993). This is an international dictionary covering *c*.10,000 makers several of which are British. Generally very short entries.

Paper Makers (see also *Book Trades*):

A.H. Shorter, *Paper Mills and Paper Makers in England, 1495-1800* (1957). Content is organised by mill site rather than by paper maker, but a name index to paper makers enables a substantial amount of biographical information to be identified.

Pewterers:

Howard H. Cotterell, *Old Pewter: Its makers and marks in England, Scotland and Ireland* (1929). This provides brief details, including address, time span, apprenticeship details and any other biographical information, of several thousand craftsmen at work from the 18th century. Sources used include livery company records, directories and trade cards. No indexes.

Carl Ricketts, *Pewterers of London, 1600-1900* (2001). This presents in column format data on several thousand London pewterers, including name, addresses, apprenticeship, time span and so on. The principal sources are records of the Worshipful Company of Pewterers and trade directories. No indexes.

Printers and Publishers (see also *Book Trades*):

David H.J. Schenck, *Directory of the Lithographic Printers of Scotland 1820-1870: their locations, periods, and a guide to artistic lithographic printers* (1999). This contains entries on *c.*500 printers at work between 1820 and 1870. Entries follow a standard format giving names, time span, addresses, other occupations and additional general information. Arranged in alphabetical order of printer. No indexes.

Michael Twyman, *Directory of London Lithographic Printers, 1800-1850* (1976). This lists *c.*500 tradesmen giving for each in brief entries name, addresses, time span as deduced from directories. No indexes.

Charles Humphries & W.C. Smith, *Music Publishing in the British Isles ..., A dictionary of engravers, printers, publishers and music sellers* (2nd edn, 1970). This contains short entries on *c.*2,000 firms covering location, time span, output, etc.

Scientific Instrument Makers:

Gloria C. Clifton, *Directory of British Scientific Instrument Makers, 1550-1851* (1995). This provides details such as name, addresses, specialisation, time span and apprenticeship in short factual entries for *c.*4,500 scientific instrument makers. Their products included calculating, navigational and surveying instruments – telescopes, microscopes, chronometers, thermometers, barometers, philosophical instruments and so on. Sources are given for each entry. Indexed by name and place.

D.J. Bryden, *Scottish Scientific Instrument Makers, 1600-1900* (1972). This gives brief details including name, addresses, specialisation and time span for *c.*225 Scottish-based scientific instruments makers at work through to 1900.

Surgical Instrument Makers:

David Wright, *An Index of London Surgical and Scientific Instrument Makers, 1736-1811* and *An Index of London Surgical Instrument Makers, 1822-1865* (unpublished typescript, Guildhall, 1988-9). These provide brief details such as address, activities and time span of many hundreds of makers. Information taken from trade directories.

b) Dictionaries of Professional People

Architects (see also *Architect Firms, p.94*):

Howard Colvin, *Biographical Dictionary of British Architects, 1600-1840* (1995). This dictionary lists *c.*7,000 individuals 'who habitually made, or may be presumed to have made, architectural designs' and includes architects as well as carpenters, master masons, civil engineers, surveyors and the like. Entries are in essay form and range from a few hundred words to several thousand. Indexed by name and place.

Antonia Brodie et al, *Directory of British Architects, 1834-1900* (1993). This provides basic facts in a standard format for *c.*10,000 architects operating in the Victorian period, supported by references to obituaries, other bibliographical sources and unpublished materials. All architects at work between 1834 and 1900 are included, although architects born after 1880 and who died after 1950 are excluded. A major source of information is the membership files of the Royal Institute of British Architects (origins date to 1834).

A. Stuart Gray, *Edwardian Architecture: A biographical dictionary* (1985). This provides essays, several lengthy, on *c*.300 architects giving biographical details, details of output and references. Indexed by name and place.

Adolf K. Placzek, *Macmillan Encyclopedia of Architects* (1982). This international encyclopaedia contains lengthy essays on many UK architects.

Other publications, dealing with architects by region, include:

J.D. Bennett, *Leicestershire Architects, 1700-1850* (1968)
Sidney M. Gold, *A Biographical Dictionary of Architects at Reading … to 1930* (1999)
Cynthia Brown et al, *Dictionary of Architects of Suffolk Buildings, 1800-1914* (1991)
Derek Linstrum, *West Yorkshire Architects and Architecture* (1978)

Designers:

Mel Byars, *The Design Encyclopaedia* (1994). This is largely an encyclopaedia of individuals and firms engaged in design and decorative activity from the last third of 19th century onwards. It is international in scope and contains *c*.3,500 entries each *c*.200 words long. No indexes.

Engineers:

A.W. Skempton et al, *A Biographical Dictionary of Civil Engineers in Great Britain and Ireland 1500-1830* (2002) and P.S.M. Cross-Rudkin & M.M. Chrimes, *A Biographical Dictionary of Civil Engineers in Great Britain and Ireland, 1830-1890* (2008). These provide essays ranging from *c*.200 to *c*.2,000 words on civil engineers working before 1890 either in Britain and Ireland or elsewhere if of British birth. Sources, works and publications are listed. Indexed by place.

David Abbott (ed.), *The Biographical Dictionary of Scientists, Engineers and Inventors* (1985). This provides biographical essays, often 500 words long, covering *c*.500 engineers and inventors, active in all branches of engineering, who were at work in Britain and other countries mostly in the 18th and 19th centuries. Indexed by name and subject.

John Marshall, *A Biographical Dictionary of Railway Engineers* (2003). This contains short essays – mostly of 200 words but sometimes considerably longer – on *c*.750 railway engineers, as well as promoters and managers provided they had an engineering background. Most are British but some worked in North America and Europe. Indexed by railway company.

Land Surveyors:

Sarah Bendall, *Dictionary of Land Surveyors and Local Mapmakers of Great Britain and Ireland, 1530-1850* (1997). This lists around 15,000 surveyors and mapmakers and gives details, when available, of address, time span, education/training, other occupations, patrons, types of map produced and counties where active. Extensively indexed.

c) Modern Business Sector Directories

Publications that serve as guides to archives are also described in the section on Locating the Archives of a Business (*see* pp.15-30).

General:

Lesley Richmond & Bridget Stockford, *Company Archives: The survey of records of the first registered companies in England and Wales* (Aldershot, 1986). This provides essays, each of *c*.100 to 500 words, on the history of *c*.700 of the 1,000 earliest registered companies on the Register of Companies in 1980. Indexed by name, place and subject.

Aircraft Manufacture:

Gunter Endres, *British Aircraft Manufacturers since 1908* (1995). This deals with *c*.75 manufacturers in short essays with a focus on output.

Bill Gunston, *World Encyclopaedia of Aircraft Manufacturers*, 2nd edn, 2005. Covers *c*.3,000 manufacturers worldwide giving key historical information in short entries with a emphasis on output.

Air Transport:

Alan J. Wright, *UK Airlines* (1998). This gives short profiles of active UK airlines.

Architecture:

Rebecca M. Bailey, *Scottish Architect's Papers: A source book* (1996). This provides detailed essays on the histories of individual firms of architects, consulting engineers and quantity surveyors operating in Scotland in the early 1990s. 114 firms are covered. Indexed by name and place but not subject.

Banking:

John Orbell & Alison Turton, *British Banking: A Guide to Historical Records* (2001). This contains essays ranging from 50 to 1,000 words on *c*.700 British banks. Indexed by name, place, bank type and repository.

Margaret Dawes & C.N. Ward-Perkins, *Country Banks of England and Wales: Private provincial banks and bankers 1688-1953* (2000). This hugely detailed work focuses in particular on individual bankers working in the provinces. Provincial banks are listed in volume two according to the city or town where their main office was located. Details of name changes, time span and sources are given, along with a list and biographical details of individual bankers associated with the bank. A single alphabetical listing of bankers is provided in volume one. Also available on CD.

F.G. Hilton Price, *A Handbook of London Bankers* (1876). This provides essays, often of several hundred words, on *c*.150 London private banks and a few joint stock banks at work in the capital before the 1870s.

G.L. Grant, *The Standard Catalogue of Provincial Banks and Banknotes* (1977). This lists private and joint stock banks by location of head office, showing for each trading name(s), legal name(s), absorbing bank and time span. Also provides details of notes issued.

Many other publications list details of banks and bankers but on a more modest scale compared with the above publication. Some are listed below:

Charles H. Cave, *A History of Banking in Bristol from 1750 to 1899* (1899)
A.S. Davies, *The Early Banks of Mid-Wales* (1935)
Francis Green, 'Early Banks in West Wales', *Transactions of the Historical Society of Mid-Wales* (1916)
L.H. Grindon, *Manchester Banks and Bankers* (1877)
John Hughes, *Liverpool Banks and Bankers 1760-1837* (1906)
Jack Parker, *Nothing for Nothing for Nobody: A History of Hertfordshire Banks and Banking* (1986)
Maberley Phillips, *History of Banks, Bankers and Banking in Northumberland, Durham and North Yorkshire ... 1755 to 1894* (1894)
Harold Preston, *Early East Anglian Banks and Bankers* (1994)
H. Ling Roth, *The Genesis of Banking in Halifax with Sidelights on Country Banking* (1914)
John Ryton, *Banks and Banknotes of Exeter* (1984)

Brewing:

Lesley Richmond & Alison Turton, *The Brewing Industry: A Guide to Historical Records* (1990). This provides essays ranging from 50 to 500 words on the history of *c.*650 British brewing companies. Extensive name and place indexes.

Several local brewery gazetteers exist, including:

C.R. Bristow, *Directory of 19th and 20th Century Suffolk Breweries* (1985). Provides short histories, sometimes only a few sentences long, of *c.*200 Suffolk breweries.

John Barge, *Gazetteer of Liverpool Breweries* (1987). Lists addresses, time spans and licensed houses. No indexes.

Brickmaking:

Several county gazetteers exist including:

James Bond et al, *The Clay Industries of Oxfordshire: Oxfordshire brickmakers* (*c.*1980)
M. Beswick, *Brickmaking in Sussex: A history and gazetteer* (2001)
Alan Cox, *Survey of Bedfordshire Brickmaking: A history and gazetteer* (1979)
Brian J. Murless, *Somerset Brick and Tile Manufacturers: A brief history and gazetteer* (2000)
Andrew Pike, *Gazetteer of Buckinghamshire Brickyards* (1995)
David N. Robinson, *Lincolnshire Bricks: History and gazetteer* (1999)

Camera Makers:

Norman Channing & Mike Dunn, *Camera Makers: An A-Z guide to companies and products* (1995). Contains short histories of *c.*400 businesses, often *c.*100 words long, sometimes much longer. Arranged in alphabetical order of business. Strong product emphasis.

Canals

www.jim-shead.com. This website contains much information per canal, including details of construction, formation, bibliography, etc.

Ceramic Manufacture and Related Trades:

R. Edwards, 'London Potters, circa 1570-1710', *Journal of Ceramic History* (6, 1974). Assemblage of known information in short entries for *c.*1,000 London potters.

Geoffrey A. Godden, *Encyclopaedia of British Porcelain Manufacturers* (1988). This lists *c.*3,000 individuals and firms involved in the manufacture of ceramics in Britain from the 1740s, when the manufacture of chinaware began, to the present day. The focus is makers' marks. Each entry includes name, location, approximate time span and specialisation – china or earthenware manufacturer, studio producer, decorator, repairer and so on.

Richard K. Henrywood, *Bristol Potters, 1775-1906* (1992). This contains details of *c.*350 businesses – address, time span, name, nature of output, etc. Essay format; some essays are lengthy.

Richard K. Henrywood, *Staffordshire Potters, 1781-1900* (2002). A gazetteer derived from contemporary directories providing brief details – name, address, nature of output, time span, etc – for *c.*4,000 businesses.

Chartered Accountancy:

Wendy Habgood, *Chartered Accountants in England and Wales: A guide to historical records* (1994). This provides essays ranging from 100 to 500 words on the history of *c.*200 firms of chartered accountants. Extensive name and place indexes.

R.H. Parker (ed.), *British Accountants: A biographical sourcebook* (1980). A compilation of obituaries and other biographical material on *c.*65 senior British accountants.

Chemical Industry:

David G. Edwards, *A Historical Gazetteer and Bibliography of By-product Coking Plants in the UK* (2001). This contains short essays on *c.*170 plants giving details of address, ownership, type of plant, etc. Indexed by owner, location and type of plant.

M.R. Fox, *Dye-Makers of Great Britain, 1856-1976: A history of chemists, companies, products and changes* (1987). Essays on leading dye-making businesses.

Coalmining:

Durham Mining Museum Database of Collieries. *See* www.dmm.org.uk. This contains extensive information for individual collieries on the Durham coalfield.

Dave Temple, *The Collieries of Durham* (2 vols, 1994, 1998). This provides essays on individual collieries (not businesses), but deals with a small proportion of the whole.

Construction:

Lawrence Popplewell, *Gazetteer of the Railway Contractors and Engineers* (1982-6). Short accounts in eight volumes, each dealing with a separate region in *c.*40 pages.

Fred Wellings, *Dictionary of British Housebuilders* (2006). Includes lengthy and rounded essays on the history of *c.*100 house-building businesses.

Cutlery:

Geoffrey Tweedale, *The Sheffield Knife Book: A history and collectors' guide* (1996). Essays, many lengthy, on *c.*125 manufacturers.

Distilling:

John Hughes, *Scotland's Malt Whisky Distilleries: Survival of the fittest* (2002). Short essays on *c.*100 active distilleries (not distillery businesses) with details of ownership, output, time span, etc.

Michael S. Moss & John R. Hume, *The Making of Scotch Whisky: A history of the Scotch whisky distilling industry* (1981). This provides a gazetteer of distilleries (not distilling businesses) giving for each details of ownership, time span, plant extensions, fate, etc. Supported by extensive indexes.

Brian Townsend, *Scotch Missed: The lost distilleries of Scotland* (3rd edn, 2004). This carries short essays on *c.*100 closed distilleries (not distilling businesses) giving details of time span, ownership, etc. No indexes.

Engineering:

⮞ *Agricultural Machinery/Steam Engines:*

Ronald H. Clark, *Steam Engine Builders of Norfolk* (1948), *Steam Engine Builders of Suffolk, Essex and Cambridgeshire* (1950), *Steam Engine Builders of Lincolnshire* (1955). Contain short essays on local manufacturers of agricultural machinery/steam engines.

⮞ *Boilermaking:*

Brian Roberts & Paul Yunnie, *A Parcel of Boilers* (2006). *See* www.hevac-heritage.org. Essays on *c.*30 leading steam and hot-water boilermakers; several entries are lengthy.

Gas Making:

E.G. Stewart, *Historical Index of Gasworks Past and Present in the Area now Covered by the North Thames Gas Board, 1806-1957* (1957) and Unknown, *Supplement to Historical Index of Gasworks* (1969). These provide short essays on over 100 gasworks giving, *inter alia*, details of ownership and time span. Organised by gasworks and not by the owning business.

Gunpowder Production:

Glenys Crocker, *Gunpowder Mills Gazetteer: Black powder manufacturing sites in the British Isles* (1988). Assemblage of known information, including ownership and time span, for gunpowder production sites (not businesses).

Heating Engineering:

Brian Roberts & Frank Ferris, *The Heat Makers* (*c.*2006). This draft proposal for a history of the Heating & Ventilating Contractors' Association, available electronically at www.hevac-heritage.org, contains a substantial gazetteer of early heating engineers. Many entries are of significant length.

Insurance:

H.A.L. Cockerell & Edwin Green, *The British Insurance Industry: A guide to its history and records* (1994). This provides brief details – date of establishment, business specialisation, time span, corporate linkages – for *c.* 300 British insurance companies.

Iron and Steel:

Philip Riden, *A Gazetteer of Charcoal-fired Blast Furnaces in Great Britain in Use since 1660* (2nd edn, 1993). This provides short essays of *c.*300 words on *c.*170 furnace sites (not owning businesses) giving details of time span, ownership and production.

Leather Goods:

Helenka Gulshan, *Vintage Leather* (1998). Essentially a product history, but with short histories (some very short) on *c.*400 makers and retailers of leather travel goods.

Locks, Keys, Safes, etc:

Jim Evans, A Gazetteer of Lock and Key Makers. *See* www.lockcollectors.eu/gazetteer. This covers *c.*200 businesses, mostly in the West Midlands. Some entries are long and detailed.

Motor and Horse-Drawn Vehicles:

Paul Braithwaite with John Carter, *A Palace on Wheels: A history of travelling showmen's living vans with an A-Z of manufacturers* (1999). Essays cover caravan makers, bodybuilders, living van builders, etc.

G.N. Georgano (ed.), *The Beaulieu Encyclopaedia of the Automobile* (2000). This international encyclopaedia provides essays on British motor car manufacturers. Strong emphasis on products, but with significant corporate detail.

G.N. Georgano (ed.), *The Beaulieu Encyclopaedia of the Automobile: Coachbuilding* (2001). This international encyclopaedia provides essays ranging from 50 to a few thousand words on coachbuilders. There is strong emphasis on products, but significant corporate details are given.

G.N. Georgano (ed.), *Complete Encyclopaedia of Commercial Vehicles* (1979). This is an international encyclopaedia of manufacturers of lorries, vans, buses, construction vehicles, etc. Each manufacturer is covered in an essay ranging from 50 to a few thousand words. Strong focus on products.

Rinsey Mills, *British Lorries, 1945-1965* (2006). This provides lengthy profiles of *c.*40 manufacturers.

Nick Walker, *A-Z of British Coachbuilders, 1919-1960* (2007). This covers a few hundred motor car body builders providing informative corporate details in short entries.

Motorcycles:

Roy Bacon & Ken Hollworth, *The British Motorcycle Directory: Over 1,100 marques from 1888* (2004). Contains broad details of makers.

Erwin Tragatsch (ed.), *The Illustrated Encyclopaedia of Motorcycles* (1983). This international encyclopaedia has good coverage of UK manufacturers. Short accounts of individual businesses focus largely on products, but significant corporate detail is given.

Pharmaceuticals:

Lesley Richmond, Julie Stepenson & Alison Turton, *The Pharmaceutical Industry: A guide to historical records* (2003). This includes essays on *c.*300 active and defunct businesses in the pharmaceutical sector varying from 100 to 1,000 words in length. Extensive name, place, subject and repository indexes.

Publishing:

Frank Kidson, *British Music Publishers, Printers and Engravers: From Queen Elizabeth's reign to George the Fourth's* (1900). This has short essays focusing on output, ranging from *c.*30 to *c.*1,000 words on *c.*500 publishers.

John A. Parkinson, *Victorian Music Publishers: An annotated list* (1990). This gives basic information – name, address, activities, time span, etc – in short entries for *c.*2,000 entities.

Jonathan Rose & Patricia J. Anderson (eds), *Dictionary of Literary Biography. Vols 106 & 112: British literary publishing houses, 1820-80 & 1881-1965* (1991). This contains essays up to *c.*6,000 words, often less, on *c.*100 houses.

Railway Equipment:

John S. Brownlie, *Railway Steam Cranes: A survey of progress since 1875 … and biography of leading member firms* (1973). Contains individual chapters on five leading crane builders plus shorter accounts of a further 19 smaller businesses.

James W. Lowe, *British Steam Locomotive Builders* (1975). This provides short accounts of several hundred locomotive builders, concentrating on output and technical detail. Extensive indexes.

Railways:

Jack Simmons & Gordon Biddle (eds), *The Oxford Companion to British Railway History from 1603 to the 1990s* (1997). This includes short essays on railway companies and sometimes lists sources on which they are based. No indexes.

Christopher Awdry, *Encyclopedia of British Railway Companies* (1990). This provides histories, *c.*150 words long, for all (*c.*1,500) British railways companies giving for each details of time span, lines, acquisitions, fate, etc. Indexed by place name.

W.P. Connolly & V.A. Vincent, *British Railways Pre-Grouping Atlas and Gazetteer* (5th edn 1972, reprinted 1997). Shows infrastructure assets – track, stations, viaducts, etc – of pre-nationalisation companies.

Road Transport:

John Armstrong et al, *Companion to British Road Haulage History* (2003). This includes essays on *c.*350 businesses associated with the British road haulage industry, either as road hauliers, commercial vehicle makers or associations connected with the industry. Average length is *c.*400 words. No indexes.

Road Transport Fleet Data Society Database. See www.fleetdata.co.uk. This gives, for each British commercial vehicle manufacturer, name, location, time span and reason for closure.

Shipbuilding:

L.A. Ritchie, *Shipbuilding Industry: A guide to historical records* (1992). This includes essays on *c.*200 shipbuilding companies varying in length from 100 to 500 words. Indexed by name, place and subject.

Norman L. Middlemiss, *British Shipbuilding Yards* (3 vols, 1993-5). This provides short profiles of individual yards.

Robert J. Winklareth, *Naval Shipbuilders of the World from the Age of Sail to the Present Day* (2003). The British section is arranged by geographical area. Businesses within areas of major shipbuilding activity are covered by individual essays. Lesser areas are each covered by a single essay covering all businesses.

Shipping:

The Ships List Database. See www.theshipslist.com. This provides potted histories of seemingly every British shipping company together with fleet lists and much more information besides. Its focus is tracing ancestors through shipping records.

Peter Mathias & A.W.H. Pearsall, *Shipping: A survey of historical records* (1971). This includes essays on the history of *c.*40 shipping companies but is very out of date. Indexed by name.

Toys:

Marguerite Fawdry, *British Tin Toys; including an A to Z of British metal toy makers* (1990). Contains, *inter alia*, short histories of several hundred metal toy makers.

Mary Hillier, *Dolls and Doll Makers* (1968). An international history but with brief details of many UK-based makers.

Veterinary Science:

Wendy Hunter, *Veterinary Medicine: A guide to historical records* (2004). This includes essays on businesses, associations and individuals. Indexed by name, place and subject.

Appendix Two

Illustrated Compendiums of Businesses

(This schedule is arranged in order of geographical area covered. Each entry provides title, publisher, date, number of businesses included, and library location, *see* pp.84-5.)

Bedford: *Where to Buy at Bedford: An illustrated local review: Premier shops, manufacturers and retailers*, Brighton, Robinson Son & Pike (1891); *c.*75 businesses; British Library.

Birmingham: *Illustrated Midland Business Review and View Album: Special edition for the district of East Birmingham with part of Aston*, Birmingham, J.G. Phelps & Co. (1897); *c.*80 businesses; British Library.

Birmingham: *Birmingham: An alphabetically arranged guide to the industrial resources of the Midlands metropolis; leading merchants and manufacturers*, Birmingham and London, British Industrial Publishing Co. (1888); *c.*600 business; Birmingham University Library.

Bristol: *Where to Buy at Bristol and Clifton: An illustrated local trades review: Premier shops, manufacturers and retailers*, Brighton, Robinson Son & Pike (1890); *c.*100 businesses; British Library.

Bristol Channel: *The Ports of the Bristol Channel* [Bristol, Cardiff, Swansea, Newport, Bath, etc], London, London Printing & Engraving Co. (1893); *c.*870 business; British Library.

Cheltenham: *Cheltenham: A review: Premier shops, wholesale and retail trades and manufacturers: Hints where to buy*, Brighton, Robinson Son & Pike (1890); *c.*150 businesses; British Library.

Coventry: *Where to Buy at Coventry: An illustrated local trades review: Premier shops, manufacturers and retailers*, Brighton, Robinson Son & Pike (1891); *c.*80 businesses; British Library.

Croydon: *Where to Buy at Croydon: An illustrated local review: Premier shops, manufacturers and retailers*, Brighton, Robinson Son & Pike (1891); *c.*90 businesses; British Library.

Dover: *Where to Buy at Dover: An illustrated local review: Premier shops, manufacturers and retailers*, Brighton, Robinson Son & Pike (1891); *c.*50 businesses; British Library.

East Anglia: *Industries of Norfolk and Suffolk Business Review: A guide to leading commercial enterprises*, London, British Industrial Publishing Co. (*c.*1890); *c.*600 businesses; Guildhall Library.

Industries of the Eastern Counties: Historical, statistical, biographical: British industry and enterprise (*c.*1890); location unknown. Essex section reprinted by Essex Libraries, 1982.

Exeter: *Where to Buy at Exeter: An illustrated local trades review: Premier shops, manufacturers and retailers*, Brighton, Robinson Son & Pike (*c.*1890); *c.*150 business; British Library.

Frome: *Where to Buy at Frome: An illustrated local trades review: Premier shops, manufacturers and retailers*, Brighton, Robinson Son & Pike (1891); *c.*40 businesses; British Library.

Glasgow: *Glasgow and its Environs: A literary, commercial and social review past and present with a description of its leading mercantile houses and commercial enterprises*, London, Stratten & Stratten (1891); *c.*250 businesses; British Library.

Glasgow: *Glasgow of Today: The metropolis of the north: An epitome of results and manual of commerce, businessmen and mercantile interests, wealth and growth: Historical, statistical, biographical*, London, Historical Publishing Co. (1888); Science Museum Library.

Glastonbury: *Where to Buy at Glastonbury: An illustrated local trades review: Premier shops, manufacturers and retailers*, Brighton, Robinson Son & Pike (1891); *c.*20 businesses; British Library.

Gloucester: *Where to Buy at Gloucester: An illustrated local trades review: The premier shops, manufacturers and retailers*, Brighton, Robinson Son & Pike (1890); *c.*150 businesses; British Library.

Great Britain: *Industrial Great Britain: A commercial review of leading firms selected from important towns of many counties*, London, Historical Publishing Co., c.2 vols (1891); c.700 businesses; Bristol University Library.

Ireland: *Industries of Ireland: Part One: Belfast and towns of the north; the provinces of Ulster and Connaught; businessmen and mercantile interests; wealth and growth; historical, statistical, biographical*, London, Historical Publishing Co. (1891); c.480 businesses; British Library.

Kingston upon Thames: *Kingston upon Thames and Surbiton in 1891: Including Norbiton, Hampton Wick and Teddington: Arts, trades and commerce*, Brighton, Robinson Son & Pike (1891); c.100 businesses; British Library.

Lancashire: *The Century's Progress: Lancashire*, London Printing & Engraving Co. (1892); c.700 businesses; Guildhall Library.

Lancashire: *Lancashire: Part One: The premier county of the Kingdom: Cities and towns: Historical, statistical, biographical: Businessmen and mercantile interests*, London, Historical Publishing Co. (1892); National Library of Scotland.

Lancashire: *Lancashire: Part Two: The premier county of the Kingdom: Cities and towns: Historical, statistical, biographical: Businessmen and mercantile interests*, London, Historical Publishing Co. (1892); c.570 businesses; British Library.

Leeds: *Leeds Illustrated: Historical and descriptive; art, commerce and trade*, Brighton, Robinson, Son & Pike (1892); c.60 businesses; British Library.

Liverpool: *Liverpool of Today: The maritime metropolis of the world: Historical, statistical, biographical*, London, Historical Publishing Co. (c.1888); c.500 businesses; British Library.

London: *Modern London, the World's Metropolis: An epitome of results, businessmen and commercial interests, wealth and growth*, London, Historical Publishing Co., 3 vols (c.1890); c.1,700 businesses; Guildhall Library. An 1887 edition is at the British Library.

London: *Descriptive Account of South London Illustrated*, Brighton, W.T. Pike & Co. (1895); c.120 businesses; British Library.

London: *Illustrated London and its Representatives of Commerce*, London, London Printing & Engraving Co. (1893); c.500 businesses; Guildhall Library.

Manchester: *Manchester of Today: Businessmen and commercial interests: Wealth and growth: Historical, statistical, biographical*, London, Historical Publishing Co. (1888); c.800 businesses; British Library.

Midlands: *Illustrated Midland Business Review: West Bromwich, Great Bridge, Smethwick, Handsworth, Walsall, Wednesbury, Cannock, Hednesford, Shifnal, Dudley, Brierley Hill,*

Stourbridge, Halesowen, Kidderminster, Droitwich, Harborne, King's Heath, Moseley; descriptive sketches, interesting historical notices and numerous illustrations, Birmingham, Industrial Publishing Co. (1896); *c.*300 businesses; British Library.

Newcastle: *A Descriptive Account of Newcastle*, Brighton, Robinson Son & Pike (189-); Newcastle University Library.

Newton Abbot: *Where to Buy at Newton Abbot: An illustrated local trades review: Premier shops, manufacturers and retailers*, Brighton, Robinson Son & Pike (1890); *c.*50 businesses; British Library.

Nottingham: *Nottingham Illustrated: Its art, trade and commerce*, London, Robinson Son & Pike (1891); Nottingham University Library.

Northampton: *Where to Buy at Northampton: An illustrated local review: Premier shops, manufacturers and retailers*, Brighton, Robinson Son & Pike (1891); *c.*115 businesses; British Library.

Oxfordshire: *British Industries Business Review: A guide to leading commercial enterprise of Oxford, Banbury, …*, Birmingham, British Industrial Publishing Co. (1891); Bodleian Library.

Paignton: *Where to Buy at Paignton: An illustrated local trades review: Premier shops, manufacturers and retailers*, Brighton, Robinson Son & Pike (1891); *c.*30 businesses; British Library.

Peterborough: *Peterborough 1892: Its history, manufactures, trade*, Brighton, Robinson Son & Pike (1892); *c.*65 business; British Library.

Sheffield: *Industries of Sheffield: Business review: An alphabetically arranged guide to the leading commercial enterprises of the town and neighbourhood*, Birmingham, British Industrial Publishing Co. (1889); Leeds University Library.

Shepton Mallet: *Where to Buy at Shepton Mallet: An illustrated local trades review: Premier shops, manufacturers and retailers*, Brighton, Robinson Son & Pike (1891); *c.*45 businesses; British Library.

South Coast: *Industries of the South Coast and West of England: Sea ports and watering places, their commercial importance and natural advantages, businesses and mercantile interests, wealth and growth*, London, Historical Publishing Co. (1891); *c.*1,000 businesses; British Library.

Southend: *Where to Buy at Southend: An illustrated local review: Premier shops, manufacturers and retailers*, Brighton, Robinson, Son & Pike (1891); *c.*50 businesses; British Library.

Taunton: *Where to Buy at Taunton: An illustrated local trades review: Premier shops, manufacturers and retailers*, Brighton, Robinson Son & Pike; *c.*95 businesses; British Library.

Torquay: *Where to Buy at Torquay: An illustrated local trades review: Premier shops, manufacturers and retailers*, Brighton, Robinson Pike & Son (1890); *c.*60 businesses; British Library.

Wales: *North Wales Illustrated Business Review: Notable business enterprises: Llandudno, Conway, Colwyn Bay, Rhyl, Abergele and Denbigh*, Birmingham, Industrial Publishing Co. (1895); *c.*110 businesses; British Library.

Watford: *Watford in 1891: Illustrated, descriptive and commercial: Including Rickmansworth: The premier shops, manufacturers and retailers*, Brighton, Robinson Son & Pike (1891); *c.*70 businesses; British Library.

Wells: *Where to Buy at Wells: An illustrated local trades review: Premier shops, manufacturers and retailers*, Brighton, Robinson Son & Pike (1891); *c.*30 businesses; British Library.

West Country: *Industries of West England Business Review: An illustrated historical and commercial guide to Ilfracombe, Barnstaple, Bideford, Torrington, South Molton, Crediton, Tiverton, Bridgwater and district manufacturers and merchants*, Birmingham, J.G. Phelps & Co. and Industrial Publishing Co. (*c.*1895); *c.*230 businesses; British Library.

Weston-super-Mare: *Where to Buy at Weston-super-Mare: An illustrated local trades review: Premier shops, manufacturers and retailers*, Brighton, Robinson Son & Pike (1890); *c.*110 businesses; British Library.

Worcester: *Where to Buy at Worcester & Malvern: An illustrated local trades review: Premier shops, manufacturers and retailers*, Brighton, Robinson Son & Pike (1891); *c.*100 business; British Library.

Yeovil: *Where to Buy at Yeovil: An illustrated local trades review: Premier shops, manufacturers and retailers*, Brighton, Robinson Son & Pike (189-); *c.*65 businesses; British Library.

Yorkshire: *Industries of Yorkshire: Leeds, Bradford, Dewsbury, Batley, Keighley, etc; England's great manufacturing centres; businessmen and mercantile interests; wealth and growth; historical, statistical and biographical*, London, Historical Publishing Co. (1888); *c.*750 businesses; Leeds University Library.

Yorkshire: *Industries of Yorkshire: York, its capital, and the great manufacturing and commercial centres of Hull, Huddersfield, Halifax, Wakefield, Middlesbrough, etc; the famous watering places of Scarborough and Harrogate and the parliamentary borough and municipality of Stockton on Tees; Durham; wealth and growth and importance*, London, Historical Publishing Co. (1890); *c.*800 businesses; Leeds University Library.

Yorkshire: *The Century's Progress, Yorkshire: Progress and commerce, 1893*, London, London Printing & Engraving Co. (1893); *c.*600 business; Leeds University Library.

PUBLISHED BIOGRAPHIES OF
BUSINESSMEN AND WOMEN

Published biographies of businessmen and women very often give insight into the businesses with which the subjects were connected and therefore can form an important source when tracing the history of a business. They relate to key individuals in the business's history – founders, chairmen, managing directors, non-executive directors, major shareholders, senior technicians and so on. These biographies – which are quite distinct from the dictionaries of tradesmen described on pp.85-92 – take many forms and include essays in biographical dictionaries, reference book entries, press obituaries and not least autobiographies.

Biographies

Biographies and autobiographies of businessmen are surprisingly numerous and some are listed in Francis Goodall, *A Bibliography of British Business Histories* (1987). Many of the earliest were published in the last decades of the 19th century but largely focus on political and social achievements and are frustratingly light on business detail. Donna Loftus, 'The self-made man? Businessmen and their autobiographies in the 19th century', *Business Archives* (2000) discusses their content. Many were privately published, had small print runs and are therefore difficult to find and sometimes absent from bibliographies and catalogues.

Of equal importance are biographical dictionaries of businessmen and women. Most notable is David J. Jeremy (ed.), *The Dictionary of Business Biography* (5 vols, 1984-6) and its Scottish equivalent by Anthony Slaven and Sydney Checkland (eds), *The Dictionary of Scottish Business Biography* (2 vols, 1986-90). The former includes essays, sometimes as long as a few thousand words but mostly very much shorter, on about a thousand British business leaders living between 1860 and the 1980s, while the latter covers 400 leaders in Scotland in the 100 years from 1860. Many entries include images of the subject and all list sources on which the entry is based. More recently, David J. Jeremy and Geoffrey Tweedale, *Dictionary of Twentieth Century British Business Leaders* (1994) has provided factual essays of around 250 words on 750 subjects. These are chairmen and/or chief executives of Britain's largest 100 businesses as measured by employment prior to 1960 and a broader range of indicators thereafter.

The recently revised *Oxford Dictionary of National Biography* (2004-) (*ODNB*), successor to the original *Dictionary of National Biography* (1885-1900 and supplements to 1990), contains 50,000 articles on people influential in all aspects of life in Britain since earliest times, although the majority lived after 1800. A few thousand of these are drawn from the worlds of business and labour and include many featured in the two dictionaries of business biography referred to above. Entries range from a few hundred to a few thousand words and each has sections dealing with sources, wealth at death, likenesses and archives relating to the subject. The ODNB is also available online (www.oup.com/oxforddnb) by subscription but most reference libraries provide access without charge.

Alongside these substantial works are smaller scale dictionaries of Scottish and Welsh biography. Rosemary Goring (ed.), *Chambers Scottish Biographical Dictionary* (1992) provides thumbnail sketches of almost 3,000 eminent Scots but business people are heavily under-represented. Thomas Thomson (ed.), *Robert Chambers' Biographical Dictionary of Eminent Scotsmen* (1870) revises a work first published in 1834 but again includes few businessmen.

271   MAC—McK

ALEXANDER MACINTYRE.

Managing Director, the Sudan Plantations, Ltd., and Kassala Cotton Company, Ltd., in Sudan. Director of Brazil Plantations, Ltd., and Parana Plantations, Ltd. After qualifying as a Civil Engineer, Mr. MacIntyre practised his profession in Scotland, principally in connection with the railways. He then became engaged in reclamation work in Egypt, subsequently joining the above Company as Manager, after some years receiving his present appointment. The firm is very extensively employed in growing cotton, and are carrying through, in conjunction with the Sudan Government, an important scheme of irrigation. Mr. MacIntyre's principal hobbies are polo, golfing, and fishing. Member Travellers' Club. (Photo : Bassano.)

SIR JAMES McKECHNIE, K.B.E.

Director, Vickers, Ltd. (with control of their Naval Construction Works, Barrow-in-Furness) ; Chairman, Ioco Rubber and Waterproofing Co., Ltd. ; Director Contraflo Condenser and Kinetic Air Pump, Co., Ltd. ; Vickers-Petters, Ltd. ; Canadian Vickers, Ltd. ; the Donaldson South American Line, Ltd., etc., etc. Sir James is a Liveryman of the Worshipful Company of Shipwrights, a Member of the Management Committee of the Engineering and Employers' Federations. During the Great War some of the largest munition factories were erected under his direction, and he initiated the great extensions of the Barrow Works, where, under his control, all classes of war vessels, and the largest types of naval gun mountings, howitzers, etc., etc., were produced. Sir James has been a life-long sportsman. Clubs : R.A.C., the Junior Carlton. (Photo : W. Barnett.)

JOHN MACKECHNIE.

As a Banker is well-known in the South of Scotland. He is a Director of several London Companies including the Grecian Marbles (Marmor), Ltd., New Broad Street, a Company owning the principal ancient Greek Marble Quarries in Greece ; The International and Balkan Trading Co., Ltd. ; J. Mackechnie & Co., Insurance Brokers, etc. Mr. Mackechnie has for many years been an ardent Freemason and as Provincial Grand Master of Dumfriesshire did yeoman service for the Craft. His artistic powers as an Artist and Horticulturist get ample scope in his fine old garden at Walton Heath, a charming spot in Surrey.

CHARLES ALEXANDER McKERROW, F.C.S.

Director, Holmwood, McKerrow & Co., Colonial, Eastern and General Merchants, 52A, Billiter Buildings, 22, Billiter Street, London, E.C.3. Earlier in his career he practised as a consulting analytical chemist and chemical engineer, being associated as technical expert with various important companies engaged in the manufacture of wool and cotton textiles, and also chemicals. During the War he was entirely employed as a technical expert to a large felt manufacturing company, who undertook large contracts for the supply of various war materials. Served in the R.A.F. for the defence of London. He was Chairman of an Overseas Panel of the Ministry of Labour for placing ex-service men in civil employment abroad and is still a member of this Panel. His education was completed at Victoria University, and he is a Fellow of the Royal Colonial Institute. Club : R.A.C. (Photo : Russell.)

18   *Biographical sources, giving details of the lives and careers of individual businessmen and women, are an important source for the history of a business. This illustration is taken from the 1927 edition of* Notable Personalities: An Illustrated Who's Who of Professional Men and Women, *which covers almost 2,000 individuals.*

Publication of an ongoing dictionary of Welsh biography, in both the Welsh and English languages, has been sponsored by the Hon. Society of Cymmrodorion since 1953. It carries around 3,000 entries, ranging from 200 to 500 words in length, and includes several business people. Access is now available online at (www.wbo.llgc.org.uk) following digitisation by the National Library of Wales. Details of the English language hard-copy volumes are

John E. Lloyd and R.T. Jenkins (eds), *The Dictionary of Welsh Biography Down to 1940* (1959) and *The Dictionary of Welsh Biography 1941-70* (2001).

Quaker businessmen are covered comprehensively in Edward H. Milligan, *Biographical Dictionary of British Quakers in Commerce and Industry, 1775-1920* (2007). This meticulously researched and detailed book has substantial essays on around 4,000 individuals engaged in a wide range of business activity.

The late Victorian and Edwardian period spawned many biographical dictionaries, mostly city or county-based, recording the lives of leading local citizens either living or recently deceased. They cover men involved in all walks of life including business but, given the spirit of the age, their focus is social, political and military and not business or wealth creation; they are also unduly congratulatory. And those business people chosen for inclusion tend to belong to the professions – architects, engineers and solicitors – rather than manufacturers and distributors.

The most objective of these publications is probably a series labelled *Pike Contemporary Biographies*, published by W.T. Pike & Co. of Brighton; often their titles include phrases such as 'at the close of the 19th century' or 'at the opening of the 20th century'. *London at the Opening of the 20th Century* (1905) is a typical example containing around 500 biographical sketches of, among others, solicitors, engineers, architects, surveyors, actuaries, accountants, company secretaries as well as clergymen, doctors and politicians. Another is *British Engineers and Allied Professions in the 20th Century* (1908), which covers around 700 individuals working in the naval, marine, rail, gas, mining, civil, water, electrical and other branches of engineering.

Many of these publications are available in local history libraries and major reference libraries. Otherwise they have probably been reproduced on microfiche as part of the *British Biographical Index and Archive* (q.v.) or the *British and Irish Biography* (q.v.). No dedicated bibliography of them exists but some titles appear in an appendix at the end of this section in order to give a sense of their range and geographical spread.

Reference Book Entries

Who's Who and *Who Was Who* are immensely useful for thumbnail sketches of a much wider constituency of business people from the late 19th century onwards. *Who's Who*, an annual publication, was first published in 1849 and took its current form in 1897. It gives details of date of birth (and of death in *Who Was Who*), occupation, education, military service, career, board appointments, connections with charities, publications, address and so on.

At the end of each decade (initially the period was longer) all *Who's Who* entries removed on account of death are republished in *Who Was Who*, although this final entry takes no account of changes made over time to earlier entries. The first volume was published in 1920 and volume nine appeared in 2001, along with a revised cumulative index for the period 1897 to 2000. *Who's Who* and *Who Was Who* are now also available online at www.ukwhoswho.com by subscription, but access is available without charge in good reference libraries.

Between the 1910s and 1930s specialist issues of *Who's Who* were published covering particular business sectors. They adopted the same format as their parent publication, and include, for example, *Who's Who in Architecture* (1914-26), *Aviation* (1928-36), *Advertising* (1924-7), *Engineering* (1920-2), *Insurance* (1924-34), *Mining and Metallurgy* (1908-10), *Motor Trade* (1934) and *Rubber* (1914). Other issues covered counties and cities such as Derbyshire

(1934), County Durham (1936), Glasgow (1909), Leicestershire (1935), Norfolk (1920), Staffordshire (1934), Warwickshire (1934) and Worcestershire (1935).

More thumbnail sketches appear in Frederic Boase, *Modern English Biography Containing Memoirs of Persons Who Have Died Since 1850* (1882-1921). Thirty thousand people who died between 1851 and 1900 are covered and these include a fair number of business people, in particular merchants, bankers, engineers, publishers and printers. Very brief biographical details are provided for each subject, including references to images and publications. Very helpfully, Boase lists his sources such as obituaries.

Early in the 20th century short-lived attempts were made to publish annual biographies of businessmen and women. Perhaps the first was Herbert H. Bassett (ed.), *Men of Note in Finance and Commerce: A biographical business directory* (1900). It was a *Who's Who* of the business world with 1,750 entries, varying in length from 200 to 300 words, on 'men who have acquired an established position in the commercial and financial world'. In 1912 Bassett returned to the charge with *Business Men at Home and Abroad: A biographical directory of partners, principals, directors and managers of important firms and institutions at home and abroad* (1912-13); it had a much larger constituency than his previous publication, with 5,000, albeit much shorter, entries. An entirely separate publication was *Notable Personalities: An illustrated who's who of professional and businessmen and women* (1923-4) which carried sketches of 2,000 individuals. Each entry was introduced by an image of the subject. An earlier publication on similar lines was *Notable Londoners* (1922).

Obituaries

These are another highly important source and are easy to locate if the date of death is known. Lengthy newspaper obituaries became the norm in the last half of the 20th century, but short obituaries have been published since at the least the beginning of the 18th century. Newspapers such as *The Times, Daily Telegraph* and *[Manchester] Guardian* are obvious places to look for them, as is the regional and local press. F.C. Roberts (ed.), *Obituaries from The Times 1951-75* (1975-9) carries 4,500 obituaries, one-third of which were British subjects absent from the first edition of the *Dictionary of National Biography*. Generally speaking the financial press, led by the *Financial Times*, is a disappointing source.

Other sources of obituaries are the trade press, house journals and magazines of schools, universities, charities and professional bodies with which the deceased businessman was associated. Appreciations delivered at memorial services are useful, but not always easy to locate.

A source of early obituaries is *The Gentleman's Magazine*, published between 1731 and 1868, although once again businessmen were included less frequently than others. Published monthly, this was Britain's first magazine-type periodical and carried literary and historical articles as well as social news – births, deaths and marriages, notices of appointments and obituaries. A number of indexes exist, most notably *An Index to the Biographical and Obituary Notices in the Gentleman's Magazine, 1731-80* (British Record Society, 1891) and Benjamin Nangle, *The Gentleman's Magazine: Biographical and Obituary Notices, 1781-1819* (1980) although the latter omits some years, seemingly in error. There is also Edward Fry, *An Index to Marriages in the Gentleman's Magazine, 1731-68* (1922). *The Annual Register* is a broadly similar publication published from 1758 and a cumulative published index exists from then until 1819.

Biographical Indexes

An index to early obituaries is William Musgrave, *Obituaries Prior to 1800: A general nomenclator and obituary with reference to the books where persons are mentioned and where some account of their character is to be found* (1899-1901). Bibliographical references are given to obituaries for many thousands of individuals, including business people led by bankers and merchants.

In recent years extremely comprehensive finding aids to biographies have been developed, notably the *British Biographical Index* (1998) and its associated *British Biographical Archive (Series I, II and III)*. The *Index* provides details of the location of biographical material relating to 350,000 individuals, most of whom are British citizens, held in over 600 English language reference books published between 1601 and 1950. The *Archive* comprises the biographies themselves, extracted from the reference books and held on microfiche. The *Index* and the *Archive* can both be consulted online as part of the World Biographical Information system (www.saur.de/wbis-online).

British and Irish Biographies 1840-1940 (1990) is a slightly less ambitious microfiche-based index and archive, differing from the *British Biographical Index and Archive* by covering a shorter period and by reproducing the reference works in whole rather than in extracted form.

APPENDIX

SELECTED BIOGRAPHICAL DIRECTORIES OF LATE 19TH AND EARLY 20TH CENTURIES

Berkshire Historical Biographical (1911)
Birmingham at the Opening of the 20th Century (1900)
Birmingham Faces and Places (1888-94)
Bristol Worthies and Notable Personalities (1907)
British Engineers and Allied Professions in the 20th Century (1908)
Cheshire Leaders (1909)
Cornwall Leaders (1909)
Derbyshire Leaders (1908)
Derbyshire Lives (1894)
Durham Lives (1900)
Essex in the 20th Century (1895)
Essex Leaders (1895)
Hampshire at the Opening of the 20th Century (1905)
Kent Historical, Biographical and Pictorial (1907)
Lanarkshire Leaders (1906)
Lancashire at the Opening of the 20th Century (1903)
Lancashire Leaders: Social and Political (1895-7)
Lancashire Lives (1898)
Leading Men of London (1895)
Liverpool and Birkenhead in the 20th Century (1911)
London at the Opening of the 20th Century (1905)
Manchester and Salford at the Close of the 19th Century (1901)
Memoirs and Portraits of 100 Glasgow Men (1886)

Men of the Period: Commerce and Industry (1901)
Men of the Period: Lancashire (1895)
Middlesex Men of Mark (1894)
Norfolk and Suffolk in East Anglia: Contemporary Biographies (1911)
North and East Ridings of Yorkshire at the opening of the 20th Century (1903)
Northamptonshire: Historical, Biographical and Pictorial (1911)
Northern Notables (1897)
Northumberland at the Opening of the 20th Century (1905)
Notable Leaders: An Illustrated Who's Who (1921-2)
Nottinghamshire, Leicestershire and Rutland: Some of their Leaders (1905)
Renfrewshire and Ayrshire Leaders (1906)
Sheffield and Neighbourhood at the Opening of the 20th Century (1901)
South Wales and Monmouthshire at the Opening of the 20th Century (1907)
Staffordshire Leaders (1907)
Suffolk Leaders (1906)
Sussex in the 20th Century (1910)
Warwickshire Leaders (1906)
Warwickshire Lives (1895)
West Riding of Yorkshire at the Opening of the 20th Century (1902)
Westmorland Lives: Social and Political (1895)
Wiltshire Lives (1907)
Worcestershire Leaders (1905)
Yorkshire Leaders (1892-3)
Yorkshire Leaders: Social and Political (1908)
Yorkshire Lives (1899)
Yorkshire Men of Mark (1893)

Annual Reports and Accounts

Printed annual reports containing accounting and descriptive information are the means by which companies report on their progress to existing and potential shareholders and creditors; the document is also frequently lodged with the Registrar of Companies. Although usually associated with registered companies formed since 1844, annual reports were also issued by earlier joint stock companies formed by royal charter or Act of Parliament if required by their constitution or deed of settlement. Some public companies also produce printed interim reports during the course of their reporting year. Clearly this is a document of real importance in understanding the history of a business. Comparison of its accounts year by year gives a view of a business's performance over time while its narrative is easily digested by the general historian.

Annual reports of public companies have changed greatly over the years, developing gradually from an undetailed balance sheet and a few sentences of introduction and explanation in the mid-19th century to the highly designed and detailed documents of today. In their more complete form they comprise in essence three elements – a balance sheet, a profit and loss account and descriptive reports by the chairman and other key executives.

The balance sheet provides a snapshot valuation of a company's assets and liabilities on the last day of its financial year while the profit and loss account provides totals for broad categories of income and expenditure together with the resulting profit or loss for the year. Attached to both accounts are substantial explanatory notes. The rest of the report comprises text that interprets the accounts, explains performance, outlines strategy, comments on outlook and reviews key events, such as new investment in plant and products, sales, acquisitions, disposals, new appointments and so on. In contrast the reports of private companies have traditionally been much briefer and to the point, often comprising little more than audited accounts and other information required by company law.

Over the years a number of factors have required companies to disclose fuller and more accurate information for the benefit of shareholders and other external parties by establishing requirements for minimum disclosure. Regulatory and market organisations such as the London Stock Exchange and professional bodies such as the different institutes of accountants have encouraged or required more and more disclosure, but the most powerful influence has been company legislation. This has been embodied mostly in a series of 'company acts' since 1844; an outline of their disclosure requirements helps in evaluating the usefulness of the annual report as an historical source.

The 1844 Joint Stock Companies Registration & Regulation Act, which enabled the general formation of joint stock companies for the first time, stipulated that a balance sheet approved by auditors had to be presented to the annual general meeting of shareholders. This obligation was made optional under the 1856 Company Act but was reintroduced in modified form by the 1907 Act. Now the audit had to be undertaken by an independent party, but there was only an implied requirement for the presentation of the audited balance sheet to shareholders at the annual general meeting. The 1928 Act was altogether more forthright. Publicly quoted companies were now required to circulate to shareholders an audited balance sheet, directors' report and audit report at least seven days prior to the annual general meeting. A profit and loss account also had to be included, but did not have to be audited. Subsequently the minimum disclosure of information within accounts was substantially increased, beginning with the notably reforming 1947 Act. However, it must be stressed that the Company Acts set down only minimum requirements; many businesses disclosed to shareholders information well in excess of what the acts required while others, especially small family businesses influenced by a tradition of excessive commercial secrecy, did not.

Companies were also legally bound to disclose information not only to their shareholders but also to the Registrar of Companies, for access by the general public, although this did not necessarily have to be the same information. As far back as 1844 a registered company was required to file with the Registrar the annual balance sheet circulated at their annual general meeting. This requirement was cancelled in 1856 but renewed in 1907. Now *public* companies had to file an annual audited balance sheet, disclosing the general nature of assets and liabilities and the basis of their valuation, but it did not have to indicate profit or loss. However, the failure of the 1907 Act to stipulate the filing of an *up-to-date* balance sheet meant that secretive companies failed to comply with the spirit of the legislation, a shortcoming only corrected in 1928. The 1947 Act required *public* companies to file all balance sheets *and* profit and loss accounts presented to shareholders.

Disclosure to the Registrar did vary between 'public' and 'private' companies, which were defined separately for the first time in 1907 (*see also* p.50); hitherto company law had made no distinction and all companies had the same status. The 1907 Act did not require private companies to file accounts and reflected once again the widely held notion that the affairs of

LIVERPOOL BOROUGH BANK.

BOARD OF DIRECTORS FOR THE YEAR 1856-7.

WILLIAM RATHBONE, Esq., Chairman.

CHRISTOPHER HIRD JONES, Esq., Deputy Chairman.

EDWARD BENN, Esq.	DUNCAN JAMES KAY, Esq.
JOHN CROPPER, Esq.	DAVID LAMB, Esq.
ROBERT CROSBIE, Esq.	JOSEPH PATER, Esq.
JOSHUA DIXON, Esq.	JAMES RYDER, Esq.
ROBERT ELLISON HARVEY, Esq.	THOMAS SELLAR, Esq.

JOHN P. GEORGE SMITH, Esq., Manager.

Report

OF THE

DIRECTORS TO THE PROPRIETORS.

According to the last Report, the paid-up Capital of the Bank was £900,000, and the Reserve Fund was £101,775 10s. 11d.

Since that date two Calls of £1 per Share have been paid upon the new Shares, making the Capital £1,000,000

The Net Profits of the past Year, after Payment of all Expenses of Management, and after deducting £45,825 2s. 1d. for Losses by bad debts incurred during the same period, amount to	.	.	£69,318	12 8
Appropriated as follows :—				
3½ per Cent. Dividend upon £950,000 .	. £33,250	0 0		
2½ „ „ „ 1,000,000 .	. 25,000	0 0		
Property Tax paid by the Bank . .	3,629	6 8		
			£61,879	6 8
Balance carried to Reserve Fund			£7,439	6 0

Nearly the whole of the losses above mentioned have been caused by the frauds of a customer.

In winding up the affairs of 1854, a year which it is well known was most disastrous to those customers of the Bank who were engaged in the Colonial Shipping Trade, heavier loss has been sustained in the realization of the assets, then taken over, by way of security, and in the liquidation of estates, then considered good, than could possibly have been anticipated.

The Directors have thought it their duty at once to reduce the Dividend to the rate of 5 per cent per annum, on the grounds that taking even the most favourable view of the liquidation of these accounts, the whole of the Reserve Fund will be required to meet the losses incurred; and that on the other hand, taking the most unfavourable view consistent with probability, the good current business of the Bank will in their opinion be sufficient to admit of the regular continuance of the Dividend, without encroaching on the Capital at the same period in the coming year.

In laying this statement before the Shareholders, the Directors desire strongly to impress upon them, that its unsatisfactory character is to be attributed to the affairs of 1854, and that apart from these, the sound and legitimate business of the Bank, would have enabled it to pay the ordinary dividends, and also to add largely to the Reserve Fund, notwithstanding the losses that have been incurred subsequently to that year. They wish also to state their confident expectation, that the change they are making in the policy and regulations of the Bank, will effectually guard against the recurrence of similar results.

Mr. SMITH having stated to the Directors, that his health would not longer permit him to undergo the labour of conducting the details of the Manager's duties, and having in consequence requested to be relieved from his office, they have with reluctance complied with his wish, and have made arrangements that Mr. THOMAS SELLAR, who is in every respect, eminently qualified for the post, shall, from the 1st August next assume the position of Manager. Mr. SMITH has, at the request of the Directors, consented to take a place at the Board, and to continue to give the Bank the aid of his valuable assistance.

The Directors who go out of office by rotation are Mr. RATHBONE, Mr. DIXON, and Mr. BENN, who are eligible for re-election.

Proprietors legally exempt from the Income Tax will be furnished with a Certificate of the proportion due on their Shares, on application to the Manager.

WM. RATHBONE,

CHAIRMAN.

19   *Annual reports vary greatly in content both over time and between public and private companies. As a source of business-related information, they are always invaluable. This report, for the year 1856-7, was issued to shareholders of the Liverpool Borough Bank and details the effect of a fraud.*

unquoted and largely family owned businesses were indeed private and not open to public scrutiny. The 1947 Act took a more rigorous view and required the filing of private company accounts unless the company could claim 'exempt company' status. This status was abolished in 1967 from when all registered companies were obliged to file full accounts.

The London Stock Exchange also introduced disclosure requirements for the proper management of public companies and functioning of the country's largest stock market. In 1906 it insisted on a printed balance sheet and directors' report being circulated to shareholders at least seven days ahead of the annual general meeting and in 1929 extended this to include a profit and loss account.

Legal and regulatory requirements for disclosure were in practice often exceeded by a company's own disclosure policy and this applied especially to public companies. At one level this policy was determined by the requirements embodied in the company's articles of association and at another by pragmatism and commonsense; investors would be more enthusiastic about a company's shares if they had reliable information about its performance. By the end of the 19th century, competition for capital and an enquiring and analytical financial press placed additional pressure on public companies to report fully to shareholders. J.R. Edwards, in an analysis of accounts published by 12 iron and steel businesses between 1900 and 1940, concluded that 'they published a great deal more financial information than the law required'.[1]

For more information about disclosure in annual accounts see J.R. Edwards, *British Company Legislation and Company Accounts 1844-1976* (1980) and *A History of Financial Accounting* (1989) and also A.J. Arnold, 'Publishing your private affairs to the world: Corporate financial disclosures in the UK, 1900-24', *Accounting, Business & Financial History* (1997). A more general account of the development of company law between 1825 and 1914 is provided in P.L. Cottrell, *Industrial Finance, 1830-1914: The finance and organisation of English manufacturing industry* (1980).

The existence and availability of annual reports might be one issue but another is their reliability. For many decades now, formidable penalties have been a powerful deterrent to the publication of misleading financial statements but in the early years of company formation a generally unregulated environment resulted in reports that often provided, *inter alia*, an over-optimistic view of a company's performance. In addition there were problems of comprehensiveness and consistency over time caused by the absence of prescription as to form and content, itself creating opportunity for manipulation and avoidance of best practice. For the historian today, this creates problems of reliability and comparability. Sheila Marriner, 'Company financial statements as source material for business historians', *Business History* (1980), reviews statements and changes in them over time and in their early days is 'particularly concerned with the dangers inherent in taking entries in such statements at face value'. More recent research has regarded this caution as overdone.

Annual reports form a key archive series and complete sets, along with those of subsidiaries, have a good chance of survival in a business's archives; they can be found either with the business or in its deposited archives. The most important collection of public company annual reports is that of the London Stock Exchange now deposited at Guildhall Library. These date from 1880-1, when the Exchange first required public companies to file annual reports, to 1964-5. Otherwise, sets of reports of public companies turn up in national and regional libraries and can be located in their online catalogues. Finding the annual reports of private companies is far more difficult as they would be circulated only to a relatively small if not tiny constituency of shareholders. Here the Registrar of Companies files are especially important although incomplete, as the retention of private company files in the National Archives has traditionally been extremely limited (*see* pp.50-3).

An important finding-aid for post-1965 annual reports is Score (Search Company Reports – www.score.ac.uk), which holds details of the collections of a small but important group of academic libraries including the London Business School, Manchester Business School and Strathclyde University in addition to the British Library. Peter N. Dunning, *Company Reports Held by the Science Reference and Information Service* (1986) lists reports held in the mid-1980s by what is now an integral part of the British Library. The National Libraries of Scotland and Wales have good collections relating to their countries. Recent annual reports are invariably available online at the website of the company issuing the report. They are also available at a price via online providers of corporate information and via the website of the Registrar of Companies/Companies House (www.companieshouse.gov.uk).

1. J.R. Edwards, *British Company Legislation and Changing Patterns of Disclosure in British Company Accounts, 1900-1940* (1981).

Prospectuses and other Shareholder Documents

From time to time public companies circulate printed documents to their shareholders and, less often, to holders of their bonds, debentures and other debt. They do so in order to report progress and annual results, call general meetings, appoint new directors, alter articles of association, change rights ascribed to securities, carry out major corporate actions such as mergers, acquisitions and takeovers, obtain shareholder support in resisting a hostile takeover, and so on. Over the years the number and length of these documents has risen substantially in line with legal and regulatory requirements; this is especially so in the last 30 years. That said, many of these documents, when distilled, contain only modest amounts of information and are of little interest to the general historian. The exceptions are annual reports, which are considered elsewhere (*see* pp.110-15), prospectuses and perhaps acquisition and defence documents issued in connection with recommended or hostile acquisitions/takeovers.

A prospectus, which is now a somewhat dated term, is of real use in tracing the history of a business and is considered here at length. It is circulated to shareholders and/or potential shareholders when a company is first floated on a stock exchange or subsequently when it needs to issue additional shares or debt. The prospectus provides sufficient information to enable the shareholder to decide whether or not to purchase the company's securities; it gives details of present value and future prospects. A useful introduction to prospectuses is provided in John Armstrong and Stephanie Jones, *Business Documents: Their origins, sources and uses in historical research* (1987).

Historically, several scenarios underlie the flotation of a company and in turn have a significant bearing on the contents of a prospectus. One is when an existing unquoted company or partnership converts to a public company in order, say, to raise additional funds, put a market value on its shares or enable existing shareholders to realise some or all of their holdings. Another is when an entirely new company is formed from scratch to develop an asset

PROSPECTUS.

Messrs. BARING BROTHERS & CO. offer for Subscription the Capital under-mentioned. The Subscription List will open on Monday, the 25th instant, and will close on or before Tuesday, the 26th, at 4 p.m.

ARTHUR GUINNESS SON & CO., LIMITED.

(Incorporated under the Companies' Acts, 1862 to 1886.)

SHARE CAPITAL, £4,500,000,

Debenture Stock, £1,500,000,

TO BE ISSUED AS FOLLOWS:—

Ordinary Shares (of £10 each)	£2,500,000
Preference Six per Cent. Shares (of £10 each) ...	2,000,000
Total Share Capital... ...	£4,500,000
Debenture Stock, bearing Interest at Five per Cent. ...	1,500,000
(Redeemable at the Company's option after the expiration of 20 years from 1st January, 1887, at 110 per Cent.)	£6,000,000

Interest on the Debenture Stock will be payable 1st May and 1st November, the first payment on 1st May, 1887. The Company will receive the profits of the business from 1st October, 1886.

One-third of the present issue of Ordinary Share Capital (being about £800,000) is reserved for the Vendor, who agrees to hold this amount for not less than five years, and the remainder, together with the Preference Shares and the Debenture Stock, are now offered severally for public subscription at **par**.

The payments for each class of security will be as follows :—

£5 per Cent.	...	on Application.
£20 ,,	...	,, Allotment.
£25 ,,	...	,, 14th December, 1886.
£25 ,,	...	,, 10th January, 1887.
£25 ,,	...	,, 8th February, 1887.

£100 per Cent.

The instalments may be paid up under discount at the rate of **4** per cent. per annum on Allotment, or on any subsequent Tuesday or Friday.

The Allotment will be made as early as possible after the Subscription is closed, and in cases where it is not practicable to make any allotment, the amount deposited on application will be returned as soon as possible.

The failure to pay any instalment when due forfeits all previous payments.

Provisional Certificates will be issued as early as possible after Allotment, and the Definitive Certificates when the payments have been completed.

The Debenture Stock will be secured by a Mortgage over the whole of the undertaking.

Trustees for Debenture Stockholders :—

The Right Honble. LORD REVELSTOKE. | The Right Honble. LORD HILLINGDON.
The Right Honble. D. R. PLUNKET, Q.C., M.P.

The Preference Shares will be entitled to a cumulative preferential dividend of 6 per cent., payable out of the profits of the Company, and will also be entitled to rank on the property and assets of the Company, in preference to the ordinary shares.

DIRECTORS.

*Sir EDWARD CECIL GUINNESS, Bart., *Chairman.*
CLAUDE GUINNESS, Esq., *Managing Director.*
REGINALD B. GUINNESS, Esq., Dublin.
Viscount CASTLEROSSE, Killarney House, Ireland.
HENRY R. GLYN, Esq., 67, Lombard Street, E.C.
HERMAN HOSKIER, Esq., Director of the Union Bank of London, Limited.
JAMES R. STEWART, Jun., Esq. (Messrs. Stewart & Kincaid), Dublin.
* Will join the Board after Allotment.

BANKERS.

Messrs. GLYN, MILLS, CURRIE & Co.

SOLICITORS.

Messrs. MARKBY, STEWART & Co., 57, Coleman Street, London, E.C.

AUDITORS.

Messrs. TURQUAND, YOUNGS & Co., 41, Coleman Street, London, E.C.

SECRETARY.

C. THEOBALD, Esq.

TEMPORARY OFFICES.

3, BISHOPSGATE STREET WITHIN, LONDON.

-(2)-

THE business was founded in 1759, and, having from that time forward steadily increased, it is now the largest Brewery in the world. It has, hitherto, been conducted as a private business, but the enormous proportions which it has attained, and its probable further growth, have determined the present proprietor to seek some relief from the constant attention and strain which his position as sole owner unavoidably entails.

Sir Edward Cecil Guinness will, however, accept the Chairmanship of the Company, retaining a large pecuniary interest in it, and Mr. Claude Guinness, who now holds an important position in the practical management of the business, will act as Managing Director.

The proportions of the business and the progress made, are attested by the following figures for successive quinquennial periods :

Quinquennial Period.	Average Sales per annum. Hogsheads.	Nett Average Profit per annum. £
1862–1866	196,125	122,119
1867–1871	263,562	130,340
1872–1876	436,691	178,571
1877–1881	589,499	308,033
1882–1886	755,235	452,294

In the above figures the nett profit of the year 1886 is estimated as the same as that of 1885, an estimate which is more than justified by the actual sales of the first nine months, and is confirmed by the following figures.

The sales for 1885 amounted to 818,984 hogsheads, and the profits to £554,327. The first quarter's profits of 1885 amounted to £113,108 14s. The second quarter's profits of 1885 amounted to £167,000 8s. 10d. In the present year, the first quarter's profits amounted to £122,832 10s. 5d. ; and the second quarter's profits amounted to £172,496 1s. The accounts of the third quarter of 1886 are not yet closed.

The annual interest on £1,500,000 Debenture Stock at 5 per cent is	£75,000
The annual dividend on £2,000,000 Preference Shares at 6 per cent.	120,000
A Dividend of, say, 10 per cent. on £2,500,000 Ordinary Shares would be	250,000
	£445,000

If the profits in the future are the same as those of the year 1885 (and judging from the results of the first half of 1886 as above stated they give promise of being larger), this would leave a surplus of £109,327 to be carried forward, or would raise the dividend on the ordinary stock to over 14 per cent.

The following comparative statement of the business done by the four leading Brewery Firms is taken from the Parliamentary Returns for each financial year :—

QUARTERS OF MALT USED.

	1881	1882	1883	1884	1885
Guinness & Co ...	254,648	294,349	270,936	310,930	334,170
The next ...	228,330	248,644	238,718	239,602	230,701
,, ...	208,059	202,647	207,026	213,547	189,312
,, ...	110,060	109,202	100,963	126,387	131,549

BARRELS OF BEER BREWED.

	1881	1882	1883	1884	1885
Guinness & Co....	1,027,764	1,198,347	1,088,762	1,253,900	1,357,592
The next ...	945,322	998,915	965,405	968,566	928,216
,, ...	814,327	795,975	813,580	824,607	737,621
,, ...	450,078	468,871	475,837	502,562	515,115

AMOUNT OF DUTY PAID.

	1881	1882	1883	1884	1885
Guinness & Co....	£321,176	£374,483	£340,238	£391,843	£424,247
The next ...	295,413	312,161	301,689	302,677	290,067
,, ...	254,477	248,742	254,243	257,689	230,506
,, ...	140,649	146,522	148,698	157,050	160,973

The following were the principal gross receipts for the year 1885 :—

For porter	£2,165,765
Grains	29,224
Yeast and Malt Dust	10,177

20   *Prospectuses issued by companies prior to their flotation as public companies provide a detailed account of their activities and performance over the previous few years. This prospectus was issued by Arthur Guinness Son & Co. Ltd in 1886 at the time of its conversion from a private partnership to a public company. A third page is not reproduced.*

or group of assets, a common 19th-century example being the development of a concession to provide, for example, a utility service, or to extract minerals. The prospectus of an entirely new company provides a snapshot of it at the time of flotation, but gives little historical information other than, perhaps, for peer businesses or the industry as a whole. That of an already-established company will detail history and performance in the recent past and be far more illuminating.

The information content of prospectuses also varies greatly over time. An early 19th-century prospectus might extend only to a dozen sentences and be frustratingly short on detail; even by the 1950s prospectuses seldom exceeded four pages of foolscap paper. By contrast, a present-day prospectus might well extend to over 100 pages, in great part the result of a much more demanding regulatory and legal environment. It is also worth pointing out that, in their very early years, prospectuses generally overstated the merits of the business being floated and should therefore be interpreted with an element of caution.

As well detailing the securities to be sold and the means of application, a prospectus gives much general information about the issuing company, such as the names, addresses and occupations of its directors; the names of some or all of its bankers, brokers, auditors and solicitors; its registered address; the activities it plans to undertake; the assets it is purchasing; its prospects; and, not least, some measure of its expected performance. If it is an established private business converting to a public company, financial data about the original business's performance over a five or even 10-year period might be included. If it is a company developing an asset from scratch, comparative financial data might be given for peer businesses in the previous few years. Some early examples taken at random illustrate the point.

The Massa-Carrara Marble Co. Ltd, formed in 1866 to purchase and develop marble quarries in Italy, sought in that year to raise a share capital of £14,000. Its prospectus outlined the company's ambitions, detailing the quarries and the nature of their marble, the assets to be acquired including saw mills and stocks, its anticipated output and profits, and the consideration to be paid to the vendor, an unnamed Italian business for which no financial data was given. Closer to home was the Marine Pier Co. Ltd, floated in 1880 to raise £100,000 to build from scratch pleasure piers at Plymouth and Torquay. Its prospectus provided the reasons for its formation and detailed the plans and specifications of the two piers, the contracts already entered into, and anticipated performance, as indicated by share price and dividend payments of peer companies in the previous five years. A far better known flotation was that of the Dublin brewers, Arthur Guinness. In 1888 the old established Guinness partnership was converted into a public company, Arthur Guinness Son & Co. Ltd, through flotation on the London Stock Exchange. Its prospectus described in detail the brewery assets and performance, in particular giving statistics for beer brewed, malt consumed and duty paid over a five-year period. Profits and sales were given for quinquennial periods from 1862. There was much more besides.

Of course, prospectuses were not inevitably linked to stock exchange flotations; they could otherwise be circulated directly to local potential investors. Hinckley Union Mill, in Leicestershire, was a case in point. This company was promoted in 1845 by local businessmen to acquire and develop an existing steam and wind-powered corn mill. They circulated a printed prospectus locally in order to attract shareholders and raise funds. There was no link whatsoever to a stock market. The prospectus is full of detail about directors and sponsors, mill premises, capacity, market and financial outlook.

Prospectuses, or detailed summaries of them, were invariably published in the national and financial press from the early 19th century and many can be located using indexes to *The Times* (*see* pp.123-4). From 1891 prospectuses published in *The Times* were included in the annual *Times Book of Prospectuses*, later known as *The Times Book of New Issues of Public Companies* and, from 1970 (following acquisition by Extel), as *The Extel Book of New Issues of Public Companies*. Each annual volume is indexed and a cumulative index, known as *Prospectuses & New Issues Cumulative Index*, covers the period from July 1939 onwards and is on microfiche. From 1984, Extel published prospectuses in microfiche format.

From the 1880s, other publications carried prospectuses including *The Economist* (established 1843), *The Statist* (1878), *The Investors' Chronicle* (established as *The Money Market Review*, 1860) and *The Financial Times* (1885). Trade publications (*see* pp.134-5) such as *Mining World* (1871), *Bradshaw's Railway Gazette* (1845) and *The Grocer* (1862) published prospectuses of relevance to their readers.

The largest collection of prospectuses is that of the London Stock Exchange lodged at Guildhall Library. It begins in 1824, the decade that saw the first significant wave of company flotations, but is incomplete before the 1880s. It excludes, of course, prospectuses of companies that were listed on provincial exchanges (*see* pp.71-5) or promoted locally without recourse to an exchange or which did not get beyond the planning stage (of which there were many). The collection is available for consultation on microfiche for the years 1824 to 1890, although paper copies are also available. Later prospectuses can be found in *The Times Book of Prospectuses* (*see* above). Guildhall Library has a cumulative index of prospectuses for 1824 to 1890 while the post-1939 period is covered by the Extel index referred to above; only the years 1891 to 1939 have no cumulative index. Otherwise prospectuses turn up in unlikely places; for example, a small group of around 100, mostly for the 1830s and 1840s, is held in the Thomas Glover collection at the British Library.

In the last couple of decades several providers of specialist information to the financial sector have emerged, establishing microfiche-based and, later, online services for the supply of shareholder documents to subscribers. These include Perfect Information (www.perfectinfo.com), which holds online prospectuses and other shareholder documents from 1990, and Europrospectus (www.europrospectus.com), whose files are of more recent origin.

Newspapers

Use of Newspapers

Newspapers are a rich and varied source of information for tracing the history of a business; their business-related content was already significant in the late 18th century. Historically the real problem in using newspapers has been a general absence of indexes as, without these, locating information about a specific business is virtually impossible unless dates of specific events are known. The rapid advance in digitisation of newspaper files, especially within the British Library, is now beginning to transform this situation and to unlock their true potential value.

The range and volume of the business-related content of newspapers is extraordinary. It includes, for example, reports on the rebuilding, extension and closure of factories, offices and other plant; the improvement of roads, the building of railways and the launching of ships; the introduction of new products, especially consumer products in the public eye; events such at Framlingham.

To MILLERS and BAKERS.

To be SOLD by AUCTION,
By JONATHAN ABBOTT,

On Tuesday the 21st of July, 1801, between the hours
of Three and Five in the afternoon, at the Swan Inn,
in Needham-Market,
IN THREE LOTS,

Lot I. A Large & substantial Post Windmill,
with a Round House to the same, in com-
plete repair; containing a capital pair of French stones,
5 feet high, flour mill, sack tackle and other apparatus,
on the newest construction, and with suitable conveniencies for laying large quantities of corn, &c. also,
a new erected Dwelling house, brick built and tiled,
at a proper and convenient distance from the mill.
  The whole of which are erected upon a piece of
    land containing nearly One Acre, most eligibly si-
    tuated for wind as well as trade, in Creeting
    St. Olaves, within half a mile of Needham-Mar-
    ket, and a smaller distance of the navigable canal
    from Stowmarket to Ipswich. The land is held
    under a lease for the term of 60 years, from Mi-
    chaelmas last, at the annual rent of 2£. 10s.
  Lot II. A convenient Dwelling-House, stucco-
fronted and sashed, in good repair, with a large bake-
office, commodious yards and garden, and many other
conveniencies for an extensive trade, which has been
carried on therein for several years past, and are plea-
santly situated in Needham-Market aforesaid.
  The above are in the occupation of Mr Richard
    Emerson, the proprietor, and possession may be
    had on the 10th day of October next.
  Lot III. Two Tenements adjoining the last lot, now
in the occupation of Mr. James Hays and Richard
Masters, as tenants at will, who have had legal notice
to quit on the 10th day of October next.
  The 2d and 3d lots are copyhold, of the Manor of
    Barking with Needham, subject to fines at the
    will of the Lords, small annual quit rents, and are
    very moderately assessed to the land tax.
  The premises may be viewed on applying to Mr.
Emerson, and further particulars had in due time, of
the auctioneer, at Needham-Market.

21 *Newspapers form a mine of business-specific information, although their full potential is only realisable when digital copy or hard-copy indexes are available. Advertisements are perhaps the single most useful category of business-specific information, even at an early date. Usually they touch on property and products and the two reproduced here, published in the* Bury Post *in 1801, are typical for the period. One relates to the sale of a milling and baking business at Needham Market, Suffolk, and the other to the marketing of anti-bilious pills made by a Mr B. Gall of Woodbridge, also in Suffolk.*

22 *(Opposite) See 21.*

as floods, fires and explosions; crimes such as fraud and robbery; litigation; the award and completion of large and/or prestigious contracts; industrial action and employee layoffs; works outings and other staff events; the retirement or death of senior managers; the business's gifts to the community; the celebration of an anniversary; and, not least so far as public companies are concerned, performance.

In addition, public notices columns convey information about business ownership such as the establishment and dissolution of partnerships; the appointment or retirement of partners; the formation or liquidation of companies; failures and bankruptcies; and so on. Here the *London Gazette* and *Edinburgh Gazette* are especially important (*see* pp.7-10). Other columns contain advertisements for the sale of consumer goods or the marketing of services. Of great importance are notices for the sale of industrial buildings, sometimes

GALL'S ANTI-BILIOUS PILLS,

AN EFFICACIOUS REMEDY

In all BILIOUS COMPLAINTS, INDIGESTION, FLATULENCY, SICK HEAD-ACHE,

HABITUAL COSTIVENESS, &c.

B. GALL having experienced for several years an encreasing demand for these Pills, considers it as the best proof of their general utility; prompted by which, and with the advice of his friends, he is now induced to offer them to the public, as a cheap and efficacious remedy in all the above complaints, and likewise to those who may find themselves uncomfortable, after an occasional excess at the table.

B. Gall takes no merit to himself for the discovery of this invaluable remedy; it was imparted to him by an eminent Surgeon, (the late Mr. Whimper, of Woodbridge) who used them for many years in his private practice, with the greatest success.

On occasions like the present, it is usual to add a long list of cases, &c. not always to be depended upon, and frequently fabricated; but B. G. has the superior advantage of having a recommendation signed by upwards of forty respectable persons. A copy of which is left at the respective venders, which he trusts will be considered by a discerning public, as a sufficient testimony of their efficacy.

They are sold wholesale and retail by the Proprietor B. Gall, Druggist, Woodbridge, in small boxes, containing 30 pills, 1s. 1½d. and large ones 80, at 2s. 9d. each; and retail by Loder, Woodbridge; S. Fitch, Ipswich; Dingle, Bury; Leatherdale, Hadleigh; Kent, Saxmundham; Knevett, Halesworth; Horth and Wales, Beccles; Fitch, Melford; Ansell and Westrop, Lavenham; Eaton, Bungay; Newson, Lowestoft; Lawrance, Stowmarket; Bowen, Norwich; Pigge, Lynn; Black, Yarmouth; Browne, Diss; Ellis, Aylsham; Barker, East Dereham; Sewell, Harleston; Johnson, Swaffham; Gee, Cambridge; Wright, Wisbeach; Thorpe, Newmarket; Jehoult and Co. No. 150, Oxford-street, and Mr. Vade, Cornhill, London and by one person in most market towns, giving detailed descriptions of capacity, dimensions, machinery, layout, construction, age and ownership.

Companies quoted on the London and provincial stock exchanges have, especially from the late 18th century, been well-covered by the financial, national and regional press, as well as by local newspapers circulating in the area of their head office or major plant. Newspapers publish details of the appointment and resignation of directors and senior executives; of annual results, performance and shareholder meetings; and of corporate events such as acquisitions, takeovers, defences, reconstructions and windings-up. They also publish, in whole or in summary form, prospectuses issued in connection with flotations or subsequent issues of securities.

Newspapers contain much about the environment in which businesses operate through reports on financial crises, adverse weather conditions, shortages or surpluses of goods, transport conditions, labour unrest and so on. Published market intelligence include commodity prices for, say, cotton at Liverpool, corn at Ipswich and tobacco at Bristol. Stock exchange prices are given. In areas of industrial specialisation, local newspapers are a bank of general information about the industry or industries concerned. *The Cornish Times*, for example, carried much about 19th-century tin and copper mining, including events on the international scene, leading one local commentator to conclude that 'this little weekly newspaper was also in effect a local *Economist*'.[1] A sense of the riches of a local newspaper for a local industry can be gleaned from Rodney Hampson, *Pottery References in the Staffordshire Advertiser, 1795-1865* (2000).

History of Newspaper Publishing

Britain's first newspapers were published in London in the early 17th century and in the provinces from around 1700. For the most part they covered national and international news, the provincial press taking much of its copy from papers published in the capital. From the mid-19th century the railways made possible a truly national press and encouraged local newspapers to focus on local news, while publishing was also stimulated by tax and production-cost reductions.

The first London newspaper of real note was the *London Gazette*, an official government publication that first appeared in 1665 as the *Oxford Gazette*. The *Daily Courant* was London's first daily newspaper to survive for a significant period until succeeded by five London dailies in the mid-18th century. Modern journalism is reckoned to have been ushered in by Britain's oldest surviving daily, *The Times*, in 1795. As a national newspaper, its chief early rivals were the *Morning Chronicle* (1770-1862) and the *Morning Post* (1772-1937). Most of London's inner suburbs had their own papers by the 1850s and the outer suburbs by the 1870s.

Lloyds List, the country's first major business newspaper published from 1726, carried news of mercantile and shipping activity; its predecessor, *Lloyds News*, had first appeared in 1696. However, the origins of the financial press appear to date to the 1680s and 1690s with the publication of the *Merchant's Remembrancer* and the *Course of Exchange*, which survived until 1889. These papers focused on stock exchange prices, shipping movements, agricultural prices and foreign exchange.

The modern daily financial press took root at the end of the 19th century and was encouraged by the rapid growth of publicly quoted companies in the late Victorian period and by the demand of investors and intermediaries for financial information about them. The *Financier* from 1870, the *Financial News* from 1884 and the *Financial Times* from 1885 dominated this sector of the press; the last two titles merged in 1945 to form the existing *Financial Times*. Together they set new standards in financial journalism by interpreting, criticising and advising as well as reporting market events and price movements. Useful insights are provided by David Kynaston, *The Financial Times: A Centenary History* (1988) and Dilwyn Porter, "'A trusted guide to the investing public": Harry Marks and the Financial News', in R.T.P. Davenport Hines (ed.), *Speculators and Patriots: Essays in business biography* (1986).

Provincial newspaper publishing began in 1690 with the appearance of the *Worcester News Sheet*, known as the *Worcester Postman* from 1709. Examples of other very early publications include the *Stamford Mercury* (1695), the *Edinburgh Gazette* (1699), which was the government's official newspaper in Scotland, the *Norwich Post* (1701) and the *Bristol Post Boy* (1702). By the end of the 18th century some 100 titles were in circulation.

A vast literature exists for British newspaper history; some 3,000 works are listed in David Linton and Ray Boston (eds), *The Newspaper Press in Britain: An annotated bibliography* (1987). Bob Clarke, *From Grub Street to Fleet Street: An illustrated history of English newspapers to 1899* (2004) is a modern account while John Westmancoat, *Newspapers* (1985) is more concise. The early provincial press is dealt with in G.A. Cranfield, *The Development of the Provincial Newspaper, 1700-1760* (1962, reprinted 1978).

Locating Newspapers and Newspaper Indexes

The British Library (www.bl.uk/collections/newspapers) has Britain's most comprehensive collection of newspapers and periodicals while the National Libraries of Scotland (www.nls.uk/collections/rarebooks) and Wales (www.llgc.org.uk), together with other copyright libraries, also have major holdings. Otherwise local record offices and local history libraries usually have comprehensive local collections. Newspapers themselves may also have retained their old files in their offices.

Annual directories detailing which newspapers circulated in which areas have been published since the mid-19th century. Compiled largely for use by advertisers, they include the *Newspaper Press Directory*, published from 1846 and known from 1976 as *Benn's Press Directory: The world's media guide*. For most of its history, it listed for each British and Irish newspaper and journal date of establishment and area of circulation. By 1900 a broad index to subject area, particularly for specialist journals, was also included. Its chief rival, *May's British and Irish Press Guide*, was first published in 1874 and known as *Willings British and Irish Press Guide* from 1890. Both directories continue to be published, as *Benn's Media* and *Willings Press Guide* respectively.

Locating historical newspapers has been greatly facilitated by two groups of British Library publications. The earliest, Charles A. Toase, *Bibliography of British Newspapers* (6 vols, 1982-91), lists the newspapers of Cornwall, Derbyshire, Devon, Durham, Kent, Northumberland, Nottinghamshire and Wiltshire. Bibliographical details and details of British and overseas library holdings are given for each title. This publication was gradually superseded by Newsplan, a far more comprehensive British Library-sponsored survey to gather information, *inter alia*, about the location of surviving newspapers. Between 1986 and 1996, the results were published in a series of 10 regional studies covering the whole of the UK and Ireland and having the generic title *Newsplan: Report on the Newsplan Project in ....*

Digitisation is now succeeding indexes as the means of realising the full potential of newspapers as a source of business-specific historical information. In this digitisation, *The*

Times has led the way. The *Times Digital Archive 1785-1985* (www.galeuk.com/times) contains 7.5 million articles that can be searched online and screen-read, providing immediate access to a vast volume of information – in fact so much for much-reported businesses that it becomes difficult to tell the wood from the trees. The *Archive* is available by subscription but can sometimes be accessed without charge in good reference libraries. The *Scotsman* (www.scotsman.com), Scotland's premier newspaper, has been digitised for the period from 1817, when it was established, to 1950. Searching is free but downloading is chargeable. Other relevant digitisation projects include the *Guardian* and *Observer* newspapers, from 1791 and 1821 respectively (www.archive.guardian.co.uk), and the *Economist* Historical Archive, 1843-2003; access to each is chargeable.

Graphic insight into what is now achievable is provided by a British Library project (www.bl.uk), the delivery of which began in late 2007, to make available digitally a wide range of British national, regional and local newspapers for the 19th century. The first release of the project covers over two million pages from almost 50 newspapers. Others will be added in 2008. The accent is on promoting political and social history but there is also much for the historian of a business. The online service is chargeable outside higher and further education establishments, but reference libraries will doubtless subscribe.

Indexes – which historically have been used for accessing information in newspapers – were published for a few national titles, most notably *The Times* from 1790. A comprehensive index to the *Financial Times* was published between 1913 and 1920 as the *Financial Times Index* but was only resumed in 1981 with the appearance of *Annual Index of the Financial Times*. Another published index is available to the *Glasgow Herald*, from 1906.

Many more, although much less elaborate, indexes exist for provincial newspapers; they are generally unpublished, are held in a variety of formats, vary greatly in their level of detail and often cover a relatively short period. Nevertheless, where they exist they have enormous value when digital copy is not available. Most are held in local record offices and local history libraries. The Colindale Newspaper Library tries to maintain a schedule of them; some indexes in book form are kept on its open shelves including ones to Chester (1960-4), Dumfries and Galloway (1777-1930), Maidstone (1830-46), Norwich (1770-9), Sherborne and Yeovil (1774-8) and Stirling (1820-1916). Some indexes are listed in the Newsplan series of publications (q.v.). In 1986, 650 indexes were reckoned to have existed in one form or another.

Although indexes are hugely helpful, information can also sometimes be pinpointed provided that dates of key events worthy of press coverage in the life of a business are known. These may include dates of the establishment or dissolution of a partnership, the formation or liquidation of a limited company, a bankruptcy, a fraud and the resulting police and court reports, the construction of new plant or closure of old ones, an accident or other disaster caused by storm, flood or fire, the announcement of annual results, industrial action, the retirement or death of senior managers and so on.

Two well-established newspaper archives are worthy of mention. That of *The Times*, maintained by News International, is described in Gordon Phillips, 'The Archives of The Times', *Business Archives* (41, 1976). The archives of the *Guardian* (formerly the *Manchester Guardian*) and the *Observer* are at the London-based Guardian Newsroom (www.guardian.co.uk/newsroom), which is open to the public.

1. Michael Murphy, *Newspapers and the Local Historian*, Chichester (1991), p.10.

TRADE DIRECTORIES: TOPOGRAPHICAL

Use of Trade Directories

Trade directories provide a small amount of vital information about a vast number of businesses from the late 18th to the mid-20th centuries, after which they were supplemented and then supplanted by other publications. The first directories were topographical, listing all or most businesses to be found in a particular county or city, giving for each business name, address and activity. Their function was to provide a means whereby customers without local knowledge could locate suppliers of goods and services and vice versa. In the third quarter of the 19th century, these topographical directories were joined by business

Hughes Henry, commission agent, 68 Gladstone st. Aston
Hughes Henry (established 1847), manufacturer of improved carriage & railway lamps, 15 Gough street & Ellis street, & 9 Upper Marshall street
Hughes Henry, shopkeeper, 86 Henry street
Hughes James, coal dealer, 13 Herbert road, Small heath
Hughes Jas. furniture remover.& coal dlr.102 New Town row
Hughes James, shopkeeper, 39 Loveday street
Hughes John, beer retailer, 35 Benacre street
Hughes John, boot maker, 49 Baldwin street,Smethwick
Hughes John, builder, Balsall Heath road, Edgbaston
Hughes John, butcher, 54 Arthur street, Coventry road
Hughes John, chimney sweeper, 39 Northwood street
Hughes John, fancy draper, silk mercer, hosier, haberdasher & wholesale & retail milliner & fringe & trimming manufacturer, 41, 42, 43 & 44 Worcester street
Hughes John, grocer, 50 Great Hampton row
Hughes John, grocer, 125 & 127 Holloway head
Hughes John, gun finisher, 18 (back of) Weaman row
Hughes John, painter &c. 205 Icknield Port road
Hughes John, shopkeeper, 39 Blucher street
Hughes John, tailor, 60 Grosvenor street west
Hughes John Joseph, artist, 37 Villa road
Hughes Joseph, baker, 93 Highgate lane, Sparkbrook
Hughes Joseph, tin plate worker, 85½ Benacre street
Hughes Joseph, tobacconist, 180 Dudley road
Hughes Joshua, stationer, 176 Sherlock street
Hughes Martin, gardnr. Chad valley, Harborne rd. Edgbstn
Hughes Mary (Mrs.), butcher, 182 Wattville rd. Hndswth
Hughes Richard, butcher, 48 Bordesley Park road
Hughes Richard Ernest, grocer & drysalter, & post office, 1 Prospect row
Hughes Robert, gun & rifle manufacturer, 100 Moland street
Hughes Samuel, pawnbroker, 93 Kyrwicks lane
Hughes Samuel, turner, 36½ Tower street
Hughes Sarah Jane (Mrs.), shopkeeper, 88 Hingeston st
Hughes Silas, coal dealer, 28 Great King street
Hughes Thomas, builder, 162 Angelina street, 59 Baker street & 80 Muntz street, Small heath
Hughes Thomas, builder, 93 to 95 Hockley hill

23   *Topographical trade directories, which relate, say, to a city or county, were first published in the mid-18th century, but only in large numbers and accurately from the early decades of the 19th. They are invaluable in giving the name, address and activity of each business and in enabling changes in time to be detected through comparison of one edition with another. Businesses were listed in early directories in alphabetical order and in later ones also by activity and address. This illustration, taken from an 1883 Birmingham directory, shows an alphabetical listing, while the one overleaf, from an 1858 Cumberland directory, shows a listing by activity.*

OFFICE TRADES DIRECTORY. 91

GROCERS & TEADEALERS—*continued.*
Swann Napthali, Windermere house, Ambleside
Swinbank A. Fish market, Kendal
Taylor J. Highgate, Kendal
Thompson J. Maulds Meaburn, Kirkby Thore
Thompson J. Ambleside
Thompson W. Highgate, Kendal
Thwaits R. Farcross bank, Kendal
Troughton J. Holme, Burton
Troughton R. Kirkby Stephen
Turner W. Kirkland, Kendal
Tyson E. Great Langdale, Ambleside
Tyson R. Orton, Shap
Wallace J. Strickland gate, Kendal
Wharton A. Temple Sowerby, Penrith
Whinerey John, Stramon gate, Kendal
Whitaker G. & Son, Milnthorpe
Whitfield J. Kirkby Lonsdale
Wildman J. Kirkby Lonsdale
Wilkinson C. Stramon gate, Kendal
Willan Mrs. J. Kirkby Lonsdale
Willan J. Shap, Penrith
Wilson J. Kirkland, Kendal
Wilson J. Milnthorpe
Wilson Mrs. M. Brough
Wilson Mrs. S. Newbiggin, Ravenstonedale, Kirkby Stephen
Winskill J. Bolton, Kirkby Thore
Winster J. Barbon, Kirkby Lonsdale
Wiseman Mrs. M. Sower pow, Kirkby Stephen
Woodburn J. Ambleside
Wright J. Wildman street, Kendal
Yeats W. F. Kirkby Lonsdale

GUANO MERCHANTS.
See Manure Merchants.

GUN & PISTOL MAKER.
Matthews Joseph, Strickland gate, Kendal

GUNSMITH,
Buckle R. Crosby Garrett, Brough

GUNPOWDER MANUFCTRS.
Elter Water Gunpowder Company, Elter water, Ambleside
Sedgwick Gunpowder Co. (R. Crooke, managing director), Milnthorpe
Wakefield W. H. & Co. Gate beck, Preston Richard, Kendal

HABERDASHERS.
Grime J. Market place, Kirkby Stephen
Lord John, Market pl. Kirkby Stephen

HAIRDRESSERS.
Birbeck J. Cloisters, St. Lawrence, Appleby
Carradus J. Highgate, Kendal
Dowker J. Finkle street, Kendal
Harrison J. Kirkland, Kendal
Kendal Mrs. I. Kirkby Stephen
Kruger S. Strickland gate, Kendal
Lodge L. Kirkby Lonsdale
Nanson J. Brough
Saul T. & W. Strickland gate, Kendal
Taylor E. Strickland gate, Kendal
Thompson T. Milnthorpe
Wharton J. Bowness, Windermere
Wilson W. Highgate, Kendal
Young Mrs. N. Kirkby Stephen

HARNESS MAKERS.
See Saddlers & Harness Makers.

HATTERS.
Blacow Mrs. J. Finkle street, Kendal
Dickinson W. Kirkby Stephen
Dixon M. Kirkby Stephen
Heap T. Finkle street, Kendal
Jordan S. Kirkby Stephen
Lord J. Market place, Kirkby Stephen
Nelson C. Ambleside
Parker & Head, Highgate, Kendal
Rigg Miss E. & M. A. Highgt. Kendal
Scott J. Brough
Smith C. Kirkby Lonsdale
Wearing J. Kirkby Lonsdale

HOOP MANUFACTURER.
Clark B. Roper Ford, Winster, Windermere

HORSE BREAKERS.
Hornby T. Church Brough, Brough
Lawson B. Kaber, Brough

HOSIERS.
Gould T. Finkle street, Kendal
Grime J. Market place, Kirkby Stephen
Johnson W. Finkle street, Kendal
Lord J. Market place, Kirkby Stephen
Mellray J. Kirkby Lonsdale
Parker & Head, Highgate, Kendal
Scott J, Brough
Wearing J. Kirkby Lonsdale

HOSIERY MANUFACTRS.
Brooks John, Stramon gate, Kendal
Edmondson Isaac & Co. Castle st. Kendal

HOTELS, *see Publicans &c.*

HOTELS—TEMPERANCE.
Brunskill J. Kelleth, Orton
Davis C. Tebay, Orton
Dickinson W. Kirkby Stephen
Harper J. Orton, Shap
Hayton E. Tebay, Orton
Kearton C. Brough
Liddle G. Milnthorpe
Wood J. Bowness, Windermere

HYDROPATHIST.
Hudson E. L. Lake Windermere hydropathic establishment, Windermere

INNS, *see Publicans &c.*

IRON FOUNDERS.
Thomson Andrew, Lowther st. Kendal
Winder Joseph, Lound foundry, near Kendal ; warehouse, Rose & Crown yard, Strickland gate, Kendal

IRON MERCHANTS.
Bindloss & Cooper, Kirkland, Kendal

IRON MINE PROPRIETOR.
See also Lead Mine Proprietor.
Bell Thomas Hodgson, Potter's hill, Kirkby Stephen ; mines, at Hartley & Nateby fells

IRONMONGERS.
Bailie & Hargreaves, Highgate, Kendal
Batty Misses H. & N. Kirkby Lonsdale
Bell J. Market place, Kirkby Stephen
Bell R. F. Ambleside
Bewley T. Market place, KirkbyStephn
Bindloss & Cooper (*who.*), Kirklnd. Kndl
Blay Mrs. S. Market pl. Kirkby Stephen
Close J. Town head, Kirkby Stephen
Davis J. B. Kirkby Stephen
Dean J. Kirkby Stephen
Gardner Charles & John, Postlethwaite, Strickland gate, Kendal
Gibson J. Kirkby Lonsdale
Moffat W. Orton, Shap
Pattinson W. Brough
Redhead Matthew, Strickland gt. Kendal
Ross W. Highgate, Kendal
Scott J. Brough
Simpson J. Orton, Shap
Waters George, Bowness, Windermere
Whittam J. Milnthorpe
Wilson G. Bridge st. St. Lawrnce. Applby
Winder T. Kirkby Lonsdale

JEWELLERS.
Lord J. Market place, Kirkby Stephen
Rhodes T. Highgate, Kendal
Robinson T. Highgate, Kendal
Scales Thomas & Henry Fawcett, Finkle street, Kendal, & at Bowness
Scott J. Strickland gate, Kendal
Tatham C. Bridge street, St. Lawrence, Appleby
Wilson G. Bridge street, St. Lawrence, Appleby

KNITTERS.
Shaw Mrs. E. Town, Ravenstonedale, Kirkby Stephen
Taylor Mrs. I. Town, Ravenstonedale, Kirkby Stephen

LAND SURVEYORS.
See also Surveyors.
Davids Richard James, Kirkby Lonsdale
Green J. Grasmere, Ambleside
Hoggarth Henry, Finkle street, Kendal

Lumb G. Lowther New town, Lowther, Penrith
Webster Crayston, Stramon gate, Kendal

LATH MAKER.
Fisher John, Strickland gate, Kendal

LAUNDRESSES.
Holden Mrs. E. Kirkland, Kendal
Rose Mrs. E. Farcross bank, Kendal

LEAD MINE PROPRIETOR.
See also Iron Mine Proprietor.
Bell Thomas Hodgson, Kirkby Stephen ; mines on Hartley & Nateby fells

LEATHER DRESSER.
Wilkinson J. Kirkby Lonsdale

LEATHER MERCHANTS.
Somervell Brothers, Netherfield, Kendal

LEATHERSELLERS.
See Curriers & Leathersellers.

LIME BURNERS.
Balmer R. Bleatarn, Warcop
Bowman R. Raisbeck, Orton
Clark R. Whassett, Milnthorpe
Ebdell I. Winton, Brough
Harrison John, Hungriggs, Bongate, Appleby
Hayton J. Orton, Shap
Mattinson R. Beastbanks, Kendal
Manson C. Stainmore, Brough
Rawes R. Plungarths, Strickland kettle, Kendal
Robinson J. Beast banks, Kendal
Taylor I. Brow head, Crosthwaite, Kendl
Thompson J. Newby end, Newby, Penrith

LINENDRAPERS.
See Drapers.

LINSEED CAKE MERCHANT.
Brunskill Stephen, Canal wharf & Strickland gate, Kendal

LINSEY MANUFACTURERS.
Ireland J. & Co. New road, Kendal
Medcalf Caleb & Sons, Highgate, Kendal
Simpson & Ireland, Kent street, Kendal

LOCKSMITHS.
See Whitesmiths &c.

LODGING & BOARDING HOUSES.
Abbott Miss F. Shap, Penrith
Abbott J. Ambleside
Askew W. Loughrigg, Ambleside
Backhouse J. Rydal, Ambleside
Bainbridge Miss M. Beast banks, Kendal
Balmer M. Hope bank, Windermere
Barrow J. Woodside cot. Windermere
Barton Mrs. M. Milnthorpe
Benson Mrs. S. Bank ter. Windermere
Bird J. Main st. St. Lawrence, Appleby
Bowness Mrs. I. Ambleside
Bowness W. Clappersgate, Ambleside
Brockbank J. Windermere bank, Windermere
Brownrigg John, North cottage, Windermere bank, Windermere
Bulman Mrs. M. Kent terrace, Kendal
Cartnell W. Windermere, Applethwaite, Ambleside
Cropper Mrs. M. Cross street, Windermere, Ambleside
Dacre Miss B. Cliffe terrace, Kendal
Dickinson J. Rose cottage, Windermere
Dobson Mrs. E. Ambleside
Dobson H. Newhouses, Patterdle. Amblsd
Dobson W. Fold head, Bowness, Windrmr
Fell D. Bank terrace, Windermere
Fell Mrs. Kent terrace, Kendal
Gardner G. Bowness, Windermere
Gillbanks J. Langdale head, Great Langdale, Ambleside
Green Mrs. M. Sand side, Beetham, Milnthorpe
Harrison Mrs. E. Ambleside
Hartley T. jun. Bowness, Windermere
Hayton R. Windermere bank, Windermere
Herd T. Windermere bank, Windermere
Holmes Mrs. A. Thorney how, Grasmere, Ambleside
Holmes J. High street, Windermere

sector directories that focused on individual industries as opposed to geographical areas (*see* pp.129-31).

The content of the earliest directories was simply an alphabetical list of businesses in a given city, town or village. By the 19th century, the business's activity and street address were also included and, by the end of the century, in a very small number of cases, details of other sites of operation, prizes awarded, agencies held, whether a government contractor, and so on.

Their regular revision and re-publication – every year for a few directories – is hugely important as it enables the historian, by comparing one issue with another, to identify changes over time. These might include alterations to trading name, implying, say, the arrival of new or departure of existing partners or conversion from a partnership to a registered company. Other changes might be in activity or in address, implying, perhaps, expansion, contraction or modernisation. Sources such as maps, census returns, bankruptcy records and published partnership details can be used to verify assumptions made on the basis of information changes in directories.

In making use of trade directories, publications such as Gareth Shaw, *British Directories as Sources in Historical Geography* (1982) and Neil Raven, 'The trade directory sources for the study of early 19th century urban economies', *Business Archives* (1997) provide useful reading.

History of Directory Publishing

Samuel Lees' *A Collection of the Names of Merchants Living In and About the City of London*, published in 1677 and listing almost 2,000 merchants, is reckoned to be the first trade directory. The next, closely resembling Lees' and also for London, appeared in 1734; thereafter at least one London directory was published each year. Other city directories followed from the 1760s, notably Birmingham (1763), Liverpool (1764), Manchester (1772) and Bristol (1775). William Bailey's *Northern Directory* (first published 1781) aimed to include every principal English town north of the River Trent and was the first attempt at a regional directory. The first national directory, *Baileys British Directory* (1784), sought to include all major towns and was followed by the *Universal British Directory* (4 vols, 1790-8). High costs and administrative effort quickly brought national directory publishing to an end but county directories flourished; the first, covering Hampshire, appeared in 1784. Altogether, between 1763 and 1790, around 50 provincial directories covering 10 cities, three counties and six larger areas were published.

Directory publishing, which had been encouraged from the mid-18th century by growth of internal trade and mobility of population, was spurred on in the early 19th century by the coming of railways and falling production costs. By the 1820s and 1830s, there was rapid growth in terms of places covered and periodicity; by the second half of the century most parts of Britain – counties, cities and major towns – had their own directories and revisions of them appeared on a regular, if not annual, basis. London long led the way; several directories were published each year for the central area and, by about the 1860s, also for the suburbs. The annual *Post Office Directory of London* was particularly important, sweeping its competitors aside and from the 1830s acting as a model for others to follow.

24 See 23, p.125.

Post Office directories, so called on account of the involvement of Post Office officials in their compilation, are reckoned more accurate than most. The first were published for Edinburgh from 1773, for London from 1800 and for cities such as Glasgow and Southampton from the 1820s. Three firms came to dominate 19th-century directory publishing – Frederic Kelly, James Pigot and William White; they merged together as the century progressed. Arrangement of data became more sophisticated over time. Gareth Shaw identifies a gradual progression from, prior to 1750, an alphabetical listing of businesses, to an additional listing by street address and, after 1800, to a further listing by activity.

The history of directory publishing is reviewed in Jane E. Norton, *Guide to the National and Provincial Directories of England and Wales Excluding London* (1984), which, *inter alia*, provides an entertaining account of both deficiencies and strengths.

Reliability of Trade Directories

The accuracy, completeness and currency of trade directories have been much debated. Early directories have obvious shortcomings with many businesses omitted on account of the high cost and poor methodology in data collection. Data collectors were untrained and not rigorous, sometimes copying data from other sources or pirating it from existing directories. By the early 19th century many of these problems had been dealt with through training data collectors, through reducing the time between data collection and publication and on account of the emergence of a new generation of directory publishers who were anxious to protect their reputation and credibility. One recognised shortcoming of directories, which has particular significance in tracing the history of a business, is the abbreviated description of business activity especially in the early period when a typical businessman carried on several activities simultaneously and when business classification was in its infancy. Very often only one activity was listed and it might not be the chief one.

Recent writers, especially those seeking to use directory data for scientific analysis, have focused on biases in coverage. Mostly this turns on under-representation of working people as opposed to businesses and is not surprising. But it does seem that businesses located in small settlements, in poor neighbourhoods, in suburbs and in backstreets as opposed to main roads were more likely than others to be excluded. Moreover, some categories of business may have been excluded simply because publishers perceived them as unimportant.

For more discussion of reliability *see* Gareth Shaw, *British Directories as Sources in Historical Geography* (1982) and also 'The content and reliability of 19th century trade directories', *The Local Historian* (1978). The latter reassuringly concludes that 'whilst directories did not cover the whole population they did, however, provide a fairly accurate picture of the number of traders and manufacturers'.

Finding Trade Directories

Local record offices and local history libraries invariably have comprehensive collections of local directories. Guildhall Library (www.cityoflondon.gov.uk/corporation) in the City of London has an especially good collection, much of which has been reproduced on microfilm as *Directories from Guildhall Library, London, 1677-1899*. It relates to all parts of Britain but especially London, and is described in Guildhall Library's publication *Historic Trade Directories in Guildhall Library* (2005). The Victoria & Albert Museum's National Art

Library's (www.vam.ac.uk/nal) collection of over 1,000 volumes is described in Michael E. Keen, *A Bibliography of the Trade Directories in the National Art Library* (1979). The British Library, the National Libraries of Scotland and Wales, the Science Museum and the London Metropolitan Archives all have notable collections.

Many directories and collections of directories are now being digitised and this massively increases the ability to search for specific pieces of information. Many are available as CD-ROM, sometimes published by local research groups.

Invaluable bibliographies giving location details are Jane E. Norton, *Guide to the National and Provincial Directories of England and Wales Excluding London Published Before 1856* (1984), P.J. Atkins, *The Directories of London 1677-1977* (1990) and Gareth Shaw and Alison Tipper, *British Directories: A bibliography and guide to directories published in England and Wales, 1850-1950, and Scotland, 1773-1950* (1997). All have useful chapters dealing with history and reliability.

Telephone Directories

Allied to trade directories are telephone directories, the first of which was published in 1880 following the introduction of telephone services in Britain. They list both private and business numbers. In 1938-9 the first business telephone directory for London was published although ones for other cities did not follow until 1968. The first *Yellow Pages*, for London, was published in 1968. British Telecom's historical archives (www.btplc.com/thegroup/bthistory/btgrouparchives) have an almost complete set of directories from 1880 and these are now available online (www.ancestry.co.uk). Leading reference libraries, local record offices and local history libraries often have good local collections, especially Guildhall Library.

Trade Directories: Business Sector

Supplementing topographical trade directories are directories focused on industries and professions. Invariably their coverage is national, sometimes international, and very much reflects the arrival of a national economy in the mid-19th century. They were published in significant numbers from the 1860s and 1870s and flourished until the Second World War; sometimes they appeared annually and otherwise less frequently. Their publishers comprised two broad categories: commercial firms, such as Kelly's, and trade associations (*see* pp.70-1).

The nature of content varies from directory to directory, depending to some extent on the industry covered and intended readership. Much of the content about individual businesses will also appear in topographical directories but business sector directories bring this information together on a national basis for a given industry. They also provide more detail about activity per individual business as well as ancillary information about the industry as a whole. However, perhaps their really useful feature is their contextual information. They identify the number, nature and location of possible competitors, trade suppliers and trade customers. In so doing, they place the business in its industry context and, through comparison of different editions, allow changes over time to be identified. Two contrasting examples provide useful illustrations.

The first is *Kelly's Directory of the Cabinet, Furniture and Upholstery Trades and Other Trades Connected Thereto*. Although not published annually, it appeared at regular intervals between

110   ENGLAND AND WALES.

CASTNER-KELLNER ALKALI COMPANY, LIMITED, Weston Point, Runcorn, Cheshire, and Wallsend-on-Tyne ; Head Office, 13 Abchurch lane, London, E.C.; T, " Muidos, Cannon, London;" T N, 5147 Bank ; P S, Runcorn, 2 m. ; G, Own Siding ; T, "Lysis, Weston Point ; " T N, 31 Runcorn ; Water facilities, by Manchester Ship and Weaver Canals : Sales Department, 257 Royal Liver buildings, Liverpool ; T, " Pegasus ; " T N, 8983 Bank (2 lines).—*Bleaching Powder, Caustic Soda, Sodium, Sodium Peroxide, Sulphate of Ammonia, Hydrogen Gas, Chlorine (Liquid) and Hydrogen Peroxide.*

CATCHPOLE (E.) & SONS, Plough Bridge, Rotherhithe, London, S.E.; T, "Catchpole, Rotherhithe, London ; " T N, 1517 New Cross (two lines) ; Water facilities, by Grand Surrey Canal.—*Coal Tar Products, Asphalte, Greases, Varnishes, Pitches, Wood Preservatives, Disinfectants, Composition for Block Floor Laying, &c., Rosin Distillers.*

CHADWICK (WILLIAM), Sling Chemical Works, The Sling, Kidderminster ; P & G S, Kidderminster, $\frac{1}{2}$ m. ; T, " Chadwick, Kidderminster ; " T N, 13 Kidderminster.—*Sulphate of Soda.*

CHANCE & HUNT, LIMITED (formerly CHANCE BROTHERS, Oldbury ; and WILLIAM HUNT & SONS, Wednesbury) ; Registered Office, Oldbury, Worcestershire ; London, 116 Fenchurch street, E.C.; T N, 4541 London Wall ; Works, Oldbury, Wednesbury and Stafford ; P S, Oldbury and Bromford Lane, L & N W R, 1 m. ; G, Oldbury, G W R, $\frac{1}{4}$ m., or Spon Lane, L & N W R, 1 m. ; T, " Chemicals, Oldbury ; " T N, Oldbury 105.—*Soda, Bicarbonate of Soda, Caustic Soda, Salts of Ammonia, Sal Ammoniac, Muriate, Carbonate, and Sulphate of Ammonia, Liquor Ammonia, Sulphuric and Muriatic Acid (Pure and Commercial), Salt, &c.*

CHEMICAL UNION, THE, LIMITED, Ipswich ; P S, Ipswich, G E R, 1 m.; G, Own Siding ; T, "Fison, Ipswich."—*Manure, Sheep Dip, Disinfectants, Insecticides, &c.*

CHEMICAL WORKS (late H. & E. ALBERT), 15 Philpot lane, E.C. ; T, "Korten, London ; " T N, 2449 Avenue.—*Phosphate of Ammonia, Phosphate of Potash, Concentrated Superphosphate, Superphosphates, Basic Slag, Lithopone.*

CHESTER (A. D.) & Co., 181 Drummond road, Bermondsey, London, S.E. ; T, " Clarifrous."—*Bisulphite of Lime, Bisulphite of Soda, Acetic and Phosphorous Acids, Brewers' Chemicals.*

25　(Opposite) Business sector trade directories are similar in content to topographical directories but they relate to a single business sector, often on a national basis. Two contrasting directories are illustrated here. The illustration opposite is from the 1914 edition of the Chemical Manufacturers' Directory, which gives especially comprehensive information about output per business. The illustration (right) is from a 19th-century edition of Kellys' Directory of the Cabinet, Furniture & Upholstery Trades & other Connected Trades, which lists by name, address and activity a mass of business involved in the different branches of the furniture trade. Such directories help to give a sense of a firm within its business-sector context.

26　See 25.

152　　ENGLAND, SCOTLAND AND WALES.

CORNICE POLE MANUFACTURERS—continued.
Kershaw Walter, Gomersal, Leeds
Liverpool Furnishing Co. (Samuel Gershon, manager), 143, 145 & 147 Islington, Liverpool
McKwen Alexander, George st. Wick, Caithness-shire
Martin C. A. 28 Wood st. Liverpool
Maw, Till, Kirke & Co. 22 & 30 Bridge st. ; 4, 5 & 6 Dock Office row & 16 Charlotte st. Hull
Mountain Charles, 26 Wellington lane, Leeds
Okell George & Co. 15, 17 & 19 Paradise st. Liverpool
Pashley William Charles, 56 Argyle st. Birken-head, Cheshire
Reid John & Sons, 47 Meadow rd. Leeds
Seapham William, Mill st. Marsh lane, Leeds. See advert. p. 23
Simms Henry James (wood), 75 Lower Essex st. Birmingham
Stone, Settle & Wilkinson, King st. brass works, King st. Hull
‡Tonks William & Sons, 201 Moseley st. Bir-mingham. See advert. p. 19
Waring Samuel James, 42, 45, 47, 49 & 53 St. Anne st. ; factory, 2 Harker pl. Liverpool
Watts & Co. Compton house, Liverpool
‡Whitehouse George, Barford st. Birmingham
Whitfield James, 38 & 39 Oxford st. Birming-ham. See advert. facing Warwickshire
‡Wilde Thomas, Charles Henry st. Birmingham
‡Williams Brothers & Co. Pershore street, Birmingham
Woodburn Miles, 45 Mount Pleasant, Liverpool
‡Youds Wm. Henry, 48 & 50 Watergate st. Chester

Cretonne & Chintz Manufacturers.
Johnson (Jabez) & Fildes, 44 Spring gardens & 39 Brown st. Manchester
Stead, McAlpin & Co. Commersdale, Carlisle

Curled Hair Manufacturers.
See Horsehair Manufacturers.

Curtain Manufacturers.
Bradshaw, Forth & Co. Hartwell st. works, Peas Hill rd. Nottingham
Carey & Son, 33 Stoney st. Nottingham
Mansergh & Son, Market pl. Lancaster ; & Queen's ter. Morecambe, Lancs
Musson Robert, 31 Stoney st. Nottingham
Pratt, Hurst & Co. Stoney st. Nottingham
Shields John & Co. Wallace works, Perth
Wells John S. & Co. 20 Stoney st. Nottingham
Wills R. C. 54A, High pavement, Nottingham

Curtain Hook Manufacturers.
Cooke Bros. 65A, Constitution hill, Birmingham
Also of fancy chair nails, drugget pins &c
Finnemore John, 9 Upper priory, Birmingham
Hart, Son, Peard & Co. Grosvenor works, Bir-mingham
Herbert George Wm. 74 Dean st. Birmingham
Hipkiss Henry & Co. 54A, Bread st. Birmingham
Hodges Rowland, jun. 3 Prospect row, Bir-mingham. See advert. p. 21
Johnson John, 36 & 37 Ashted row, Birmingham

Jones & Askin, 22, 23 & 24 Lower Loveday st. Birmingham
Jullien J. H. 134 Balsall Heath rd. Birmingham
Linnett Edward, 40 Lombard st. Birmingham
Rowley Chas. & Co. 24 Newhall st. Birmingham
Whitfield James, 38 & 39 Oxford st. Birming-ham. See advert. facing Warwickshire

Curtain Ring Manufacturers.
Barton Samuel (wood), 32 Bishop st. Birmingham
Cooke Bros. 65A, Constitution hill, Birmingham
Ernest Charles, Shambles, York
Geldert George, Corporation st. Sheffield
Gibbon Ebenezer (cornish), 37 Ludgate hill, Birmingham
Hart, Son, Peard & Co. Grosvenor works, Bir-mingham
Herbert George Wm. 74 Dean st. Birmingham
Hipkiss Henry & Co. 54A, Bread st. Birmingham
Hodges Rowland, jun. 3 Prospect row, Bir-mingham. See advert. p. 21
Hopkins Joseph, 23 Augusta st. Birmingham
Jones & Askin, 22, 23 & 24 Lower Loveday st. Birmingham
Jones Brothers, 69 Moland st. Birmingham
Longmore Frederick Peter, 60 Cambridge st. Birmingham
Martin C. A. 28 Wood st. Liverpool
Nicklin & Co. 166 Gt. Charles st. Birmingham
Parker William, 114 Lionel st. Birmingham
Seapham William, Mill st. Marsh lane, Leeds. See advert. p. 23
Snow Samuel, Upper Highgate st. Birmingham
Whitehead William, 200 Bristol st. Birmingham
Whitfield James, 38 & 39 Oxford st. Birming-ham. See advert. facing Warwickshire

Daylight Reflector Manufacturers.
Adams Joseph Benjamin & Co. 9 Church lane, Liverpool
Gratrix Samuel, jun. & Brothers, 25 & 27 Al-port town, Deansgate & Philip's Park rd. Bradford, Manchester
Hepton William & Son, Hunslet lane & South Brooke st. Leeds
London & Manchester Daylight & Gaslight Reflector Co. 179 Gt. Ducie st. Strangeways, Manchestr
Neillings John, 26 Percival st. Chorlton-upon-Medlock, Manchester
Revill Edwin, 17½ Constitution hl. Birmingham
Rigby John & Son, 15 Piccadilly, Manchester

Dining Table Manufacturers.
Atkinson T. National store, Saltburn-by-the-Sea, Yorks
Blackburn Richard Stead, Market pl. & Salter row, Pontefract, Yorks
Brindle Thomas & Son, 82 Market st. Chorley, Lancs
Brown & Brough, 12 & 14 Moss st. London rd. Liverpool
Creddle & Smith, 16 King st. Truro, Cornwall
Crosby Robert & Sons, 8 Cases st. ; 63 Great George st. ; 9A, Elliott st. ; factory, 58 Rath-bone st. Liverpool

---

1885 and 1936, in which time its structure remained remarkably consistent. It catered for a wide range of activities – antique furniture dealers, antique furniture makers, art furniture manufacturers, art pottery manufacturers, artistic designers, baize manufacturers, bath chair makers and bed tick manufacturers to name but a few. Its chief contents comprised two schedules, one of businesses arranged by county/town/activity and the other of businesses arranged by activity. Most individual business entries are restricted to name, address and activity/activities but occasionally there is much more. The entry for Charles Field of Oldham, for example, reads 'Charles Field, cotton and woollen flock manufacturer; fan fly blowings, clean waste and mill puffs. Home, colonial and foreign governments and railways stores contractor; works at Blackridings Mill, Oldham; established 1842.' More generally, the directory enables the researcher to obtain a sense of the number and distribution of competitor businesses and of potential suppliers.

A somewhat esoteric example is *The Ice and Cold Storage Trades Directory and Handbook*, published annually by the Ice & Cold Storage Trades Association between 1900 and 1932. It illustrates well the more varied and informed content of trade association directories relative to the directories published by commercial firms such as Kelly's. It provides an alphabetical listing of all businesses in the sector, giving for each name, address and activities, and also a listing by business activity. This ranges from butter factories to meat importers, from refrigerator manufacturers to makers of ice-making machines, and from cold-storage companies to ice factories. Presentation therefore closely resembles that of a Kelly's directory although in this instance coverage is international as businesses as far away as South America, the Far East and Australasia are included. However, in this directory other types of business-specific information are given, such as patents registered and businesses newly registered. The latter embraced objectives and reasons for establishment, status, capital, directors and their addresses and so on. A further section deals with cold stores, giving for each capacity, system of refrigeration, year opened, types of goods stored, etc. Numerous trade advertisements give further business-specific details, while trade bodies and their members are also listed.

Many specialist directories are listed in Gareth Shaw and Allison Tipper, *British Directories: A bibliography and guide to directories published in England and Wales (1850-1950) and Scotland (1773-1950)* (1997) and in P.J. Atkins, *The Directories of London 1677-1977* (1990). Another source is the *Waterloo Directory of English Newspapers and Periodicals 1800-1900* (2003), which is also available online at www.victorianperiodicals.com. *Willings Press Guide* and *The Newspaper Press Directory* (*see* p.123) may also be helpful.

The following short schedule is given as a means of indicating the wide range of specialist directories available. Dates of publication are given in brackets and titles may have changed, often more than once, during the directory's history. The titles are taken from Shaw and Tipper, *British Directories:*

Bill Posters' Directory (1880-1950)
Bourne's Insurance Directory (from 1889)
Chemical Manufacturers' Directory of England, Wales and Scotland (from 1867)
Directory of Shipowners, Shipbuilders and Marine Engineers (from 1903)
Directory of the Tobacco Trade in Great Britain and Ireland (1883-1922)
Exporters' Directory (1871-81)
Gas and Water Companies' Directory (1877-1930)
Hardware Trades Year Book (1919-40)
International Mercantile Directory (1881-1930)
Kelly's Directory of Building Trades (1870-1939)
Kelly's Directory of Manufacturers of Textile Fabrics (1880-1928)
Kelly's Directory of the Leather Trades (1871-1940)
Kelly's Directory of the Watch and Clock Trades (1871-1937)
Kelly's Directory of the Wine and Spirit Trades, Brewers and Maltsters (from 1877)
Paper Makers' Directory of all Nations (from 1884)
Pott's Mining Register and Directory of Coal and Ironstone Trades of Great Britain and Ireland (1888-1915)
Pottery Gazette and Glass Trade Review Directory (from 1905)
Ryland's Iron, Steel and Allied Trades Directory (from 1881)
Ryland's List of Merchant Exporters (1888-1906)
Soap Makers' Directory of Great Britain (from 1888)
United Kingdom Stock and Share Brokers' Directory (1881-1940)

HOUSE JOURNALS

Businesses publish house journals and other publications for distribution among employees and external parties such as customers, suppliers, shareholders and institutions including local libraries, professional bodies and employer organisations. Sometimes one publication serves all but, in the case of big businesses, different publications might serve separate groups. Content of house publications is invariably non-confidential but, for the historian, comprises a rich seam of business-specific information simply not available elsewhere. These publications are therefore enormously useful in tracing the history of a business.

This section focuses in particular on house journals, i.e. newsletters or magazines circulated to staff, but much of it applies equally to house publications distributed to other groups. Few businesses of even average size will not have some form of staff publication, especially today when the costs of electronic publication are so relatively small. Traditionally, at one end of the house journal spectrum were publications made up of photocopied or duplicated sheets while, at the other, were the glossy magazines of big corporations. The earliest appeared at the end of the 19th century and they proliferated after 1945. Content and appearance very much depended upon the size, nature and distribution of the workforce; customers and products; and, not least, the culture and resources of the business itself.

The function of internal house journals is to inform employees of events and change and to encourage their identification with the business that employs them. More specifically they report and interpret financial performance, strategy, new products, structural changes, expansion, contraction, marketing initiatives, new investment, new appointments, staff events and so on. Much of this information is of obvious value to the historian, although it tends to be sanitised and selective, an issue touched on by John Griffiths, 'Exploring corporate culture: The potential of company magazines for the business historian', *Business Archives* (1999).

Journals intended for external circulation may be directed at actual or potential customers, suppliers, agents, dealers, wholesalers, shareholders, technical groups, pensioners and the wider community including the trade press, chambers of commerce, libraries and so on. Content, of course, is determined by function and readership. Prestige magazines dealing with products, contracts, plant and contribution to the community are intended for general circulation. Journals conveying technical and research information are circulated to professional bodies, academia, research institutions and the like. Sales magazines produced by manufacturers or retailers of high-value consumer goods – motor vehicles are an excellent example – circulate to potential customers. Sales and product-focused publications are directed at agents, dealers and wholesalers. The list is as long as it is broad.

House journals first appeared in the late 19th century; that of the Great Western Railway, published in 1862-3, is often cited as the first. Other early staff publications include Rowntree & Co.'s *CWM: A journal in the interests of the employees of Rowntree & Co.* (from 1902) and Westminster Bank's *The Westminster* (from 1907). Numbers expanded during and after the First World War, contracted between 1939 and 1945 and stormed ahead thereafter. The *Newspaper Press Directory* listed 165 titles in 1951 and 650 in 1976, after which the listing was discontinued. In the mid-1960s the British Association of Industrial Editors reckoned that nationwide some 1,800 internal and external journals were in circulation, rising to 2,300 ten years later.

Another early staff-orientated journal was Lever Brothers' *Progress*. First published in 1900, it aimed at 'intercommunication between the head office and works at Port Sunlight, the branch offices in the United Kingdom and the offices and agencies, oil mills and affiliated companies abroad'. Much content touched on staff issues such as social activities, promotions, benefits, bonuses and profit-sharing but management philosophy, the opening and closure of plant, new products, advertising initiatives and other business-related subjects figured. *Metal Box News*, the house journal of Metal Box Ltd, had similar content. Staff matters apart, its first issue, in 1952, carried articles on the chairman's visit to subsidiaries in Australia and India, participation in the annual packaging exhibition, the business's 50-year association with Worcester, the commissioning of a new strip mill, a recent business acquisition and the closure of old plant. Other articles explained current issues, such as the introduction of standard accounting procedures, new pension arrangements for widows and the value of education and training in the workplace.

Locating house journals is no easy matter. No national collection exists, no institution has specialised in their collection and there is no specialist bibliography. On account of being privately published, copyright libraries such as the British Library did not collect them as a matter of routine. That said, the British Library has large numbers, many collected via the former Science Reference Library, as do the National Libraries of Scotland and Wales. Peter M. Dunning and David E. Sawyer, *House Journals Held by the Science Reference Library* (1985) lists some 800 British and foreign titles being added to the British Library's collections in the 1980s. A library survey in 1985, called *Trade Literature in British Libraries*, noted that local reference libraries tended to hold house journals of local companies as part of their permanent collections.

About a thousand journals are recorded in *British House Journals* (1956, 2nd edition 1962), published by the British Association of Industrial Editors, which makes this the most comprehensive listing for this period. The annual *Newspaper Press Directory* listed house journals from about 1951 in a separate section headed 'House Magazines of the UK'. Other useful bibliographical guides are the *Waterloo Directory of Victorian Publications* and the *British Union Catalogue of Periodicals*.

Isobel J. Haberer, *House Journals: A bibliographical study* (Library Association thesis, 1965), which is available in the British Library, provides an analysis of house journal publishing. It includes, *inter alia*, an extensive directory of external journals giving for each date of establishment. A somewhat dated but nevertheless useful introduction to the production and content of house journals is John W. Hazzlewood, *House Journals* (1963) and Charles Mann, *Editing for Industry* (1974).

TRADE PRESS

Since well into the 19th century the business community has been served by a seemingly vast trade press published mostly as periodicals for use by business managers. Most publications are the output of commercial publishers but some are produced by trade and employer associations and by market organisations for distribution to their members. Several often exist for the same industry, differentiated by their commercial and technical content or by the management level at which they are pitched.

The trade press contains a wide range of information about the industry it serves as well as about particular member firms and has huge value for the historian, although very often its potential is significantly reduced for want of indexes. Content embraces such matters as corporate change, including new businesses setting up from scratch; mergers and acquisitions; business failures; new technology; legal cases and issues; Parliamentary news; company performance; new investment in plant; trade conditions; commodity prices; new appointments; contracts announced; labour issues; overseas competition; and so on. Some have the feel of a newspaper, others that of a yearbook. Invariably, throughout their history titles change several times, often as a result of merger with allied publications.

Examples taken at random well illustrate the range of content. *The Country Brewers' Gazette*, published between 1877 and 1931 and latterly known as *The Brewers' Gazette and Wine and Spirits Trades' Journal*, contained in 1900 reports of company annual meetings; law case reports touching on the brewing industry and involving specific businesses; share price performance of quoted brewers; obituaries of leading figures in the industry; details of newly registered patents and trade marks; technical articles on the brewing process; advertisements placed by suppliers to the industry; and so on.

The short-lived *Draper and Clothier*, published between 1859 and 1862, was designed as 'an organ of intercommunication and permanent record of news, advertisements and information for … all manufacturers or dealers in textile fabrics'. A typical issue for 1859 contained, *inter alia*, details of 'new inventions and improvements'; law reports; lists of bankruptcies and dissolutions, presumably taken from *The London Gazette*; and advertisements including 'a list of drapery businesses and premises for disposal', giving such details as location, stock value, rental, 'returns', lease and sale price – unfortunately business name is not given!

Rubber Information differs in both period and readership. First published in 1930, it was directed at technical managers but much content is of general interest, including schedules of new trade marks; supplier advertisements; classified list of manufacturers and suppliers to the industry; tables detailing plantation companies and giving for each the value of issued capital, profit or loss, acreage, crop outturn, etc. Much of the latter was presumably extracted from annual reports.

The British Library and the other copyright libraries have comprehensive holdings of the trade press while other holdings are in good general reference and academic libraries. Two annual press guides list current trade publications, namely *Benn's Media* and *Willings Press Guide*. The former was first published in 1846 as *Newspaper Press Directory* and the latter followed in 1874 when known as *May's British & Irish Press Guide*. For most of their history they have listed trade press publications and in their current form give short summaries of content and readership. *Willings* alone gives date of first publication.

An important source of cumulative information is the *Waterloo Directory of English Newspapers and Periodicals 1800-1900* (2003), which is also available electronically, and the *Waterloo Directory of Scottish Newspapers and Periodicals 1800-1900* (1989). Both include periodicals *first published* between 1800 and 1900, so their content is more wide-ranging than their titles suggest, and both have extensive subject, issuing body and other indexes. Others titles appear in *The British Union Catalogue of Periodicals*.

Some trade publications are indexed but invariably these are annual or otherwise periodic rather than cumulative; the British Library's Newspaper Library maintains a paper-based schedule of indexed periodicals known to them as 'hidden indexes', while references to indexes are sometimes recorded in its online catalogue. Important published indexes include, for example, C.E. Procktor, *The Engineer Index, 1856-1959* (1964) and Ruth Richardson and Robert Thorne, *The Builder Illustrations Index, 1843-1883* (1994).

27   Many businesses published trade catalogues as a means of marketing their output. These give details and, invariably, illustrations of each product made. Sometimes prices are given. Pages from two contrasting catalogues are reproduced here. One is from an 1870 catalogue published by Williams' Perran Foundry Co. of Cornwall, which manufactured capital goods. The other is from a 1920 catalogue of James Lyne Hancock & Co. of London, which manufactured a vast range of small-scale rubber goods including washers and gaskets.

28   See 27.

Trade Catalogues

Trade catalogues form a major part of what libraries generally call 'trade literature' or publications privately printed by a business and circulated to customers as part of its marketing, advertising, sales and servicing effort. Closely related are price lists, instruction manuals, publicity brochures and the like, but trade catalogues are probably the most interesting so far as the historian of a business is concerned.

Trade catalogues are, in effect, handbooks describing and illustrating the product range of a business, sometimes also giving prices, although more often these were included in a separate price list accompanying the catalogue. For the historian, catalogues show at a glance the product range of a business and, when revised and reprinted over a number of years as often happened, they enable identification of change in the business's mix of products. For historians of design, technology and buildings they have obvious relevance, as David Yeomans points out in 'Trade literature sources in design history', *Construction History Society Newsletter* (1999).

Catalogues were circulated most frequently by manufacturers but also by wholesalers and from time to time by retailers, especially mail-order businesses. The products advertised embraced every conceivable item of equipment including architectural ironmongery, fireplaces, furniture, handling machinery, heating appliances, machine tools, photographic equipment, sanitary ware, scientific instruments, sports equipment, table silver, textiles and so on. Catalogues circulated by capital goods manufacturers often show plant in situ. Retailers such as Army & Navy Stores illustrated their entire range of goods. Illustrations of the business's premises, stressing size and capacity, were often included to impress customers.

The earliest modern trade catalogues are reckoned to have been circulated in the mid-18th century by dynamic businessmen such as Thomas Chippendale and Josiah Wedgwood, Midlands-based brass founders and manufacturers of Sheffield plate. However trade catalogue publishing did not really get into its stride until 100 years later, the result of reduced printing and paper costs. Theodore R. Crom, *Trade Catalogues 1542 to 1842* (1989) provides a general introduction to the subject and is heavily illustrated with early examples.

Although trade catalogues very much resemble books – sometimes hard-backed and several inches thick – the fact that they were privately published and so narrowly focused meant that they did not find their way to copyright libraries as a matter of course. At the same time businesses did not have to retain copies long term for legal or commercial reasons. Both factors result in somewhat patchy survival, especially so far as complete sets are concerned. Nevertheless, large numbers can to be found, especially in national and leading academic and local reference libraries and sometimes also in record offices.

No bibliography or dedicated catalogue of trade catalogues exists; they are much needed. The Trade Literature Collection of the British Library's Business and Intellectual Property Section (the former Science Reference Library) (www.bl.org.uk) includes many trade catalogues (as well as technical manuals, price lists, etc) dating to the early 19th century. It is probably the major UK collection but much is not yet listed in the library's integrated catalogue, so manual finding aids must be used.

The National Art Library at the Victoria & Albert Museum (www.vam.ac.uk/collections/prints_books/trade_catalogues/index.html) also has significant holdings, especially in its Jobbing Printing Collection, EKCO Collection and Liberty Department Store Collection.

Most items can be located in the library's online book catalogue (http://ipac.nal.vam.ac.uk) but some material may still be manually catalogued. A select of catalogues has been published on microfiche as *Trade Catalogues in the Victoria & Albert Museum* (1986), while others are detailed in J. Brunston, *A Bibliography of 120 Pattern Books and Trade Catalogues in the Library of the Victoria & Albert Museum* (1971) and Elizabeth McMurray, *At Home in the Thirties: The EKCO Collection of trade catalogues* (1995).

Another very large accumulation is in the Science Museum Library, although much of this is still to be added to the library's online catalogue (www.imperial.ac.uk/library/resources/cataccess. htm). Complementing this is the library's exhibition literature collection, which contains catalogues and other publications connected with public exhibitions of industrial and decorative products, for example, the 1851 Great Exhibition. Additional information about these collections is available at www.sciencemuseum.org.uk. Parts of Manchester Metropolitan University Library's large collection (www.library.mmu.ac.uk) are described in two exhibition catalogues, *Historical Trade Catalogues* (1978) and Gaye Smith, *Trade Catalogues: A hundred years 1850-1949* (1992).

Other collections reflect the industrial specialisation of the institutions that hold them. Oxford's Museum of the History of Science has many catalogues relating to scientific instruments, Sheffield Central Library is strong on silver plate and cutlery, as is Keele University on Josiah Wedgwood ceramics and the Wellcome Library on medical/surgical equipment and pharmaceuticals. For the latter *see* Michael Jones & Jean Taylor, *A Handlist of Trade Catalogues in the Wellcome Museum of the History of Medicine* (1984). Local record offices often have large groups dispersed through their collections, good examples being those of James Gibbons Ltd, locksmiths and gunsmiths of Wolverhampton, at Staffordshire Record Office, Stafford, and of Platt Saco Lowell, textile machinery manufacturers of Accrington, at Lancashire Record Office. A somewhat dated and generalised summary of library holdings is *Trade Literature in British Libraries* (1985) based on a British Library survey.

PARLIAMENTARY PAPERS AND OTHER OFFICIAL PUBLICATIONS

'Official publications' is the term used to describe British government publications issued either by the Houses of Parliament or by government departments and agencies. These cover legislation, Parliamentary activity and government policy as well as research reports, annual reports, statistical data and the like. A complete set of them from the 17th century would probably total well in excess of 250,000 items; in addition there are an unknown number of unofficial publications. Given the interest of the legislature and of government departments in the performance, regulation and well-being of the economy and of business and industry, official publications are of obvious interest to business historians.

The most significant historical component of official publications for business history is British Parliamentary Papers, which were either laid before Parliament or produced at its command. They were printed as a matter of routine and, historically, fell into three groups, viz.: reports of committees of members of both houses; reports of royal commissions or departmental committees appointed by the Crown or ministers; and accounts and papers comprising a wide variety of accounts, returns, estimates and bills ordered to be presented to Parliament, sometimes on a regular annual basis. Public bills are included but not private ones. The latter often relate to specific individuals, businesses and other institutions and are available in the Parliamentary Archives (q.v.). Parliamentary Papers are held by the national libraries, leading academic and good reference libraries and can be located via BOPCRIS (q.v.). The British Library and the London School of Economics have particularly good collections.

The practice of holding British Parliamentary Papers in a bound set began in 1801 although until 1833 many presented papers were bound in a separate series called House of Commons Journals. Papers for each Parliamentary session were bound into a discrete set of volumes and by 1925 some 7,000 volumes existed. From 1807 onwards an annual subject index was included, which was subsequently supported by periodic cumulative indexes. Many pre-1801 Parliamentary Papers were brought together retrospectively in the 19th century. Initially a selection of papers for the years 1715 to 1801 was reprinted and bound in 15 volumes; it is known as 'first series'. Subsequently further papers were selected and bound in 111 volumes; it is known as the 'Abbott Collection'. In the 1970s, all these, plus others not earlier reprinted, were published in facsimile in Sheila Lambert (ed.), *House of Commons Sessional Papers of the 18th Century* (147 vols, 1975-6). Some unprinted papers, for the Lords from 1531 and for the Commons from 1851, exist in the Parliamentary Archives.

The huge diversity of Parliamentary Papers makes summarising their business history content in broad categories quite difficult. Bills and the reports and evidence of select committees and royal commissions contain much information about the environment in which businesses operated, about production, exports and imports, taxes paid, market processes and about general performance. In the 19th century, trading in commodities such as grain, tobacco, sugar, cocoa, coffee, timber, cotton and wool received much attention from Parliament and is well covered. So are extractive industries such as coal and tin-mining, transport industries including canals, railways and shipping, distilling and brewing, fishing, gas production, shipbuilding and the textile industries. The evidence submitted by leading individual businessmen and industrial bodies to committees and commissions is of particular interest.

Business-specific information is not as plentiful and often appears as data ordered to be presented to Parliament, sometimes on an ongoing annual basis, following the introduction of related legislation. In other words, it allowed Parliament to keep watch on the effects of the legislation it had passed. In the 19th century it includes, for example, schedules of stamp duty paid by named fire insurance offices; returns of named assurance companies; numerous schedules relating to named joint stock and private banks; details of gas companies; schedules of newly registered joint stock companies; and so on. In the 20th century there is much information about businesses in public ownership or subject to particular public scrutiny, especially water, gas, electricity, coal and iron and steel.

In the 20th century the rigorousness with which papers of relevance to Parliament were filed as Parliamentary Papers diminished. Prior to 1921 few papers of importance were omitted but thereafter changes in the practice of distribution meant the exclusion of papers deemed to be inessential, a term that was only very loosely defined. These included, for example, many annual reports and other publications of government-appointed bodies, nationalised industries and the like, many of which have significant interest to business historians. The number of these non-Parliamentary Papers has grown significantly over the years and they are far more difficult to locate.

Several helpful guides to official publications exist. Useful starting points are Richard H.A. Cheffins, *How to Find Information: Official publications* (2004), which provides an excellent overview, and the more specialised but dated Peter and Grace Ford, *Guide to Parliamentary*

Papers: What they are, how to find them, how to use them (1972). Others include Frank Rodgers, *A Guide to British Government Publications* (1980), Stephen Richard, *Directory of British Official Publications: A guide to sources* (1984) and David Butcher, *Official Publications in Britain* (1991), which also deals with local government.

In recent years, access to Parliamentary Papers has been significantly enhanced by digitisation and, earlier, by reprinting. In the late 1960s Irish University Press reprinted papers of importance to historical research in a 1,000-volume series grouped by broad subject category. These include ports and telegraphs (8 vols), shipping (9 vols), trade and industry (11 vols), insurance and friendly societies (10 vols), monetary policy including banks (31 vols), and transport (22 vols); despite digitisation these remain highly useful for browsing. Nineteenth *and* 20th-century papers have also been published in microfiche format by Chadwyck-Healey, the 19th-century component supported by a comprehensive subject index. More recently, digitisation has made a major impact with several projects underway. The most significant are Chadwyck Healey's digitisation and indexing of House of Commons Parliamentary Papers (HCPP) from 1801 to the present, which can be accessed on a subscription basis (www.parlipapers.chadwyck.com), and BOPCRIS's Parl18C (www.bopcris.ac.uk), which covers 18th-century Parliamentary publications generally, including Parliamentary Papers. Access to this resource is restricted to higher and further education institutions and other key libraries.

In locating official publications BOPCRIS (British Official Publications Collaborative Reader Information Service) (www.bopcris.ac.uk) is helpful. It covers around 40,000 key publications from 1688 to 1995, providing bibliographical details and usually an abstract. It also carries details of holdings of individual libraries. Much of its content is based on the painstaking work of indexing and abstracting by Peter and Grace Ford and their successors and published in hard-copy form between 1951 and 1989. Hard-copy cumulative subject indexes to House of Commons papers cover the periods 1801-52, 1852-99, 1900-49 and at decennial intervals thereafter. Less complete indexes exist for House of Lords 19th-century papers and to 18th-century papers generally.

The Houses of Lords and Commons archives are held in the Parliamentary Archives (sometime House of Lords Record Office) (www.parliament.uk) and include papers created by or presented to Parliament. These include British Parliamentary Papers but much else besides. Of particular importance are private and personal bills and acts, most of which have been digitised (www.bopcris.ac.uk), and related papers. Many of these are business-specific and include especially extensive maps, plans and committee evidence accumulated as a result of the promotion of private acts for the construction of canals, railways, roads and other utilities. The Parliamentary Archives' website holds a guide to its collections and provides access to its catalogue. Parts of the catalogue are available via the A2A initiative. A comprehensive hard-copy guide is Maurice F. Bond, *Guide to the Records of Parliament* (1971).

MAPS AND PLANS

The Use of Maps

Large scale maps, defined here as one inch or more to the mile, are a little used resource for tracing the history of a business but can be especially useful for 18th- and early 19th-century research when so few sources exist. A huge number and range of maps exist, far more varied than is generally appreciated.

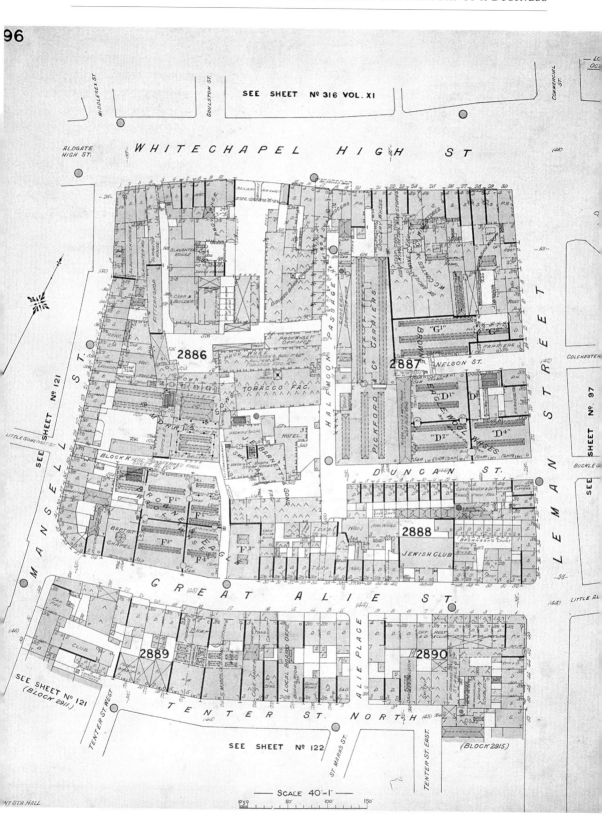

Maps show the physical environment in which a business operated. Such contextual information includes nearby transport facilities; for example, turnpike roads, canals, railways and ports; raw material supplies from nearby mines and quarries; neighbouring businesses that may have been competitors or suppliers; sources of demand when goods were produced for local consumption; sources of labour in neighbouring towns and villages; and so on. The comparison of one map with another reveals changes over time.

Particularly large-scale maps and plans, which usually date from the second half of the 19th century, show the footprint of buildings and might mark features such as function, floor size and sometimes even height and materials used in construction. Once again comparison of different maps shows what additions, demolitions or modifications to premises were made over time. For this purpose, large-scale maps are certainly more helpful than earlier small-scale maps, but even the latter mark windmills and watermills, often along with their function, as well as coal pits; iron, tin and lead mines; salt works; forges; lime works; and so on.

Paul Hindle, *Maps for Historians* (1998) considers the value of maps as a source for historians, while Catherine Delano-Smith and Roger J.P. Kain, *English Maps: A history* (1999) provides a useful overview of the history of mapmaking.

Early County and Town Maps

Large-scale mapmaking in Britain dates back to the 16th century, when county maps on scales varying from 1 inch/1.5 miles to 1 inch/5 miles were published. Christopher Saxton, the leading cartographer at this time, mapped over 30 counties and his work was not surpassed until the 18th century and the publication of a new generation of county maps, surveyed by the likes of Thomas Jefferys and Benjamin Dodd. By 1800 only Cambridgeshire among English counties had not been resurveyed. Invariably scales were 1 inch/1 mile but sometimes to 2 miles. Another generation of similar county maps, by Christopher Greenwood and Andrew Bryant, appeared in the 1820s and 1830s. The production of maps on a county basis was an enduring feature of British mapmaking until the appearance of Ordnance Survey maps shortly after 1800.

E.M. Rogers, *The Large Scale County Maps of the British Isles, 1596-1850* (2nd edn, 1972) provides a schedule of these early maps while David Smith, 'The representation of industry on large scale maps of England and Wales, 1700-c1840', *Industrial Archaeology Review* (1990) provides an excellent assessment of their accuracy and comprehensiveness with regard to the marking of industrial sites. Significant landscape features in rural areas, such as watermills, windmills, mines and quarries, were much more likely to be marked than non-specialist industrial buildings, which were the norm at this early time. Transport infrastructure, such as turnpikes, other roads and canals, was well depicted. One recurring issue affecting the

29   *Large-scale maps and plans show business premises and, through comparison, how the footprint of these premises changed over time. Smaller-scale maps show the geographical area in which a business operated. The plans of Charles Goad, such as the one of Shoreditch, London, reproduced here, are especially valuable in giving details of footprint and business environment.*

accuracy of early maps is the time delay, sometimes measured in years, between dates of survey and publication.

Town maps and plans, of more help to historians on account of their larger scale and greater level of detail, date back to the 16th century but were published in much greater numbers from the 18th century. London led the way, with almost 200 maps appearing in the 100 years after 1700; as many again were published in the next 50 years. Some were of particularly large scale, such as Richard Horwood's 26 inch/1 mile map published between 1792 and 1799; it extended to four editions. Other cities and towns were not nearly as well catered for until after 1800, when the greatest demand came from the relatively wealthy and rapidly expanding centres of industry. John West, *Town Records* (1983) provides a useful gazetteer of many hundreds of town maps arranged by name of town. James Howgeyo, *Printed Maps of London circa 1553-1850* (1978) lists maps of the capital.

Ordnance Survey Maps

The Ordnance Survey, which came to dominate the market for general topographical maps, started to publish in 1801. Its maps were initially on a scale of 1 inch/1 mile, were much more accurate than earlier maps and broke the tradition of publishing on a county basis. The earliest ones, known as Old Series, were for South-East and South-West England and East Anglia; by 1844 90 per cent of England and Wales had been mapped with the last sheets appearing in 1873-4. Scotland was further behind, its first 1 inch maps being published between 1856 and 1887. Well before the completion of the first mapping programme, early sheets of Old Series were initially revised on an ad hoc basis and then updated periodically and republished in new editions. The earliest Old Series sheets have been reprinted in book format under the title *The Old Series Ordnance Survey Maps of England and Wales, Scale 1 Inch to 1 Mile* (8 vols, 1975-92).

The field surveys on which the Old Series sheets were based are lodged in the British Library's Map Library. These original historical documents are usually on a larger scale than 1 inch, sometimes being 2, 3 or 6 inches/1 mile, and have a greater level of detail than their published counterparts. Microfiche copies are available. As with other early maps, dates of survey and publication vary significantly, especially early on. Dating is further complicated by dates of ad hoc revision not being printed on Old Series sheets, which continued to carry original date of publication.

Demand soon existed for larger-scale maps, so from the early 1840s future field surveys were on a scale of 6 inches/1 mile; progressively between 1854 and 1863 this was upgraded to 25 inches/1 mile. Therefore, the final Old Series sheets, including all those for Scotland, were based on much more detailed surveys than hitherto. Yorkshire and Lancashire were chosen for the first 6-inch surveys undertaken from 1840; the first 25-inch surveys, which began in 1854, were of the four most northerly counties. Eventually 6-inch maps were published for the whole of Britain and 25-inch maps for most of it, with the exception of sparsely populated areas. By 1900 some 15,000 6-inch sheets and 50,000 25-inch sheets existed. Revision and republishing were subsequently undertaken regularly.

These large-scale surveys show the function and footprint of buildings in clear detail and, when one edition is compared with another, show changes in premises layout and function over time. For urban areas this level of detail was further enhanced with the publication of very large-scale town plans on scales of 5 feet/1 mile from about 1843,

10 feet/1 mile from about 1850 and 10.56 feet/1 mile from about 1855. Manchester and Leeds in about 1843 were probably the first cities to be dealt with; by 1850 plans on a scale of 5 feet/1 mile existed or were in progress for 40 cities and towns. The 10.56-feet series proved to be the most enduring one, with 400 cities and towns mapped in this way between 1855 and 1895.

It should be added that the early history of Ordnance Survey maps is a good deal more complicated than the above account suggests. It is well related by J.B. Harley, *The Historian's Guide to Ordnance Survey Maps* (1964), while Richard Oliver, *Ordnance Survey Maps: A Concise Guide for Historians* (1993) provides a more detailed discussion and has useful schedules of town plans and larger-scale maps. Paul Hindle, *Maps for Historians* (1998) provides an excellent overview.

Maps for Special Purposes

A vast range of other large-scale maps exists, very often in manuscript form and dating from the early 19th century. Among these, some broad categories can be identified, which are fully explored in Paul Hindle, *Maps for Historians*.

One is estate maps, which were commissioned by country landowners to facilitate management of their estates. They show rural industrial sites such as watermills, windmills and mines, but from time to time also cover urban areas when towns had encroached upon the landowner's estate. Another category, relating to rural areas, is enclosure maps commissioned to assist the enclosure and redistribution of land within parishes as a step to agricultural improvement. These date from the mid-18th to the mid-19th century, by which time 5,000 enclosure awards had been granted, covering 20 per cent of England's land surface. Another group is tithe maps commissioned following the 1836 Tithe Commutation Act that reorganised the basis of tithe payments to the Church of England. Now tithes would be paid by landowners on the basis of acreage and quality of land, and maps were required for their calculation. Local record offices have fine collections of all these maps, while tithe maps are also in the National Archives and the National Library of Wales. For more about tithe maps *see* Roger J.P. Kain and Hugh C. Prince, *Tithe Surveys for Historians* (2000), and for enclosure maps *see* Steven Hollowell, *Enclosure Records for Historians* (2000).

Town maps and plans were also made for special purposes. These include landownership maps commissioned by urban landowners such as the Church of England, educational institutions, local authorities, livery companies, charities, property companies and railway companies for the management of their estates. Another group is parochial assessment maps drawn up in the 1840s following rating reform that linked rates to property value; some 4,000 were produced. A third group is improvement and planning maps commissioned for the approval and construction of railway, canal, road, tramway, port, utility and similar projects that caused huge change to the townscape.

Of particular interest are town plans produced for risk assessment by fire insurance companies. In densely built urban/industrial areas, an insurance company's actual risk/exposure could only be accurately assessed by reference to risks in the neighbourhood as a whole and not just on its customer's premises. In order to assess this risk, fire insurance companies used particularly large-scale plans showing in great detail the footprint and construction of buildings. The earliest ones were produced by insurance companies but few survive. Of much greater importance are the plans of Charles Goad (1848-1910) and his firm, Chas E. Goad Ltd, which were made for leasing to fire insurance companies on a long-term basis. Between about 1885 and the late 1960s, they produced plans, generally on a scale of 1 inch/40 feet, for 53 urban areas comprising 126 central retail and industrial districts; revisions were made every five years or so. Individual properties are clearly labelled with business name, product line, dimensions, construction details and particular hazards such as steam engines and boilers. Cross sections and isometric projections are sometimes included. Large collections of Goad plans exist at the British Library, Guildhall Library, London Metropolitan Archives, Manchester Central Library and other important reference libraries and local record offices. Others remain in the ownership of Goads and are described in Chas E. Goad Ltd, *Goad Fire Insurance Plan Catalogue: Part A, British Isles* (1984). For an overview *see* Gwyn Rowley, 'British fire insurance plans: The Goad productions c1885-c1970', *Archives* (1985) and for details of their location *see* Gwyn Rowley, *British Fire Insurance Plans* (1984).

The categorisation of maps into a limited number of well-defined categories should not mask the sheer diversity of British map collections. The collections of the National Archives (www.catalogue.nationalarchives.gov.uk) and of the National Archives of Scotland (www.nas.gov.uk) well illustrate the point. The former's collection dates mostly from the 16th century and relates largely to the day-to-day work of government departments. It includes tithe maps, which form part of the Tithe Commission's archives, land valuation maps (created for the calculation of estate duty) of the Valuations Office, maps of pre-nationalisation railway and canal companies, maps required for the management of assets of the Crown Estate and the Duchy of Lancaster, maps deposited in courts for litigation purposes, and so on. More details are available in *Maps and Plans in the Public Record Office* (1967).

Locating Maps

The major map collections in Britain are at the British Library (www.bl.com), the National Library of Scotland (www.nls.uk/collections/maps), the National Library of Wales (www.llgc.org.uk), the National Archives (www.catalogue.nationalarchives.gov.uk), the National Archives of Scotland (www.nas.gov.uk) and the Royal Geographical Society (www.rgs.org). Catalogues to their collections can be accessed online. A somewhat unlikely source is the Parliamentary Archives (www.parliament.uk), which holds maps deposited in connection with private bills for canal building from 1794 and for railway building from 1803 and especially from 1836. *See* Maurice F. Bond, *Guide to the Records of Parliament* (London, 1971).

Helen Wallis and Anita McConnell (eds), *Historian's Guide to Early British Maps* (1994) provides general descriptions of the holdings of a wide range of repositories in Britain and has useful short essays on different map types. It has now been succeeded by the Directory of UK Map Collections, compiled in 2000 by Joan Chibnall and accessed via the British Cartographic Society's website (www.cartography.org.uk).

Geoff Armitage provides useful cartobibliographies of both county and town maps in a series of four articles, viz.: G. Armitage, 'County Cartobibliographies of England and Wales', *The Map Collector* (1990, 1995) and 'Cartobibliographies of City and Town Plans of England and Wales', *The Map Collector* (1994). For Scotland *see* John N. Moore, *The Historical Cartography of Scotland: A guide to the literature of Scottish maps and mapping prior to the Ordnance Survey* (2nd edn, 1991).

PERSONAL RECORDS

Private Papers

The private papers of former chairmen, directors, major shareholders and the like, as well as those of founding families, may well be of great value in tracing the history of a business. This is because they relate in summary form to every aspect of a business's activities, in particular dealing with performance and strategy.

For the most part, private papers of senior managers form a discrete group within a business's archives largely on account of their confidentiality. However, sometimes some become detached from the main archive, perhaps when senior people on retirement take them home. There they may be added to as a result of non-executive work during retirement. Whatever the case, private papers accumulate away from the business and may eventually pass into the ownership of descendants. They become especially useful if the business, along with its archives, subsequently disappears.

Such papers may include board and other committee minutes, papers submitted to the board, files of correspondence with the chairman and other senior managers, brochures, photographs and so on. In the case of a founder, or a direct descendant of a founder, papers may be more wide-ranging, reflecting the family's contribution to the business's establishment and early success. The papers of a major shareholder may include annual reports, shareholders' circulars, statements made at general meetings and brokers' reports. Retired members of a partnership might keep partnership deeds and accounts.

Less senior staff may accumulated at home papers such as house journals, photographs of staff events, details of pension funds, newspaper cuttings and so on. Once again these might be passed down to descendants.

A starting point in locating such private papers is, of course, the business itself, if it still survives, or its pension fund. They may well be in touch with past executives or their families and be prepared to forward to them letters requesting assistance. If the whereabouts of any papers are known to the National Register of Archives (www.nationalarchives.gov.uk/nra) or the National Register of Archives for Scotland (www.nras.gov.uk) reference to them will be made in their online registers. Failing this, the task of locating descendants will require common sense and detective work.

As a postscript, it is worth stating that detached private papers relating to a particular business may also turn up in the archives of another business with which the person in question was also connected and there are many precedents for this. The most likely location is the business with which the person was most closely associated. The annual *Directory of Directors*, first published in 1880, is useful in discovering directorships held by an individual in major businesses.

Wills and Related Documents

The Use of Wills

Wills and associated documentation are especially helpful in shedding light on businessmen and women and through them their businesses, and this is especially so before the 19th century when few documentary sources are available to the historian. In particular, wills name relatives, friends, executors and witnesses and therefore provide some notion of the deceased's

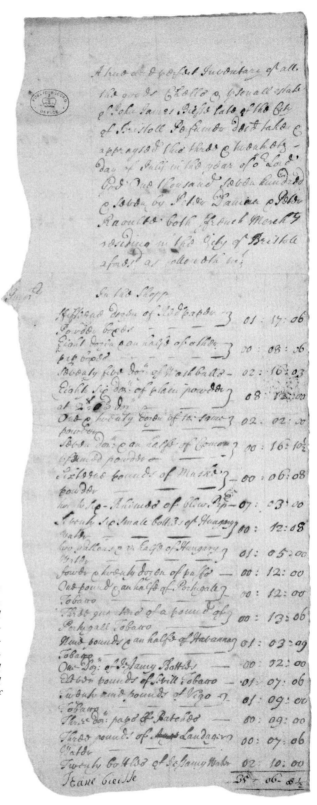

30   *A useful source of information about businesses and businessmen and women are wills and associated inventories, especially as many date back to a period when few other sources exist. Probate inventories are especially useful, providing lists and values of property. This one is dated 1707 and relates to the estate of John Bieisse, perfumer of Bristol.*

business network. Addresses of town, country and overseas residences may be given and household goods, chattels, securities and real estate referred to. Charities and educational institutions with which the deceased was associated may be listed as beneficiaries, shedding light on origins and interests. Perhaps even more important, these tiny pieces of information suggest routes to other sources.

Documentation associated with wills includes inventories and/or valuations that detail items making up an estate, and are of real help to historians. Other related documentation includes national probate calendars from 1858 that, for English and Welsh estates, provide a total valuation of the deceased's estate, although good reasons exist for treating the accuracy of this figure with caution.

Its also worth noting that a large proportion of the population did not make wills, while not all wills were processed; even by 1858 only 10 per cent of deceased people left a will, although the figure for businessmen and women is bound to be higher in view of their more valuable and complex estates.

History of Will-Making

The history of will making is long and complicated, dating back to Anglo-Saxon times. Before 1858 the proving of wills was largely undertaken by a variety of local courts, mostly connected with the established church. At one stage over 200 such courts existed and a will was usually proved in the court in whose jurisdiction the deceased died, but also in others if the estate was geographically dispersed. For example, if an estate exceeded £5 (for provincial estates) or £10 (for London estates) in more than one diocese, the will would be proved in either the Prerogative Court of Canterbury or the Prerogative Court of York, or both if there was property in both archdioceses. Otherwise the will would be dealt with in a lower court such as that of a bishop or archdeacon. The £5 and £10 qualifications did not change over time and so more and more wills were proved in the Courts of Canterbury and York.

Probate inventories were required by the courts in order to make the administration of wills as transparent as possible and to ensure that debts were paid off ahead of the distribution of the estate to beneficiaries. Sometimes an account detailing the administration of the estate was attached to the inventory. Such records are, of course, of great interest to the historian of a business; they might give a value for each item listed and provide fascinating insight into the nature of an early businessman's assets. Inventories are discussed in several publications, but Barrie Trinder and Jeff Cox, *Yeomen and Colliers in Telford* (1980) gives interesting perspective by reproducing and analysing some 250 estates, most of which belonged to tradesmen. Another important archive series sometimes kept by the courts is probate registers into which wills were copied; they are obviously useful if the original will has not survived.

The role of ecclesiastical courts in proving wills was swept away in January 1858 by a new national Court of Probate, supported by a network of district registries. Hitherto proved wills had been stored or otherwise recorded in probate registers or both by the different ecclesiastical courts. From 1858 they would be stored centrally, making their present-day location vastly easier and ensuring their survival. They were recorded in probate calendars, which give a total valuation for most estates, although this figure should be treated with some caution.

In Scotland the probate process was somewhat different, although the information to be derived from the resulting documentation is similar. Between 1515 and 1823 probate was obtained via a network of secular commissary courts. These were abolished, mostly in the 1820s, and replaced by sheriff courts that still retain a probate function.

Karren Grannum and Nigel Taylor, *Wills and Other Probate Records* (2004) and, on a smaller scale, Jane Cox, *Affection Defying Death: Wills, probate and death duty records* (1998) provide excellent accounts of will documentation. Scottish wills are well dealt with in Alwyn James, *Scottish Roots: The step by step guide to tracing your Scottish ancestors* (2002).

Locating Wills

Because pre-1858 wills were proved in so many courts, those that survive are well-scattered. Many ended up in diocesan record offices and have invariably been transferred to local record offices. The most important early groups are wills proved in the Prerogative Courts of Canterbury (PCC) and York (PCY), which today are lodged in the National Archives (www.nationalarchives.gov.uk) and the University of York's Borthwick Institute (www.york.ac.uk/inst/bihr) respectively. The PCY records include most original wills from 1660 onwards, many original inventories from 1688 and most probate registers (which also include inventories) from 1389. PCC records include many original wills from around 1650, some registered copies of wills from 1383, and inventories from 1417 although from 1710 only required in the event of litigation.

The location of English and Welsh wills and letters of administration proved from January 1858 is far simpler. Both the original and a copy were stored centrally while an additional copy was retained in the district registry where the will was proved. From 1858, the Principal Registry of the Court of Probate compiled an annual schedule of proved wills in the National Probate Calendar; this has been done on an annual basis ever since. The calendar, along with wills, can be consulted at Principal Registry of the Family Division, London.

Copies of wills accumulated by the post-1858 district registries have been transferred to local record offices. These also sometimes hold microfiche copies of the calendar and, in a few cases, paper copies, also transferred from district registries. Scottish wills and associated documentation are in the National Archives of Scotland and Welsh wills are in the National Library of Wales. A number of useful guides exist to the location of wills, including Jeremy Gibson and Else Churchill, *Probate Jurisdictions: Where to look for wills* (2002) and Anthony J. Camp, *Wills and their Whereabouts* (1974).

Locating wills is being made easier by digitisation and availability online. In this the National Archives and the National Archives of Scotland have led the way. One million PCC wills, proved between 1383 and 1858, have been digitised by the National Archives and can be accessed at www.documentsonline.nationalarchives.gov.uk. Scottish wills between 1500 and 1901 can be accessed at www.scottishdocuments.com. In both cases searching is free but downloading is chargeable. Otherwise, finding individual wills has been greatly facilitated by indexes to local record office holdings drawn up by, say, local history societies. These are available in a variety of formats – card indexes, publications and online – and are described in Gibson and Churchill and in Camp (*see* above).

Estate Duty Registers

These registers, available in the National Archives, cover the years 1796 to 1903 and relate to taxes paid on deceased estates; strictly speaking they are not probate records but records of a government tax department. They embrace a surprisingly large proportion of estates; for example, perhaps 75 per cent of the total between 1805 and 1815 and all those valued in excess of £20 after 1857. No registers survive for the post-1903 period.

The registers are held in the National Archives in series IR26 and indexes to the registers are in series IR27. They give details of the deceased, of his or her executors or administrators, of bequests and beneficiaries and also provide a valuation, although for reasons considered earlier this should be used with caution; much of this information will be in the will. However, for smaller estates such details may not have been recorded. As working records they were often annotated with additional information. To facilitate access, the registers are in the process of digitisation, those for the years 1796 to 1811 having been covered by early 2008. As an aside, the indexes to the registers, which are arranged by name of the deceased, show the place at which the will was proved thereby providing a useful if unintended means of locating wills proved in ecclesiastical courts prior to 1858. There are other series relating to estate duties that are referred to in a useful National Archives research guide, 'Death Duty Records from 1796' but many are subject to a 75-year closure period. Death duty archives for Scotland are held in the National Archives of Scotland. Grannum and Taylor, above, provide a detailed account of them.

Valuation of Estates

The accuracy of valuations of estates appearing in probate inventories, probate calendars, estate duty registers, etc, has been much debated and it is clear that they cannot be taken as an accurate reflection of the deceased's wealth. Sometimes, for example, wealth was disposed of prior to death to avoid taxation, while at other times valuations may simply have been inaccurate. More importantly, debts were excluded, as were certain categories of land. On balance, these factors point to under-valuation.

William D. Rubenstein and Daniel H. Duman, 'Probate valuations', *The Local Historian* (11, 1974) provides a succinct account of issues so far as probate calendars are concerned. Valuations in estate duty registers are rigorously debated in Barbara English, 'Probate valuations and the death duty registers', *Bulletin of the Institute of Historical Research* (1984) and in Barbara English, 'Wealth at death in the 19th century' and M.L. Collinge, 'Probate valuations and the death duty registers', *Bulletin of the Institute of Historical Research* (1987). Nancy Cox and Jeff Cox, 'Probate inventories: The legal background', *The Local Historian* (2 parts, 16, 1984) deals well with the issues underpinning the content and reliability of probate inventories.

Interviews

The recollections of directors, partners, managers and other employees make a significant contribution to tracing the history of a relatively modern business, filling gaps in documentary evidence and providing new interpretations that might not necessarily have been, or needed to have been, committed to paper. Interviews have played a key part in the writing of many recent corporate histories such as David Kynaston, *Cazenove & Co.: A history* (1991); Edgar Jones, *The Business of Medicine: The extraordinary history of Glaxo* (2001); and T.R. Gourvish, *British Railways* (2 vols, 1986, 2002) which the last writer briefly alludes to in 'Writing British Rail's history', *Business Archives* (1991). Some publications have relied almost entirely on interviews, such as Leonard Spacek, *The Growth of Arthur Andersen & Co, 1928-73: An oral history* (1989) where discussions between Spacek, a retired senior partner of Andersens, and his business associates, explain the emergence of this now defunct force in international accountancy.

Wives, partners, widows and children also have their story to tell, especially when they were in direct contact with the business. A recent HSBC Group project, for example, reviewed the role of wives and family in supporting branch and other senior managers of Hongkong & Shanghai Banking Corp when working overseas between the 1930s and 1990s.

The work of the National Life Stories Collection (NLSC) (www.bl.uk/collections/sound-archive/nlsc.html), an independent charity operating within the oral history section of the British Library Sound Archive, is an especially interesting resource for business historians. Established in 1987, its mission is to 'record first-hand experiences of as wide a cross-section of present-day society as possible' and much of its output has been workplace-related and supported by the associated industry body. Over the years an interview bank has accumulated through such projects as *Architects' Lives*, *Book Trade Lives*, *City Lives*, *Food: From Source to Salespoint*, *Lives in Steel*, *Lives in the Oil Industry* and *An Oral History of the Post Office*; several remain in progress. Each project very roughly comprises 100 interviews with people drawn from all strata of the industry, although the tendency is to focus on senior management. Interviews, along with summaries and transcripts, are accessible via the National Sound Archives' website. The City Lives project formed the basis of Cathy Courtney and Paul Thompson, *City Lives: The changing voices of British finance* (1996). NLSC's annual reports give good coverage of developments.

Another project in a broadly similar vein, funded by the Institute of Chartered Accountants in England & Wales, comprised 70 interviews with retired or long-serving chartered accountants and dealt with the changing nature of the company audit. Transcriptions, along with introductory chapters on interview techniques and lessons learnt, are contained in D. Mathews and J. Pirie, *Auditors' Talk: An oral history of a profession from the 1920s to the present day* (2001). Other useful insight may be got from Peter Pagnamenta and Richard Overy, *All Our Working Lives* (1984), a social and industrial history of Britain based extensively on interviews.

Although it may appear straightforward at first glance, effective interviewing is far from easy in practice. Paul Thompson, *The Voice of the Past: Oral History* (1988) provides sound practical advice on the interviewing process and on establishing an interviewing project, and also explores and evaluates the effectiveness of interviews. Robert Perks and Alistair Thomson (eds), *The Oral History Reader* (1998) adopts a more wide-ranging textbook approach while Margaret Brooks, 'A beginner's guide to establishing an oral history archive', *Proceedings of the Annual Conference of the Business Archives Council* (1987) provides a short summary of issues. A key requirement is the development of an effective interviewing technique and questioning strategy ahead of the event in order to maximise an opportunity that might not return.

Census Records

Census records provide only a tiny amount of information but are invaluable when used with sources such as trade directories, apprenticeship records, wills and the like to construct a profile of a small businessman. Apart from giving personal details, census records provide information about his family and address, his neighbours and his neighbourhood, and even his apparent affluence as judged by, say, the number of his live-in servants or workers.

Census returns become more detailed over time, but generally from 1841 they name, on the night of the census, all people at a particular address and for each give age, occupation and relationship to the head of the household. Details are also given of employees such as servants, shop workers and apprentices.

A census of the UK population was first held in 1801 and subsequent censuses have taken place every 10 years. However, only those census records more than 100 years old are available for public inspection while those prior to 1841 give only population totals and therefore are not helpful in tracing the background of a particular person.

Records for all censuses have survived and originals for England and Wales are held in the National Archives; those for Scotland are in Edinburgh at the General Register Office for Scotland. Access and searching have become vastly easier with the digitisation of census records, which can be accessed at www.nationalarchives.gov.uk/census for England and Wales and at www.gro-scotland.gov.uk for Scotland.

Susan Lumas, *Making Use of the Census* (2002, reprinted 2004) is a standard guide to census records in England and Wales. Cecil Sinclair, *Jock Tamson's Bairns: A history of the records of the General Register Office for Scotland* (c.2000) covers census records in Scotland.

Visual Sources

Industrial Archaeology

Visits to the surviving factories, other plant and offices of a business can provide useful insight into the scale and nature of its activities; the general environment in which it operated; its proximity to transport facilities, markets and raw materials; its access to sources of labour and the houses in which its workers and managers may have lived in; and its size relative to neighbouring businesses. Even when buildings have not survived, site visits can still be informative.

Close observation might enable the dating of individual buildings and the sequence of plant expansion to be understood. Original machinery and artefacts are unlikely to survive in situ, but the scale, complexity and nature of the work process can be discovered through visits to industry, technology and transport museums, where similar plant can be examined.

Industrial archaeology surveys are obviously especially useful when the buildings they deal with have not survived. Here much excellent work has been carried out by groups of enthusiasts in collaboration with academic specialists. Many are organised in local societies and publish newsletters and local guides. Sometimes they hold, or have access to, surveys by individual members. Reports are complemented by a growing literature on the architecture of industrial buildings and districts, for example Lynn Pearson, *British Breweries: An Architectural History* (London, 1999) and John Cattell, Sheila Ely and Barry Jones, *The Birmingham Jewellery Quarter: An architectural survey of the manufactories* (Swindon, 2002).

An umbrella organisation for industrial archaeology is the Association for Industrial Archaeology (www.industrial-archaeology.org.uk), which since 1976 has published the *Industrial Archaeology Review*. This deals with surveys, excavations, industrial development, particular sites and processes and local guides. Abstracts and an index to articles appear on its website. IA Recordings (www.iarecordings.org) is concerned with recording on film industrial processes; its website, as well as dealing with this, provides linkages to a large number of sites of institutions and groups concerned with industrial archaeology. Another publication of relevance is *Industrial Archaeology: The journal of the history of industry and technology*, which appeared between 1964 and 1980.

Important central sources of information about industrial archaeology sites are English Heritage's National Monuments Record (www.english-heritage.org.uk), the Royal Commission on the Ancient and Historical Monuments of Scotland (www.rcahms.gov.uk) and the Royal Commission on Ancient and Historical Monuments of Wales (www.rcahmw.gov.uk). Science, technology, transport and industrial museums also have relevant resources.

Useful introductions to industrial archaeology are Kenneth Hudson, *Industrial Archaeology: An Introduction* (London, 1963) and R.A. Buchanan, *Industrial Archaeology in Britain* (3rd edition, Harmondsworth, 1982). Process recording – i.e. the recording of industrial processes or the 'archaeology of work' – is considered in Brian Malaws, 'Process Recording at Industrial Sites' and in Richard Hayman, 'The Archaeologist as Witness: Matthew Harvey's Glebeland Works, Walsall', both are in *Industrial Archaeology Review* (19, 1997). Barrie Trinder (ed.), *Blackwell Encyclopedia of Industrial Archaeology* (Oxford, 1992), covers the years 1650 to 1950 and provides useful basic information. The 20th century is surveyed in Michael Stratton and Barrie Trinder, *20th Century Industrial Archaeology* (2000). A vast literature exists for industrial archaeology in the UK and a finding aid to it is the online British & Irish Archaeological Bibliography (www.biab.ac.uk).

Images: Photographs, Films, Prints, Drawings

Images include, on the one hand, photographs, prints, drawings and paintings and, on the other, moving images. They record information about a business's buildings, people, processes and products as well as the environment in which it operated. Their importance in illustrating publications and presentations is obvious and they supplement information available from sources such as maps and industrial archaeology surveys.

Photography was invented in the late 1830s and had been widely adopted by the late 19th century. Prior to photography, illustrations for printing were derived from engravings, which themselves may have been copied from pencil or watercolour drawings or oil paintings. The first routine use of images by businesses may well have been as illustrations in trade catalogues and advertisements; the earliest photographs in a business's archives are nearly always of the goods it produced. Particular subjects covered by images include portraits of the founder and other senior managers; the streets and neighbourhoods in which the business was based; the plant it used and the products it sold; its offices and factories, especially at the time of opening; interiors of factories, shops and offices showing work processes; and employees especially when participating in events such as parties and outings.

Moving images also shed light on work processes and environment. British businesses were some of the first to realise the potential of film; an 1899 promotional film by the matchmakers Bryant & May about the supply of matches to troops fighting in the Boer War is an early surviving example. Early on, business films had three functions – to advertise products, to promote the business's image, and to instruct and motivate staff. Some of the first image promotion films were commissioned by the likes of Lever Brothers in 1898 to show work and life at its giant Port Sunlight soap factory; by Peek Frean in 1906 to show off its biscuit factory in Bermondsey; and in 1903 by the North Borneo Co. to give its British shareholders insight in to its activities overseas. Advertising films of the 1920s relate to products as far removed as Daimler cars and Coleman pastry products, while staff-oriented films include the 1955 'Home and Away' by Glasgow engineers Babcock & Wilcox, and 'Ingot Pictorial' by steelmakers Richard Thomas & Baldwin.

Museums, record offices and local history libraries hold photograph collections, while others are with long-established commercial photography studios and private collectors. Towns of significant size were usually served by at least one professional photographer by the late 19th century and some of the earliest are described in Bernard and Pauline Heathcote, *A Faithful Likeness: The first photographic portrait studios in the British Isles, 1841 to 1855* (2002); their early photographs of local scenes and personalities are hugely valuable. Sometimes their photograph libraries are lodged in local record offices but otherwise remain with the business if it survives. A helpful if somewhat dated guide is John Wall, *Directory of British Photographic Collections* (London, 1977), which lists about 1,600 collections arranged in 10 subject categories. Other hard-copy guides are Hilary and Mary Evans, *The Picture Researcher's Handbook* (6th edition, London, 1996) and Rosemary Eakins, *Picture Sources UK* (London, 1985). PhotoLondon (www.photolondon.org.uk) is a gateway to collections held in London-based museums, record offices and libraries and provides broad details of content. Photographiclibraries (www.photographiclibraries.com) is a gateway mostly to commercial picture agencies, but also includes some museums and galleries as well as major libraries outside Britain.

Particularly useful sources of building photographs are the collections of the National Monuments Record held by English Heritage (www.english-heritage.org.uk) at Swindon; the National Monuments Record of Scotland, which is part of the Royal Commission on Ancient & Historical Monuments of Scotland (www.rcahms.gov.uk); and the Royal Commission on Ancient & Historical Monuments of Wales (www.rcahmw.gov.uk) at Cardiff. The National Monuments Record holds a particularly large collection of aerial photographs. The Royal Institute of British Architects (www.riba.org) holds another significant collection relating to buildings and architecture. The archive of London's National Portrait Gallery (www.npg.org.uk) focuses on eminent individuals.

Major initiatives are underway to make collections available online through digitisation. These include the collections of the National Monuments Record (*see* above) (www.english-heritage.org.uk), Guildhall Library (www.cityoflondon.gov.uk), the British Library (www.imagesonline.bl.uk), London Metropolitan Archives (www.cityoflondon.gov.uk) and the Science Museum/National Railway Museum/National Museum of Photograph, Film and Television (www.scienceandsociety.co.uk). Of emerging importance is Images of England (www.imagesofengland.org.uk), an initiative of the National Monuments Record and the Heritage Lottery Fund to establish online a free access library of images of listed buildings; it already holds images of many industrial buildings.

The British Film Institute's National Film & Television Archive (www.bfi.org.uk) owns the country's leading collection of moving images. It comprises some 500,000 items, including documentary and fiction, amateur and professional films and, since 1990, much of the output of the BBC and commercial television. Other important sources are the Scottish Screen Archive (www.scottishscreen.com) based at Glasgow; the National Screen & Sound Archive of Wales (www.screenandsound.llgc.org.uk) at Aberystwyth; and the North West Film Archive at Manchester (www.nwfa.mmu.ac.uk). Their catalogues can be searched online.

Ephemera

Ephemera are quite difficult to define. Maurice Rickards' definition as 'minor transient documents of everyday life' is as good as any but he is first to admit that not every item of ephemera is either minor or transient.[1] Put another way, ephemera are documents disposed of shortly after use; they are useable only once or are otherwise soon outdated and in need of renewal. Their retention is often unintended except, of course, by collectors. Yet for the historian of a business, these documents add colour to an otherwise plain story of decision-making, performance and like issues. Certainly ephemera are at their most important when the output of the business lacks a tangible form.

Ephemera are wide-ranging – trade cards, textile labels, timetables, bus tickets, greeting cards, fruit wrappers, beer mats, account book labels, price lists, hotel tariffs and passenger liner lists to name but a few. Their diversity is highlighted by Maurice Rickards and Michael Twyman (ed.), *The Encyclopaedia of Ephemera: A guide to the fragmentary documents of everyday life for the collector, curator and historian* (2000).

At one level ephemera are valuable as illustrations for text, as they often have strong visual impact. At another they can contain significant information about products, activities, plant and design. Beer mats, for example, might show trade marks, brand names and images of breweries. Passenger lists identify at a glance the nature of the customer base of a shipping company and the entertainment and other services provided to it. Greeting cards illustrate the output, design capability and innovativeness of a printing business. Tickets and timetables are the only evidence of the especially transient services of bus services. Fruit wrappers are all that remains of the products distributed by fresh fruit wholesalers. Prospectuses and tariffs are the most enduring evidence of the premises and services of hotels. Picture postcards, some issued by firms, show premises, work processes, aerial views, street scenes with retail premises, advertising and so on. Potential uses of ephemera are explored in Kenneth Hudson, 'Printed ephemera and the industrial historian', *Industrial Archaeology* (1977). Janice Anderson and Edmund Swinglehurst, *Ephemera of Travel and Transport* (1981) is a well-illustrated introduction to the ephemera of its subjects.

Important ephemera collections include the University of Reading's Maurice Rickards and John Lewis Collections (www.reading.ac.uk); Manchester Metropolitan University's (www.mmu.ac.uk) collections of greeting cards and ladies albums; Middlesex University's Silver Studio Collection (www.moda.mdx.ac.uk); the British Library's Evaniou Collection (www.bl.uk); and the Bodleian Library's (www.bodley.ox.ac.uk/johnson) one million item-strong John Johnson Collection. This is described in *The John Johnson Collection: Catalogue of an exhibition* (Oxford, 1971) and *A Nation of Shopkeepers: Trade ephemera from 1654 to the 1860s in the John Johnson Collection* (Oxford, 2001). The Victoria & Albert Museum's Archive of Art & Design (www.vam.ac.uk/nal) collects ephemera on a systematic basis, which is briefly referred to in Elizabeth Lomas, *Guide to the Archives of Art and Design, Victoria & Albert Museum* (2001). The History of Advertising Trust (www.hatads.org.uk) has much ephemera embedded in its collections of marketing and business archives but maintains no dedicated collection. Reading University's Centre for Ephemera Studies publishes *Register of Ephemera Collections in the United Kingdom* (2003), which lists about five hundred collections held in public institutions (excluding national collections).

Many distinguished and highly specialised collections have been built by private collectors. Many of these collectors will probably belong to the Ephemera Society, which is able to introduce researchers to owners. This energetic society has, since 1975, published each quarter *The Ephemerist*, a journal carrying articles about different categories of ephemera.

Of all categories of ephemera, printed trade cards are of particular importance as an information source for early businesses. Their name is somewhat misleading as trade cards, for much of their existence, were not printed on card and could measure as much as 12 inches

Thomas Atkins Stationer,
at the Queens Head & Half Moon,
against Broad Street in Cheapside
London.
· Makes & Sells all Sorts of Merchants and other
Acco.t Books of yͤ best Paper neatly Bound wͭʰ
all Stationary Wares, Wholesale & Retail
at Reasonable Rates.

31 *Ephemera comprise a vast range of material. Perhaps the most useful are trade cards, which give name, address and other details of individual businesses, such as this one used by Thomas Atkins, a stationer of London.*

across. They were originally produced as a marketing document for distribution to customers or potential customers, but along the way they developed other functions such as being used as memorandum slips, invoices, posters, labels and even price lists. Makers of products such as furniture, picture frames and scientific instruments often pasted them to the underside or reverse of their products.

Trade cards invariably carried the name, occupation and address of the tradesman or business and, most importantly, a varying amount of information about products made or sold and about services offered. They were elaborately designed in order to be eye-catching but, as Kenneth Hudson (*see above*) points out, the artistic licence of designers and engravers could result in substantial exaggeration and inaccuracy, especially when it came to illustrating premises. Ambrose Heal, *London Tradesmen's Cards of the XVIII Century: An account of their origin and use* (1925) provides many illustrations as well as historical background.

A significant limitation of trade cards is that often they carry no date. Their heyday was in the 100 years from 1720, although the first ones appeared around 1600. They therefore predate other sources, such as trade directories, which give brief details about a mass of individual businesses. Providers of luxury goods and premium services, such as milliners and hosiers, stationers and cabinet makers, grocers and fishmongers, made the most use of them, especially those based in London. They were seldom used by the likes of millers and founders, horticulturists and animal keepers.

The Prints & Drawings Department of the British Museum (www.thebritishmuseum.ac.uk) possesses two major trade card collections comprising, in total, about 15,000 items collected by Sir Ambrose Heal and Sarah Banks. Guildhall Library in the City of London (www.cityoflondon.gov.uk) has around 4,000 cards and the Science Library (www.sciencemuseum.org.uk/library) has a strong collection relating to scientific instrument makers. The latter group is described in H.R. Calvert, *Scientific Trade Cards in the Science Museum Collection* (1971). Other important collections are the John Johnson Collection at the Bodleian Library (*see* above) and the Pepys Library of Magdalene College, Cambridge (www.magd.cam.ac.uk).

1. Maurice Rickards & Michael Twyman, *The Encyclopaedia of Ephemera* (2000).

BIBLIOGRAPHY

BOOKS

Abbott, D. (ed.), *Biographical Dictionary of Scientists, Engineers and Inventors* (1985)

Anderson, Janice and Swinglehurst, Edmund, *Ephemera of Travel and Transport* (1981)

Aitkins, P.J., *The Directories of London, 1677-1977* (1990)

Aldcroft, Derek H. and Oliver, Michael J., *Trade Unions and the Economy, 1870-2000* (2000)

Aldis, H.G. et al, *A Dictionary of Printers and Booksellers in England, Scotland and Ireland and of Foreign Printers of English Books, 1557-1640*,

Anon., *Advertising Art of J. & J. Colman: Yellow, red and blue* (1977)

Anon., *Faculty of Advocates in Scotland, 1532-1943* (1944)

Anon., *Index to the Biographical and Obituary Notices in the Gentleman's Magazine, 1731-80* (1891)

Anon., *International Directory of Company Histories*, Chicago, 74 vols, 1988-2005, ongoing

Anon., *Notable Londoners* (1922)

Anon., *Notable Personalities: An illustrated who's who of professional and businessmen and women* (1923-4)

Anon., *Old Series Ordnance Survey Maps of England and Wales, Scale 1 Inch to 1 Mile*, 8 vols (1975-92)

Anon., *Records of the Glasgow Stock Exchange Association* (1927)

Anon., *Register of Ephemera Collections in the United Kingdom* (2003)

Anon., *Story of Sunlight: Centenary of a famous soap* (1984)

Armstrong, John, Aldridge, John, Boyes, Grahame, Mustoe, Gordon and Storey, Richard, *Companion to British Road Haulage History* (2003)

Armstrong, John and Jones, Stephanie, *Business Documents: Their origins, sources and use to the historian* (1987)

Awdry, Christopher, *Encyclopedia of British Railway Companies* (1990)

Bailey, De Witt, *British Board of Ordnance Small Arms Contractors, 1689-1840* (1999)

Bailey, De Witt and Nie, Douglas A., *English Gunmakers: The Birmingham and provincial gun trade in the 18th and 19th centuries* (1978)

Bailey, Rebecca M., *Scottish Architects' Papers: A source book* (1996)

Baillie, G.H., *Watchmakers and Clockmakers of the World*, 3rd edn (1951)

Baillie, G.H., Ilbert, Courtenay and Clutton, Cecil, *Britten's Old Clocks and Watches and their Makers*, 9th edn (1982)

Bain, G.S. and Bennett, J.D., *Bibliography of British Industrial Relations, 1971-79* (1985)

Bain, G.S. and Woolven, G.B., *Bibliography of British Industrial Relations* (1979)

Banfield, Edwin, *Barometer Makers and Retailers, 1660-1900* (1991)

Barriskill, D.T., *Guide to the Lloyd's Marine Collection and Related Marine Sources at Guildhall Library*, 2nd edn (1994)

Bassett, Herbert H. (ed.), *Business Men at Home and Abroad: A biographical directory of partners, principals, directors and managers of important firms and institutions at home and abroad* (1912-13)

Bassett, Herbert H. (ed.), *Men of Note in Finance and Commerce: A biographical business directory* (1900)

Beard, Geoffrey and Gilbert, Christopher, *Dictionary of English Furniture Makers, 1660-1840* (1986)

Bellamy, Joyce M., *Yorkshire Business Histories: A bibliography* (1970)

Bellamy, Joyce M. and Saville, John (eds), *Dictionary of Labour Biography*, 11 vols (1972-2003)

Bendell, Sarah, *Dictionary of Land Surveyors and Local Mapmakers of Great Britain and Ireland, 1530-1850*, 2nd edn, 1997

Bennett, J.D., *Leicestershire Architects, 1700-1850* (1968)

Bennett, John and Storey, Richard (eds), *Trade Union and Related Records*, 6th edn (1991)

Benson, John, Neville, Robert G. and Thompson, Charles H., *Bibliography of the British Coal Industry: Secondary literature, parliamentary and departmental papers, mineral maps and plans and a guide to sources* (1981)

Beresford, Maurice, *Leeds Chamber of Commerce* (1951)

Beswick, M., *Brickmaking in Sussex: A history and gazetteer* (2001)

Bezdek, Richard H., *Swords and Sword Makers of England and Scotland* (2003)

Blackmore, Howard L., *Dictionary of London Gunmakers, 1350-1850* (1986)

Blackmore, Howard L., *Gunmakers of London Supplement* (1999)

Boalch, Donald H. and Mould, Charles (eds), *Makers of the Harpsichord and Clavichord, 1440-1840*, 3rd edn (1995)

Boase, Frederic, *Modern English Biography Containing Memoirs of Persons Who Have Died Since 1850*, 6 vols (1882-1921); 2nd impression, 6 vols (1965)

Bodleian Library, *Nation of Shopkeepers: Trade ephemera from 1654 to the 1860s in the John Johnson Collection* (2001)

Bond, James et al, *Clay Industries of Oxfordshire: Oxfordshire brickmakers* (c.1980)

Bond, Maurice F., *Guide to the Records of Parliament* (1971)

Booker, John, 'Access Policy', in Turton, Alison (ed.), *Managing Business Archives* (1991)

Booker, John, *Temples of Mammon: The architecture of banking* (1990)

Boyes, Graham, Searle, Matthew and Steggles, Donald, *Ottley's Bibliography of British Railway History*, 2nd supplement (1998)

Braithwaite, Paul with Carter, John, *Palace on Wheels: A history of travelling showmen's living vans with an A-Z of manufacturers, 1860-1960* (1999)

Bristow, C.R., *Directory of 19th and 20th Century Suffolk Breweries* (1985)

British Association of Industrial Editors, *British House Journals* (1956), 2nd edn (1962)

British Library, *Trade Literature in British Libraries* (1985)

Brockman, H.A.N., *British Architect in Industry 1841-1940* (1974)

Brodie, Antonia, Felstead, Alison, Franklin, Jonathan, Pinfield, Leslie and Oldfield, Jane, *Directory of British Architects, 1834-1900*, 2nd edn, 2 vols (1993)

Brown, Cynthia, Haward, Birkin and Kindred, Robert, *Dictionary of Architects of Suffolk Buildings, 1800-1914* (1991)

Brown, Philip A.H., *London Publishers and Printers, c1800-1870* (1982)

Brownlie, John S., *Railway Steam Cranes: A survey of progress since 1975 ... and Biography of Leading Member Firms* (1973)

Brunston, J., *Bibliography of 120 Pattern Books and Trade Catalogues in the Library of the Victoria & Albert Museum* (1971)

Bryden, D.J., *Scottish Scientific Instrument Makers, 1600-1900* (1972)

Bryon, Rita V. and Bryon, Terence N., *Maritime Information: A guide to libraries and sources of information in the United Kingdom*, 3rd edn (1993)

Burg, Judith A., *Guide to the Rowntree and Mackintosh Archives, 1862-1969* (1997)

Burns, Edward, *Scottish Brewery Trade Marks, 1876-1900, and 1900-1976*, 2 vols (1986-7)

Butcher, David, *Official Publications in Britain*, 2nd edn (1991)

Byars, Mel, *Design Encyclopaedia* (1994)

Calderdale Archives, *Calderdale Archives, 1964-1989: An illustrated guide to Calderdale District Archives* (1990)

Calvert, H.R., *Scientific Trade Cards in the Science Museum Collection* (1971)

Camp, Anthony, *Wills and their Whereabouts*, 4th edn (1974)

Cave, Charles H., *History of Banking in Bristol from 1750 to 1899* (1899)

Channing, Norman and Dunn, Mike, *British Camera Makers: An A-Z guide to companies and products* (1995)

Chapman, Stanley D., *Devon Cloth Industry in the 18th Century: Sun Fire Office inventories of merchants' and manufacturers' property, 1726-70* (1978)

Chapman, Stanley D., *Rise of Merchant Banking* (1984)

Chartered Insurance Institute, *Sources of Insurance History: A guide to historical material in the CII library* (1990)

Checkland, S.G., *Scottish Banking: A history, 1695-1973* (1975)

Cheffins, Richard H.A., *How to Find Information: Official publications* (2004)

Clark, Christine and Munting, Roger, *Suffolk Enterprise: A guide to the county's companies and their historical records* (2000)

Clarke, Bob, *From Grub Street to Fleet Street: An illustrated history of English newspapers to 1899* (2004)

Clarke, William M., *How the City of London Works: An introduction to its financial markets*, 6th edn (2004)

Clegg, H.A., Fox, A. and Thompson, A.F., *History of British Trade Unions, 1889-1951*, 3 vols (1964-94)

Clifton, Gloria C., *Directory of British Scientific Instrument Makers, 1550-1851* (1995)

Clinkscale, Martha N., *Makers of the Piano*, 2 vols (1993 and 1999)

Cockerell, H.A.L. and Green, Edwin, *British Insurance Business: A guide to its history and records*, 2nd edn (1994)

Collingwood, Judy, *Guide to Resources for Canadian Studies in the UK and Ireland*, 3rd edn (c.1998)

Colvin, Howard, *Biographical Dictionary of British Architects, 1600-1840*, 3rd edn (1995)

Colwell, Stella, *Family Records Centre*, 2nd edn (2002)

Copsey, Tony, *Book Distribution and Printing in Suffolk, 1534-1850* (1994)

Corfield, Penelope, *Power and the Professions in Britain, 1700-1850* (1995)

Cotterell, Howard H., *Old Pewter: Its makers and marks in England, Scotland and Ireland* (1963)

Cottrell, P.L., *Industrial Finance, 1830-1914: The finance and organisation of English manufacturing industry* (1980)

Courtney, Cathy and Thompson, Paul (eds), *City Lives: The changing voices of British finance* (1996)

Cox, Alan, *Survey of Bedfordshire Brickmaking: A history and gazetteer* (1979)

Cox, Jane, *Affection Defying Death: Wills, probate and death duty records* (1998)

Cranfield, G.A., *Development of the Provincial Newspaper, 1700-1760* (1978)

Creaton, Heather, *Bibliography of Printed Works on London History to 1939* (1994)

Crisp Jones, Kenneth, *Silversmiths of Birmingham and their Marks, 1750-1980* (1981)

Crocker, Glenys, *Gunpowder Mills Gazetteer: Black powder manufacturing sites in the British Isles* (1988)

Crom, Theodore R., *Trade Catalogues, 1542 to 1842* (1989)

Crookham, Alan, *Trades Union Congress Archive, 1960-1970* (1998)

Crookham, Alan, Wilcox, Michael et al, *Confederation of British Industry and Predecessor Archives* (1997)

Cross-Rudkin, P.S.M. and Chrimes, M.M., *Biographical Dictionary of Civil Engineers in Great Britain and Ireland. vol 2, 1830-1890* (2008)

Culme, John, *Directory of Gold and Silversmiths, Jewellers and Allied Trades, 1838-1914*, 2 vols (1987)

Cushion, John P., *Handbook of Pottery and Porcelain Marks*, 4th edn (1980)

Davenport, Neil, *United Kingdom Patent System: A brief history* (1979)

Davies, A.S., *Early Banks of Mid-Wales* (1935)

Davies, Jim, *Book of Guinness Advertising* (1998)

Dawes, Margaret and Ward-Perkins, C.N., *Country Banks of England and Wales: Private provincial banks and bankers, 1688-1953*, 2 vols (2000)

Delano-Smith, Catharine and Kain, Roger J.P., *English Maps: A history* (1999)

Dennett, Laurie, *Slaughter & May: A short history* (1989)

Donnelly, Tom and Durham, Martin, *Labour Relations in the Coventry Motor Industry, 1896-1939: A guide to the records of the AUEW* (c.1988)

Douglas, James, *Scottish Banknotes* (1975)

Gordon Duff, E., *Century of the English Book Trade: Short notices of all printers, stationers, bookbinders and others connected with it from the issue of the first dated book in 1457 to the incorporation of the Company of Stationers in 1557* (1948)

Duffield, Sarah and Storey, Richard, *Trades Union Congress Archive, 1920-60* (1992)

Dumbell, Stanley, *Centenary Book of the Liverpool Stock Exchange* (1936)

Dunning, Peter M., *Company Reports held in the Science Reference and Information Service* (1986)

Dunning, Peter M. and Sawyer, David E., *House Journals Held by the Science Reference Library* (1985)

Edwards, Cliff, *Railway Records: A guide to sources* (2001)

Edwards, David G., *Historical Gazetteer and Bibliography of By-product Coking Plants in the UK* (2001)

Edwards, J.R., *British Company Legislation and Company Accounts, 1844-1976* (1980)

Edwards, J.R., *Company Legislation and Changing Patterns of Disclosure in British Company Accounts 1900-1940* (1981)

Edwards, J.R., *History of Financial Accounting* (1989)

Elizabeth James, I., *The Goldsmiths of Aberdeen* (1981)

Elvin, Laurence, *Family Enterprise: The story of some North Country organ builders* (1986)

Elvin, Laurence, *Pipes and Actions: Some organ builders in the Midlands and Beyond* (1995)

Evans, Angela, *Index to the Dictionary of English Furniture Makers* (1990)

Farrugia, Jean, *Guide to Post Office Archives* (1987)

Fawdry, Marguerite, *British Tin Toys; including an A to Z of British metal toy makers* (1990)

Ffoulkes, Charles, *Gun Founders of England* (1937)

Ford, Peter and Grace, *Guide to Parliamentary Papers: What they are, how to find them, how to use them* (1972)

Forrer, L., *Biographical Dictionary of Medallists, Coin, Gem and Seal Engravers, Mint Masters, etc, Ancient and Modern, with Reference to their works*, 6 vols (1904-16)

Foster, Janet and Sheppard, Julia (eds), *British Archives*, 4th edn (2002)

Fox, M.R., *Dye-Makers of Great Britain, 1856-1976: A history of chemists, companies, products and changes* (1987)

Fry, Edward, *Index to Marriages in the Gentleman's Magazine, 1731-68* (1922)

Gardner, Robert E., *Small Arms Makers: A directory of fabricators of firearms, edged weapons, crossbows and polearms* (1963)

Gerhold, Dorian, *Courts of Equity: A guide to Chancery and other legal records* (1994)

Gibson, Jeremy and Churchill, Else, *Probate Jurisdictions: Where to look for wills*, 5th edn (2002)

Giles, Colum and Goodall, Ian H., *Yorkshire Textile Mills 1770-1930* (1992)

Gill, Margaret A.V., *Directory of Newcastle Goldsmiths* (1980)

Chas E. Goad Ltd, *Goad Fire Insurance Plan Catalogu: Part A, British Isles* (1984)

Godden, Geoffrey A., *Encyclopaedia of British Porcelain Manufacturers* (1988)

Gold, Sidney M., *Biographical Dictionary of Architects at Reading … to 1930* (1999)

Goodall, Francis, *Bibliography of British Business Histories* (1987)

Goodall, Francis, Gourvish, Terry and Tolliday, Steven (eds), *International Bibliography of Business History* (1997)

Goodison, Nicholas, *English Barometers, 1680-1860: A history of domestic barometers and their makers and retailers*, 2nd edn (1977)

Goring, Rosemary (ed.), *Chamber's Scottish Biographical Dictionary* (1992)

Gourvish, T.R., *British Rail, 1974-97: From integration to privatisation* (2002)

Gourvish, T.R., *British Railways, 1948-73* (1986)

Grace, D.R. and Phillips, D.C., *Ransomes of Ipswich: A history of the firm and guide to its records* (1975)

Grannum, Karren and Taylor, Nigel, *Wills and Other Probate Records* (2004)

Grant, G.L., *Standard Catalogue of Provincial Banks and Banknotes* (1977)

Grant, Wyn and Marsh, David, *Confederation of British Industry* (1997)

Green, Jennifer, Ollerenshaw, Philip and Wardley, Peter, *Business in Avon and Somerset: A survey of archives* (1991)

Grimwade, A.G., *London Goldsmiths, 1697-1837: Their marks and lives from the original registers at Goldsmiths' Hall and other sources*, 3rd edn (1990)

Grindon, L.H., *Manchester Banks and Bankers* (1877)

Guildhall Library, *City Livery Companies and Related Organisations: A guide to their archives in Guildhall Library*, 3rd edn (1989)

Guildhall Library, *Historic Trade Directories in Guildhall Library* (2005)

Gulshan, Helenka, *Vintage Leather* (1998)

Gunston, Bill, *World Encyclopedia of Aircraft Manufacturers* (1993)

Habgood, Wendy, *Chartered Accountants in England and Wales: A guide to historical records* (1994)

Hadley, Peter (ed.), *History of Bovril Advertising* (1972)

Hampson, Rodney, *Pottery References in the Staffordshire Advertiser, 1795-1865* (2000)

Handover, P.M., *History of the London Gazette, 1665-1965* (1965)

Harding, Herbert, *Patent Office Centenary: A story of 100 years in the life and work of the Patent Office* (1975)

Harley, J.B., *Historian's Guide to Ordnance Survey Maps* (1964)

Harrison, Royden, Woolven, Gillian B. and Duncan, Robert, *Warwick Guide to British Labour Periodicals, 1790-1970: A Checklist* (1977)

Harvey, Brian, *The Violin Family and its Makers in the British Isles: An illustrated history and directory* (1995)

Hawkings, David T., *Fire Insurance Records for Family and Local Historians, 1696 to 1920* (2003)

Hawkins, R.N.P., *Dictionary of Makers of British Metallic Tickets, Checks, Medalets, Tallies and Counters, 1788-1910* (1989)

Hayward, P.A., *Hayward's Patent Cases, 1600-1883: A compilation of the English patent cases for those years*, 11 vols (1987)

Hazzlewood, John W., *House Journals* (1963)

Heal, Ambrose, *London Goldsmiths, 1200-1800: A record of the names and addresses of the craftsmen, their shop signs and trade cards* (1935)

Heal, Ambrose, *London Tradesmen's Cards of the XVIII Century: An account of their origin and use* (1925)

Heathcote, Bernard and Pauline, *A Faithful Likeness: The first photographic portrait studios in the British Isles, 1841-1855* (2002)

Henley, William, *Universal Dictionary of Violin and Bow Makers*, 7 vols (1959-69)

Hennessy, Elizabeth, *Coffee House to Cyber Market: 200 years of the London Stock Exchange* (2001)

Henry, Brian, *British Television Advertising: The first thirty years* (1986)

Henrywood, Richard K., *Bristol Potters, 1775-1906* (1992)

Henrywood, Richard K., *Staffordshire Potters, 1781-1900: A comprehensive list assembled from contemporary directories* (2002)

Hillier, Mary, *Dolls and Doll Makers* (1968)

Hilton-Price, F.G., *Handbook of London Bankers* (1970)

Hindle, Paul, *Maps for Historians* (1998)

Hinton, R.W.K., *Port Books of Boston in the Early 17th Century* (1956)

Hocking, Charles, *Dictionary of Disaster at Sea during the Age of Steam, 1824-1962*, 2 vols (1969)

Holden, Roger N., *Stott & Sons: Architects of the Lancashire cotton mill* (1998)

Hollowell, Steven, *Enclosure Records for Historians* (2000)

Honeyman, William C., *Scottish Violin Makers: Past and present* (1910)

Hook, Elizabeth, *Guide to the Papers of John Swire & Sons Ltd* (1977)

Hoppit, Julian, *Risk and Failure in English Business, 1700-1800* (1987)

Howe, Ellic, *List of London Bookbinders, 1648-1815* (1950)

Howgego, James, *Printed Maps of London circa 1553-1850* (1978)

Hudson, Pat, *West Riding Wool Textile Industry: A catalogue of business records from the 16th to the 20th century* (1975)

Hughes, John, *Scotland's Malt Whisky Distilleries: Survival of the fittest* (2002)

Hughes, John, *Liverpool Banks and Bankers, 1760-1837* (1906)

Humphries, Charles and Smith, W.C., *Music Publishing in the British Isles …. A dictionary of engravers, printers, publishers and music sellers …*, 2nd edn (1970)

Hunter, Pamela, *Veterinary Medicine: A guide to historical records* (2004)

Ilersic, A.R., *Parliament of Commerce: The story of the Association of British Chambers of Commerce* (1960)

Irving, Joe, *The City at Work* (1981)

Jalovec, Karel, *Encyclopedia of Violin Makers* (1968)

James, Alwyn, *Scottish Roots: The step by step guide to tracing your Scottish ancestors* (2002)

James, Philip B., *Early Keyboard Instruments from their Beginnings to the Year 1820* (1930)

Jenkins, D.T., *Indexes of Fire Insurance Policies of the Sun Fire Office and the Royal Exchange Assurance, 1775-87* (1986)

Jenkins, D.T., 'Practice of insurance against fire, 1750-1840, and historical research' in Westall, Oliver M., *The Historian and the Business of Insurance* (1984)

Jeremy, David J. (ed.), *Dictionary of Business Biography*, 5 vols (1984-6)

Jeremy, David J. and Tweedale, Geoffrey, *Dictionary of Twentieth Century British Business Leaders* (1994)

Jones, Charles, *Britain and the Dominions: A guide to business and related records in the United Kingdom concerning Australia, New Zealand and South Africa* (1978)

Jones, E.L., Porter, S. and Turner, M., *Gazetteer of English Urban Fire Disasters, 1500-1900* (1984)

Jones, Edgar, *Accountancy and the British Economy 1840-1980: The evolution of Ernst & Whinney* (1981)

Jones, Edgar, *The Business of Medicine: The extraordinary history of Glaxo* (2001)

Jones, Edgar, *Industrial Architecture in Britain 1750-1939* (1985)

Jones, Geoffrey, *British Multinational Banking 1830-1990* (1993)

Jones, Michael and Taylor, Jean, *Handlist of Trade Catalogues in the Wellcome Museum of the History of Medicine* (1984)

Kahl, William F., *Development of London Livery Companies: An historical essay and select bibliography* (1959)

Kain, Roger J.P. and Prince, Hugh C., *Tithe Surveys for Historians* (2000)

Keen, Michael E., *Bibliography of the Trade Directories in the National Art Library* (1979)

Kennard, A.N., *Gunfounding and Gunfounders: A directory of cannon founders from the earliest times to 1850* (1986)

Kennett, Annette M. (ed.), *Archives and Records of the City of Chester: A guide to the collections in the Chester City Record Office* (1985)

Kidson, Frank, *British Music Publishers, Printers and Engravers; from Queen Elizabeth's reign to George the Fourth's* (1967)

Kirk, H., *Portrait of a Profession: A history of the solicitor's profession, 1100 to the present day* (1976)

Knight, R.J.B. (ed.), *Guide to the Manuscripts of the National Maritime Museum, vol 2: Public records, business records and artificial collections* (1980)

Kynaston, David, *Cazenove & Co.: A history* (1991)

Kynaston, David, *The Financial Times: A centenary history* (1988)

Lambert, Sheila (ed.), *House of Commons Sessional Papers of the 18th Century*, 147 vols (1975-6)

Lane, Joan, *Apprenticeship in England 1600-1914* (1996)

Lane, Joan, *Register of Business Records of Coventry and Related Areas* (1977)

Langwill, Lyndesay G. and Boston, Noel, *Church and Chamber Barrel Organs: Their origin, makers, music and location* (1970)

Lees, Samuel, *A Collection of the Names of Merchants Living In and About the City of London* (1677)

Levitt, Sarah, *Victorians Unbuttoned: Registered designs for clothing, their makers and wearers, 1839-1900* (1986)

Ling Roth, H., *Genesis of Banking in Halifax with Sidelights on Country Banking* (1914)

Linstrum, Derek, *West Yorkshire Architects and Architecture* (1978)

Linton, David and Boston, Ray (eds), *The Newspaper Press in Britain: An annotated bibliography* (1987)

Lloyd, John E. and Jenkins, R.T. (eds), *Dictionary of Welsh Biography Down to 1940* (1959)

Lloyd, John E. and Jenkins, R.T. (eds), *Dictionary of Welsh Biography 1941-70* (2001)

Lomas, Elizabeth, *Guide to the Archives of Art and Design, Victoria & Albert Museum* (2001)

Loomes, Brian, *Early Clockmakers of Great Britain* (1981)

Loomes, Brian, *Watchmakers and Clockmakers of the World* (1976)

Lowe, James W., *British Steam Locomotive Builders* (1989)

Lowe, Jane, *Guide to Sources in the History of the Cycle and Motor Industries in Coventry, 1880-1939* (1982)

Lumas, Susan, *Making Use of the Census* (2004)

Mace, Angela, *Architecture in Manuscript, 1601-1996: Guide to the British Architectural Library manuscripts and archives collection* (1998)

Mace, Angela, *The Royal Institute of British Architects: A guide to its archives and history* (1986)

Manchester Metropolitan University, *Historical Trade Catalogues* (1978)

Mander-Jones, Phyllis, *Manuscripts in the British Isles relating to Australia, New Zealand and the Pacific* (1972)

Mann, Charles, *Editing for Industry* (1974)

Markham Lester, V., *Victorian Insolvency: Bankruptcy, imprisonment for debt and company winding up in 19th century England* (1995)

Marsh, Arthur and Ryan, Victoria, *Historical Directory of Trade Unions*, Aldershot, 4 vols (1980-94)

Marshall, John, *Biographical Dictionary of Railway Engineers*, 2nd edn (2003)

Martin, Janet D. (ed.), *Guide to the Lancashire Record Office: A supplement, 1977-1989* (1992)

Marton, J.S., *Index to Biographical Dictionary of Medallists by L. Forrer* (1987)

Mathias, Peter, 'The lawyer as businessman in 18th century England' in Coleman, D.C. and Mathias, Peter (eds), *Essays in Honour of Charles Wilson* (1984)

Mathias, Peter and Pearsall, A.W.H., *Shipping: A survey of historical records* (1971)

Matthews, D. and Pirie, J., *Auditors' Talk: An oral history of a profession from the 1920s to the present day* (2001)

Matthews, Noel and Doreen Wainwright, M., *Guide to Manuscripts and Documents in the British Isles Relating to Africa* (1971)

Matthews, Noel and Doreen Wainwright, M., *Guide to Manuscripts and Documents in the British Isles Relating to the Far East* (1977)

Matthews, Noel and Doreen Wainwright, M., *Guide to Manuscripts and Documents in the British Isles Relating to the Middle East and North Africa* (1980)

Matthews, Noel and Doreen Wainwright, M., *Guide to Western Manuscripts and Documents in the British Isles Relating to South and South East Asia* (1965)

Maxted, Ian F., *British Book Trades, 1710-1777: An index of the masters and apprentices recorded in Inland Revenue registers at the Public Record Office* (1983)

Maxted, Ian F., *London Book Trades, 1735-1775: A checklist of members in trade directories and Musgrave's Obituary* (1984)

Maxted, Ian F., *London Book Trades, 1775-1800: A preliminary checklist of members* (1977)

Maxted, Ian F., *British Book Trades, 1775-1787: An index of insurance policies* (1992)

McIvor, Arthur J., *Organised Capital: Employers' associations and industrial relations in northern England, 1880-1939* (1996)

McMurray, Elizabeth, *At Home in the Thirties: The EKCO collection of trade catalogues* (1995)

Mendenhall, John, *British Trade Marks of the 1920s and 1930s* (1989)

Mercer, Tony, *Chronometer Makers of the World; with extensive list of makers and craftsmen*, 2nd edn (2004)

Meredith Morris, W., *British Violin Makers: A biographical dictionary of British makers of stringed instruments and bows and a critical description of their work* (1920)

Michie, Ranald, *London Stock Exchange: A history* (1999)

Michie, Ranald, *Money, Mania and Markets: Investment, company formation and the stock exchange in 19th century Scotland* (1981)

Middlemiss, Norman L., *British Shipbuilding Yards*, 3 vols (1993-5)

Modern Records Centre, *Confederation of British Industry and Predecessor Archives* (1997)

Modern Records Centre, *Trades Union Congress Archive, 1920-60* (1992)

Modern Records Centre, *Trades Union Congress Archive, 1960-70* (1998)

Moore, John N., *Historical Cartography of Scotland: A guide to the literature of Scottish maps and mapping prior to the Ordnance Survey*, 2nd edn (1991)

Morris, Peter J.T. and Russell, Colin A., *Archives of the British Chemical Industry, 1750-1914: A handlist* (1988)

Morrison, Kathryn A., *English Shops and Shopping: An architectural history* (2003)

Moss, Michael, *Building of Europe's Largest Mutual Life Company: Standard Life, 1825-2000* (2000)

Moss, Michael and Russell, Iain, *An Invaluable Treasure: A history of the TSB* (1994)

Murless, Brian J., *Somerset Brick and Tile Manufacturers: A brief history and gazetteer* (2000)

Murphy, Michael, *Newspapers and the Local Historian* (1991)

Musgrove, William, *Obituaries Prior to 1800: A general nomenclator and obituary with reference to the books where persons are mentioned and where some account of their character is to be found*, 6 vols (1899-1901)

Myers, Robin, *Stationers' Company Archive: An account of the records, 1554-1884* (1990)

Nangle, Benjamin, *The Gentleman's Magazine: Biographical and obituary notices, 1781-1818* (1980)

National Archives of Scotland, *Guide to the National Archives of Scotland* (1995)

National Archives of Scotland, *Tracing Scottish Local History: A guide to local history research in the Scottish Record Office* (1994)

National Archives of Scotland, *Tracing Your Scottish Ancestors: A guide to ancestry research in the National Archives of Scotland*, 3rd edn (2003)

Nevett, T.R., *Advertising in Britain: A history* (1982)

Newton, David C., *Trade Marks: An introductory guide and bibliography* (1991)

Norton, Jane E., *Guide to the National and Provincial Directories of England and Wales excluding London*, 2nd edn (1984)

Oliver, Richard, *Ordnance Survey Maps: A concise guide for historians* (1993)

Orbell, John and Turton, Alison, *British Banking: A guide to historical records* (2001)

Orbell, John, *Guide to the Baring Archive at ING Barings* (1997)

Ottley, George, *Bibliography of British Railway History*, 2nd edn (1983); Supplement (1988); Second Supplement (1998)

Oxford Dictionary of National Biography, 60 vols (2004)

Packer, Maurice, *Bookbinders of Victorian London* (1991)

Pagnamenta, Peter and Overy, Richard, *All Our Working Lives* (1984)

Parker, Jack, *Nothing for Nothing for Nobody: A history of Hertfordshire banks and banking* (1986)

Parker, R.H., *British Accountants: A biographical sourcebook* (1980)

Parkinson, John A., *Victorian Music Publishers: An annotated list* (1990)

Patent Office, *A Century of Trade Marks* (1976)

Payne, P.L., *The Early Scottish Limited Companies, 1856-1895* (1980)

Payne, P.L., *Studies in Scottish Business History* (1967)

Pearson, Lynne, *British Breweries: An architectural history* (1999)

Pearson, Robin, *Insuring the Industrial Revolution: Fire insurance in Great Britain, 1700-1850* (2004)

Perks, Robert and Thomson, Alistair (eds), *Oral History Reader* (1998)

Phillips, Maberley, *History of Banks, Bankers and Banking in Northumberland, Durham and North Yorkshire … 1755 to 1894* (1894)

Pike, Andrew, *Gazetteer of Buckinghamshire Brickyards* (1995)

Plomer, Henry R., *Dictionary of the Booksellers and Printers Who Were at Work in England, Scotland and Ireland from 1641 to 1667* (1907)

Plomer, Henry R., *Dictionary of Printers and Booksellers who were at Work in England, Scotland and Ireland from 1668 to 1725* (1922)

Plomer, Henry R., Bushnell, G.H. and Dix, E.R.McC., *Dictionary of the Printers and Booksellers who were at Work in England, Scotland and Ireland from 1726 to 1775* (1932)

Popplewell, Lawrence, *Gazetteer of the Railway Contractors and Engineers [c1830-1914]*, 8 vols (1982-6)

Porter, Dilwyn, "'A trusted guide to the investing public.' Harry Marks and the Financial News', in Davenport-Hines, R.T.P. (ed.), *Speculators and Patriots: Essays in business biography* (1986)

Powell, Christopher, *The British Building Industry since 1800*, 2nd edn (1996)

Pressnell, L.S., *Country Banking in the Industrial Revolution* (1956)

Preston, Harold, *Early East Anglian Banks and Bankers* (1994)

Price, Roger and Swift, Fraser, *Catalogue of 19th Century Medical Trade Marks, 1800-1880* (1988)

Procktor, C.E., *The Engineer Index, 1856-1959* (1964)

Public Record Office, *Maps and Plans in the Public Record Office* (1967)

Raimo, John W., *Guide to Manuscripts Relating to America in Great Britain and Ireland* (1979)

Ramsden, Charles, *London Bookbinders, 1780-1840* (1987)

Ramsden, Charles, *Bookbinders of the United Kingdom (Outside London), 1780-1840* (1987)

Raymond, Stuart A., *Family History on the Web: An internet directory for England and Wales*, 3rd edn (2004)

Raymond, Stuart A., *Occupational Sources for Genealogists*, 2nd edn (1996)

Raynes, Harold E., *History of British Insurance*, 2nd edn 1964

Reader, W.J., *A House in the City: A study of the City and of the Stock Exchange based on the records of Foster & Braithwaite, 1825-1975* (1979)

Reader, W.J. and Kynaston, David, *Phillips & Drew: Professionals in the City* (1998)

Reading University, *Historical Farm Records: A summary guide to manuscripts* (1973)

Richard, Stephen, *Directory of British Official Publications: A guide to sources*, 2nd edn (1984)

Richardson, Ruth and Thorne, Robert, *The Builder Illustrations Index 1843-1883* (1994)

Richmond, Lesley, Stevenson, Julie and Turton, Alison, *Pharmaceutical Industry: A guide to historical records* (2003)

Richmond, Lesley and Stockford, Bridget, *Company Archives: The survey of the records of 1,000 of the first registered companies in England and Wales* (1986)

Richmond, Lesley and Turton, Alison, *Brewing Industry: A guide to historical records* (1990)

Richmond, Lesley and Turton, Alison (eds), *Directory of Corporate Archives*, 4th edn (1997)

Rickards, Maurice and Twyman, Michael (ed.), *Encyclopedia of Ephemera: A guide to the fragmentary documents of everyday life for the collector, curator & historian* (2000)

Ricketts, Carl, *Pewterers of London, 1600-1900* (2001)

Riden, Philip, *Gazetteer of Charcoal-fired Blast Furnaces in Great Britain in Use since 1660*, 2nd edn (1993)

Ritchie, L.A., *Shipbuilding Industry: A guide to historical records* (1992)

Robinson, David N. et al, *Lincolnshire Bricks: History and gazetteer* (1999)

Rodgers, F., *Guide to British Official Publications* (1980)

Rogers, E.M., *Large Scale County Maps of the British Isles, 1596-1850*, 2nd edn (1972)

Room, Adrian, *Dictionary of Trade Name Origins* (1983)

Rose, Jonathan and Anderson, Patricia J. (eds), *Dictionary of Literary Biography: British literary publishing houses, vol 106, 1820-1880, vol 112, 1881-1965* (1991)

N.M. Rothschild and Sons Ltd, *Rothschild Archive: A guide to the collection* (2000)

Rowe, J.J., *Northern Business Histories: A bibliography* (1979)

Rowley, Gwyn, *British Fire Insurance Plans* (1984)

Royal Bank of Scotland, *Guide to the Historical Records of the Royal Bank of Scotland* (2000)

Royal Commission on Historical Manuscripts, *Records of British Business and Industry, 1760-1914: Metal processing and engineering* (1994)

Royal Commission on Historical Manuscripts, *Records of British Business and Industry, 1760-1914: Textiles and leather* (1990)

Russell, Iain, *Sir Robert McAlpine: The early years* (1986)

Ryton, John, *Banks and Banknotes of Exeter* (1984)

Schenck, David H.J., *Directory of the Lithographic Printers of Scotland, 1820-1870: Their locations, periods, and a guide to artistic lithographic printers* (1999)

Sharpe France, R., *Guide to the Lancashire Record Office*, 3rd edn (1985)

Shaw, Gareth and Tipper, Alison, *British Directories: A bibliography and guide to directories published in England and Wales, 1850-1950 and Scotland, 1773-1950*, 2nd edn (1997)

Shorter, A.H., *Paper Mills and Paper Makers in England, 1495-1800* (1957)

Simmons, Jack and Biddle, Gordon (eds), *Oxford Companion to British Railway History from 1603 to the 1990s* (1997)

Sinclair, Cecil, *Jock Tamson's Bairns: A history of the records of the General Register Office for Scotland* (2000)

Skempton, A.W., *British Civil Engineering 1640-1840: A bibliography of contemporary printed records, plans and books* (1987)

Skempton, A.W., Chrimes, M.M., Cox, R.C., Cross-Rudkin, P.S.M. and Ruddock, E.C., *Biographical Dictionary of Civil Engineers in Great Britain and Ireland, vol 1, 1500-1830* (2002)

Slaven, Anthony and Checkland, Sydney (eds), *The Dictionary of Scottish Business Biography*, 2 vols (1986-90)

Slinn, Judy, *Clifford Chance: Its origins and development* (1993)

Slinn, Judy, *History of Freshfields* (1984)

Smallbone, Linda and Storey, Richard (ed.), *Employers' and Trade Associations' History* (1992)

Smith, Gaye, *Trade Catalogues: A hundred years, 1850-1949* (1992)

Southwick, Leslie, *London Silver Hilted Swords: Their makers, suppliers and allied trades; with directory* (2001)

Spacek, Leonard, *Growth of Arthur Andersen & Co, 1928-73* (1989)

St George, Andrew, *History of Norton Rose* (1995)

St John Thomas, David, *Three Victorian Telephone Directories* (1970)

Storey, Richard, *Automotive History Sources in Coventry Archives* (1996)

Storey, Richard (ed.), *Employers' and Trade Associations' History* (1992)

Storey, Richard (ed.), *Rubery Owen Holdings Ltd Archive* (1997)

Stratton, Michael and Trinder, Barrie, *20th Century Industrial Archaeology* (2000)

Stuart Gray, A., *Edwardian Architecture: A biographical dictionary* (1985)

Swann, Brenda and Turnbull, Maureen, *Records of Interest to Social Scientists, 1919-1939* (1971)

Syed, Isabel, *Eagle Star: A guide to its history and archives* (1997)

Taylor, Nicholas, *Monuments of Commerce* (1968)

Temple, Dave, *Collieries of Durham*, 2 vols (1994, 1998)

Thomas, W.A., *Provincial Stock Exchanges: Their history and their function* (1973)

Thompson, Paul, *Voice of the Past: Oral history*, 2nd edn (1988)

Thompson, Thomas (ed.), *Robert Chamber's Biographical Dictionary of Eminent Scotsmen*, 3 vols (1971)

Toase, Charles A., *Bibliography of British Newspapers*, 6 vols (1982-91)

Todd, William B., *Directory of Printers and Others in Allied Trades, London and Vicinity, 1800-1840* (1972)

Townsend, Brian, *Scotch Missed: The lost distilleries of Scotland*, 3rd edn (2004)

Trinder, Barrie and Cox, Jeff, *Yeomen and Colliers in Telford* (1980)

Turton, Alison (ed.), *Managing Business Archives* (1991)

Tweedale, Geoffrey, *National Archive for the History of Computing Catalogue* (1990)

Tweedale, Geoffrey, *Sheffield Knife Book: A history and collectors' guide* (1996)

Twyman, Michael, *Directory of London Lithographic Printers, 1800-1850* (1956)

van Dulken, Stephen, *British Patents of Invention, 1617-1977: A guide for researchers* (1999)

Victoria & Albert Museum, *Trade Catalogues in the Victoria & Albert Museum* (1986)

Walker, Stephen P. and Mitchell, Falconer, *Trade Associations and Uniform Costings in the British Printing Industry, 1900-1963* (1997)

Wallis, Helen and McConnell, Anita (eds), *Historian's Guide to Early British Maps* (1994)

Walne, Peter (ed.), *Guide to Manuscript Sources for the History of Latin America and the Caribbean in the British Isles* (1973)

Walter, John, *Greenhill Dictionary of Guns and Gunmakers* (2001)

Walters, H.B., *Church Bells of England* (1977)

Watts, Christopher T. and Watts, Michael J., *My Ancestor was a Merchant Seaman*, 2nd edn (2002)

Watts, Christopher T. and Watts, Michael J., *Records of Merchant Shipping and Seamen* (1998)

Weedon, Alexis and Bott, Michael, *British Book Trade Archives, 1830-1939: A location register* (1996)

Wellings, Fred, *Dictionary of British House Builders: A 20th century history* (2006)

Wellings, Fred and Gibb, Alistair, *Bibliography of Banking Histories*, 2 vols (1995-7)

Welsh, Charles, *History of the Cutlers' Company of London and the Minor Cutlery Crafts with Biographical Notices of Early London Cutlers*, 2 vols (1916-23)

West, John, *Town Records* (1983)

Westmancoat, John, *Newspapers* (1985)

Whitelaw, Charles E., *Scottish Arms Makers: A biographical directory of makers of firearms, edged weapons and armour working in Scotland from the 15th century to 1870* (1977)

Woodcroft, Bennet, *Alphabetical Index of Patentees of Inventions from 1617 to 1852* (1969)

Woodcroft, Bennet, *Chronological Index of Patents of Invention from 1617 to 1853*, 2 vols (1854)

Woodcroft, Bennet, *Subject Matter Index of Patents of Invention, 1617 to 1852*, 2 vols (1857)

Woodcroft, Bennet, *Reference Index of Patents of Invention from 1617 to 1852* (1862)

Wright, Alan J., *UK Airlines* (1998)

Wyke, Terry and Rudyard, Nigel (eds), *Cotton: A select bibliography on cotton in North West England* (1997)

Zarach, Stephanie, *British Business History: A bibliography*, 2nd edn (1994)

Articles

Adams, Barbara, 'Ceramic insurance in the Sun Company, 1766-74', *English Ceramic Circle Transactions*, 10 (1976)

Armitage, G., 'Cartobibliographies of city and town plans of England and Wales', *The Map Collector*, 66-7 (1994)

Armitage, G., 'County cartobibliographies of England and Wales', *The Map Collector*, 52 (1990), 73 (1995)

Armstrong, John, 'An annotated bibliography of the British coastal trade', *International Journal of Maritime History*, 7 (1995)

Arnold, A.J., 'Publishing your private affairs to the world: Corporate financial disclosures in the UK, 1900-24', *Accounting, Business and Financial History*, 7 (1997)

Baker-Jones, T.E., 'Archives of WH Smith & Son Ltd', *Business Archives*, 54 (1987)

Bamford, Francis, 'Dictionary of Edinburgh wrights and furniture makers, 1660-1840', *Furniture History*, 19 (1983)

Beresford, Maurice, 'Building history from fire insurance records', *Urban History Yearbook* (1976)

Brooks, Margaret, 'A beginner's guide to establishing an oral history archive', *Proceedings of the Annual Conference of the Business Archives Council* (1987)

Campbell McMurray, H., 'Records of the Shipbuilders' & Repairers' National Association', *Business Archives*, 45 (1979)

Collinge, M.L., 'Probate valuations and the death duty registers', *Bulletin of the Institute of Historical Research*, 60 (1957)

Cooper, C.R.H., 'Archives of City of London livery companies and related organisations', *Archives*, 72 (1984)

Edwards, J.A., 'Publishers' archives at Reading University', *Business Archives*, 45 (1979)

Edwards, R., 'London Potters, circa1570-1710', *Journal of Ceramic History*, 6 (1974)

English, Barbara, 'Probate valuations and the death duty registers', *Bulletin of the Institute of Historical Research*, 58 (1884)

English, Barbara, 'Wealth at death in the 19th century', *Bulletin of the Institute of Historical Research*, 60 (1987)

Gawne, Eleanor, 'A not so unusual place to find company records. Business archives at the Archive of Art and Design', *Business Archives*, 69 (1995)

Gourvish, T.R., 'Writing British Railways' history', *Business Archives*, 62 (1991)

Green, Edwin and Kinsey, Sara, 'Archives of HSBC Group', *Financial History Review*, 3 (1996)

Green, Francis, 'Early banks in West Wales', *Transactions of the Historical Society of Mid-Wales*, 6 (1916)

Griffiths, John, 'Exploring corporate culture: The potential of company magazines for the business historian', *Business Archives*, 78 (1999)

Hadfield, Charles, 'Sources for the history of British Canals', *Journal of Transport History*, 2 (1955-6)

Hare, Susan M., 'Records of the Goldsmiths' Company', *Archives*, 72 (1984)

Harvey, Charles, 'Business records at the Public Record Office', *Business Archives*, 52 (1986)

Higgins, David and Tweedale, Geoffrey, 'Asset or Liability? Trade marks in the Sheffield cutlery and tool trades', *Business History*, 37 (1995)

Holden, Roger N., 'The architect and the Lancashire cotton textile industry, 1850-1914: The example of Stott & Sons, *Textile History*, 23 (1992)

Hollier, Anita, 'British Petroleum Archive: What's in it for you?', *Business Archives*, 76 (1998)

Johnson, L.C., 'British Transport Commission Archives: Work since 1953', *Journal of Transport History*, 5 (1962)

Johnson, L.C., 'Historical records of the British Transport Commission', *Journal of Transport History*, 1 (1953-4)

Koerner, Steve, 'Business archives relating to the British motorcycle industry', *Business Archives*, 80 (2000)

Levitt, Sarah, 'Uses of registered design samples in the Public Record Office, Kew, for the study of 19th century clothing manufacturers', *Business Archives*, 50 (1984)

Loftus, Donna, 'The self-made man? Businessmen and their autobiographies in the 19th century', *Business Archives*, 80 (2000)

Marriner, Sheila, 'Company financial statements as source material for business historians', *Business History*, 22 (1980)

Mitchell, Karen, 'ICI: A brief history and guide to the archives', *Business Archives*, 60 (1990)

Moss, Michael, 'Forgotten ledgers, law and the business historian: Gleanings from the Adam Smith Business Records Collection', *Archives*, 16 (1984)

Myers, Robin, 'Records of the Worshipful Company of Stationers and Newspaper Makers, 1554-1912', *Archives*, 69 (1983)

Orbell, John, 'Note on Series J90 in the Public Record Office', *Business Archives* (1983)

Orbell, John, 'Uses of business archives', *Record Aids* (1984)

Phillips, Gordon, 'Archives of The Times', *Business Archives*, 41 (1976)

Rath, T., 'Business records in the Public Record Office in the age of the Industrial Revolution', *Business History*, 17 (1975)

Raven, Neil, 'Trade directory sources for the study of early 19th century urban economies', *Business Archives*, 74 (1997)

Read, Gordon, 'The BICC archive and artefact collection', *Business Archives*, 58 (1989)

Rees, Liz, Tyrell, David and Wood, Sue, 'Picks and pistons: The industrial history of the North East online', *Business Archives*, 85 (2003)

Richmond, Lesley, 'The records of the Registrar of Companies', *Business Archives*, 64 (1992)

Ritchie, L.A., 'Business history and the National Register of Archives', *Business Archives*, 80 (2000)

Rowley, Gwyn, 'British fire insurance plans: The Goad productions, c1885-c1970', *Archives*, 8 (1985)

Russell, Iain, 'Researching a company history: The McAlpine project', *Construction History*, Vol. 2 (1986)

Sampson, Karen and Green, Katy, '"Pounds, shillings and sense." History and sources of the Trustee Savings Bank', *Business Archives*, 76 (1998)

Schwarzkopf, Stefan, 'Sources for the history of advertising in the United Kingdom: The records of the advertising agencies and related advertising material at the History of Advertising Trust', *Business Archives*, 90 (2005)

Shaw, Gareth, 'Content and reliability of 19th century trade directories', *The Local Historian*, 13 (1978)

Shaw, Gareth, Curth, Louise and Alexander, Andrew, 'A new archive for the history of retailing: The Somerfield Collection', *Business Archives* (2002)

Sime, J.H., 'The records of engineering firms and their treatment in the Scottish Record Office', *Archives*, 16 (1983)

Slinn, Judy, 'Histories and records of firms of solicitors', *Business Archives*, 58 (1989)

Smith, David, 'Representation of industry on large scale maps of England and Wales, 1700-c1840', *Industrial Archaeology Review*, 12 (1990)

Stockford, Bridget, 'Burmah Oil Co. Ltd: History and archives', *Business Archives*, 58 (1989)

Suddards, R.W., 'The lawyer and the archivist went down to the filing room', *Archives*, 15 (1981)

Symons, Leonore, 'Archives and records of the Institution of Electrical Engineers', *Archives*, 16 (1983)

Thoms, David, 'Bank records and the early history of the Coventry motor car industry', *Business Archives*, 64 (1992)

Turton, Alison, 'Babcock & Wilcox Ltd: An engineering company's archive', *Scottish Industrial History* (1992)

Turton, Alison, 'Archives of the House of Fraser', *Business Archives*, 45 (1980)

Tweedale, Geoffrey, 'Records of Hadfields Ltd', *Business Archives*, 45 (1980)

Watts, Christopher T. and Watts, Michael J., 'Company records as a source for the family historian', *Genealogists' Magazine*, 21 (1983)

Winship, Brian, 'Patents as an historical source', *Industrial Archaeology*, 61 (1981)

Yeomans, David, 'Trade literature sources in design history', *Construction History Society Newsletter*, 52 (1999)

OTHER SOURCES

Anon., *Gloucester Port Books Database, 1575-1765 on CD-ROM* (1998)

Bodleian Library, *John Johnson Collection: Catalogue of an Exhibition*, a monograph (1971)

Guildhall Library, *Directories from Guildhall Library, London, 1677-1899*, East Ardsley, microfiche, 166 reels

Haberer, Isobel J., 'House Journals: A bibliographical study', Library Association thesis (1965)

Kelly, Serena, 'Report of a Survey of the Archives of British Commercial Computer Manufacturers, 1950-70', unpublished typescript (1985)

National Archives, 'Apprenticeship records as sources for genealogy', *National Archives Research Guide*, www.nationalarchives.gov.uk

National Archives, 'Chancery masters and other exhibits: Sources for economic and social history', *National Archives Research Guide*, www.nationalarchives.gov.uk

National Archives, 'Chancery proceedings: Equity suits from 1558', *National Archives Research Guide*, www.nationalarchives.gov.uk

National Archives, 'Inventions: Patents and specifications, *National Archives Research Guide*, www.nationalarchives.gov.uk

National Archives, 'Lawyers: Records of attorneys and solicitors', *National Archives Research Guide*, www.nationalarchives.gov.uk

National Archives, 'Merchant shipping: Agreements and crew lists, 1747-1860', *National Archives Research Guide*, www.nationalarchives.gov.uk

National Archives, 'Merchant shipping: Agreements and crew lists after 1861', *National Archives Research Guide*, www.nationalarchives.gov.uk

National Archives, 'Merchant shipping: Registration of ships', *National Archives Research Guide*, www.nationalarchives.gov.uk

National Archives, 'Port books, 1565-1799', *National Archives Research Guide*, www.nationalarchives.gov.uk

National Archives, 'Railways: An overview', *National Archives Research Guide*, www.nationalarchives.gov.uk

National Archives, 'Registration of companies and businesses', *National Archives Research Guide*, www.nationalarchives.gov.uk

National Archives, 'Stationers' Hall copyright records', *National Archives Research Guide*, www.nationalarchives.gov.uk

Shaw, Gareth, *British Directories as Sources in Historical Geography*, Historical Geography Research Group Papers, 8 (1982)

Gareth Shaw, *British Directories as Sources in Historical Geography*, Historical Geography Research Group Papers (1982)

Wright, David, *Index of London Surgical and Scientific Instrument Makers, 1736-1811*, unpublished typescript (1988-9)

Wright, David, *Index of London Surgical Instrument Makers, 1822-1865*, unpublished typescript (1988-9)

ADDRESSES

Bank of England Archives Threadneedle Street London EC2R 8AH www.bankofengland.co.uk	British Library 96 Euston Road London NW1 2DB www.bl.uk
Bodleian Library Broad Street Oxford OX1 3BG www.bodley.ox.ac.uk	British Museum Great Russell Street London WC1B 3DG www.thebritishmuseum.ac.uk
Bolton Archives & Local Studies Central Library Le Mans Crescent Bolton BL1 1SE www.bolton.gov.uk	British Records Association c/o Finsbury Library 245 St John's Street London EC1V 4NB www.britishrecordsassociation.org.uk
Borthwick Institute University of York Heslington York YO10 5DD www.york.ac.uk	Centre for Business History in Scotland Bute Gardens University of Glasgow Glasgow G12 8RT www.gla.ac.uk/centres/businesshistory
British Architectural Library Victoria & Albert Museum Cromwell Road London SW7 2RL www.vam.ac.uk/collections/architecture	Chartered Insurance Institute 20 Aldermanbury London EC2V 7HY www.cii.co.uk
British Film Institute National Library 21 Stephen Street London W1T 1LN www.bfi.org.uk	Companies House Crown Way Maindy Cardiff CF14 3UZ www.companieshouse.gov.uk

Construction History Society c/o Chartered Institute of Building Englemere Kings Ride Ascot Berkshire SL5 7TB	Institution of Mechanical Engineers 1 Birdcage Walk London SW1H 9JJ www.imeche.org
Glasgow University Archives 13 Thurso Street Glasgow GE11 6PE www.gla.ac.uk/archives	Keele University Keele Staffordshire ST5 5BG www.keele.ac.uk
Guardian Newsroom 60 Farringdon Road London EC1R 3GA www.guardian.co.uk/newsroom	Manchester City Archives Central Library St Peter's Square Manchester M2 5PD www.manchester.gov
Guildhall Library Aldermanbury London EC2P 2EJ www.cityoflondon.gov.uk	Manchester Metropolitan University Library All Saints Manchester M15 6BH www.library.mmu.ac.uk
History of Advertising Trust 12 Raveningham Centre Norwich Norfolk NR14 6NU www.hatads.org.uk	Manchester Museum of Science & Industry Liverpool Road Castlefield Manchester M3 4FP www.msim.org.uk
Institute of Chartered Accountants in England & Wales Chartered Accountants' Hall PO Box 433 London EC2P 2BJ www.icaew.co.uk	Memorial University of Newfoundland St John's Newfoundland NL A1C 5SJ Canada www.mun.ca/mha
Institute of Chartered Accountants of Scotland 21 Haymarket Yards Edinburgh EH12 5BH www.icas.org.uk	Middlesex University Silver Studio Collection Cat Hill Campus Barnet Hertfordshire EN4 8HT www.moda.mdx.ac.uk
Institution of Civil Engineers One Great George Street London SW1P 3AA www.ice.org.uk	Modern Records Centre University of Warwick Coventry CV4 7AL www.warwick.ac.uk
Institution of Engineering & Technology Savoy Place London WC2R 0BL www.theiet.org	Museum of English Rural Life Whiteknights University of Reading Reading RG1 5EX www.merl.org.uk

National Archives Ruskin Avenue Kew Richmond Surrey TW9 4DU www.nationalarchives.gov.uk	National Register of Archives National Archives Ruskin Avenue Kew Richmond Surrey www.nationalarchives.gov.uk/nra
National Archives of Scotland HM General Register House Princes Street Edinburgh EH1 3YY www.nas.gov.uk	National Register of Archives for Scotland National Archives of Scotland HM General Register House Princes Street Edinburgh EH1 3YY www.nas.gov.uk/nras
National Art Library Victoria & Albert Museum Cromwell Road London SW7 2RL www.vam.ac.uk/nal	National Screen & Sound Archive of Wales National Library of Wales Aberystwyth Ceredigion Wales SY23 3BU www.screenandsound.llgc.org.uk
National Library of Scotland George IV Bridge Edinburgh EH1 1EW www.nls.uk	North West Film Archive Manchester Metropolitan University 47-49 Chorlton Street Manchester M1 3EU www.nwfa.mmu.ac.uk
National Library of Wales Aberystwyth Ceredigion Wales SY23 3BU www.llgc.org.uk	Oldham Local Studies & Archives 84 Union Street Oldham OL1 1DN www.oldham.gov.uk
National Life Stories Collection British Library 96 Euston Road London NW1 2DB www.bl.uk	Parliamentary Archive Houses of Parliament London SW1A 0PW www.parliament.uk
National Maritime Museum Greenwich London SE10 9NF www.nmm.ac.uk	Pepys Library of Magdalene College Cambridge CB3 0AG www.magd.cam.ac.uk
National Monuments Record Centre Kemble Drive Swindon SN2 2GZ www.english-heritage.org.uk	Public Record Office of Northern Ireland 66 Balmoral Avenue Belfast BT9 6NY www.proni.gov.uk
National Railway Museum Leeman Road York YO26 4XJ www.nrm.org.uk	Reading University Library Whiteknights Reading RG6 6AE www.reading.ac.uk

Royal Air Force Museum Grahame ParkWay London NW9 5LL www.rafmuseum.org.uk	Scottish Screen Archive 39-41 Montrose Avenue Hillington Park Glasgow G52 4LA www.ssa.nls.uk
Royal Commission on Ancient 　　& Historical Monuments in Scotland John Sinclair House 16 Barnard Terrace Edinburgh EH8 9NX www.rcahms.gov.uk	Sheffield Central Library Surrey Street Sheffield S1 1XZ www.sheffield.gov.uk
Royal Commission on Ancient 　　& Historical Monuments in Wales Plas Crug Aberystwyth Wales SY23 1NJ www.rcahmw.gov.uk	The Times Archive News International 1 Virginia St London E98 1ES
Royal Geographical Society 1 Kensington Gore London SW7 2AR www.rgs.org	Tyne & Wear Archives Services Blandford House Blandford Square Newcastle upon Tyne NE1 4AJ www.tyneandweararchives.org.uk
Royal Institute of British Architects 66 Portland Place London W1B 1AD www.architecture.com	University College, London Gower Street London WC1E 6BT www.ucl.ac.uk
Royal Institution of Chartered Surveyors 12 Great George Street London SW1P 3AD www.rics.org	Wellcome Library 183 Euston Road London NW1 2BE www.wellcome.ac.uk
Science Museum Library Imperial College Road London SW7 5NH www.sciencemuseum.org.uk	Worshipful Company of Stationers Stationers' Hall Ave Maria lane London EC4M 7DD www.stationers.org
Scottish Brewing Archive Glasgow University Archives 13 Thurso Street Glasgow GE11 6PE www.gla.ac.uk/sba	

INDEX

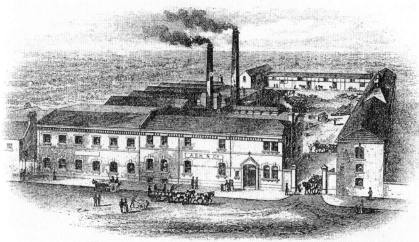

ASH & Cº

BREWERS, CANTERBURY.

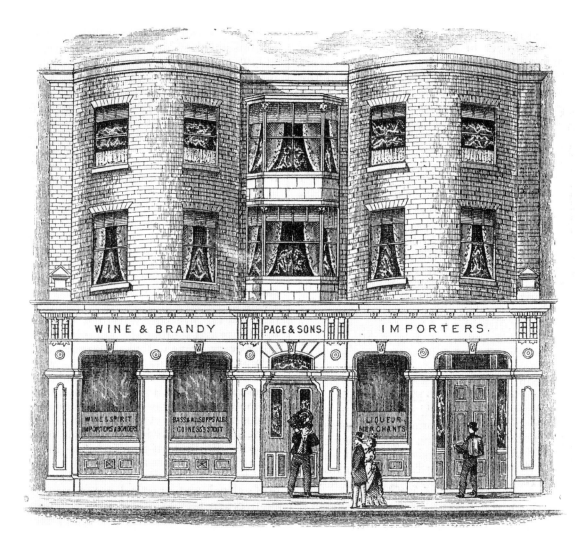

WINE & BRANDY PAGE & SONS. IMPORTERS.

WINE & SPIRIT IMPORTERS & BONDERS   BASS & ALLSOPPS ALES GUINESS STOUT   LIQUEUR MERCHANTS